Suitcase 44
Suitcase 53
Suitcase 72
Suitcase 79
Suitcase 74
Suitcase 67
Suitcase 50
Suitcase 31

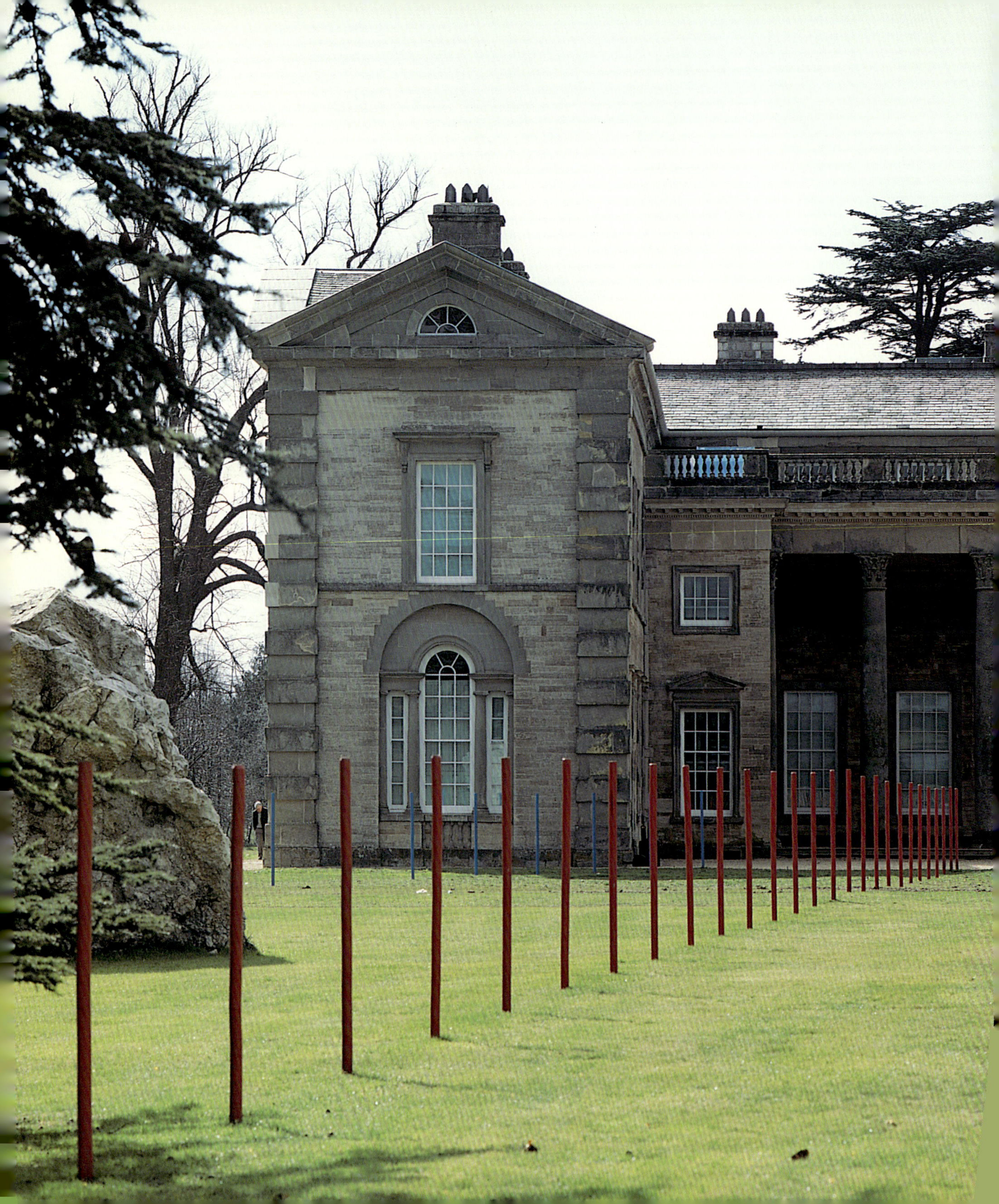

Luper at Compton Verney

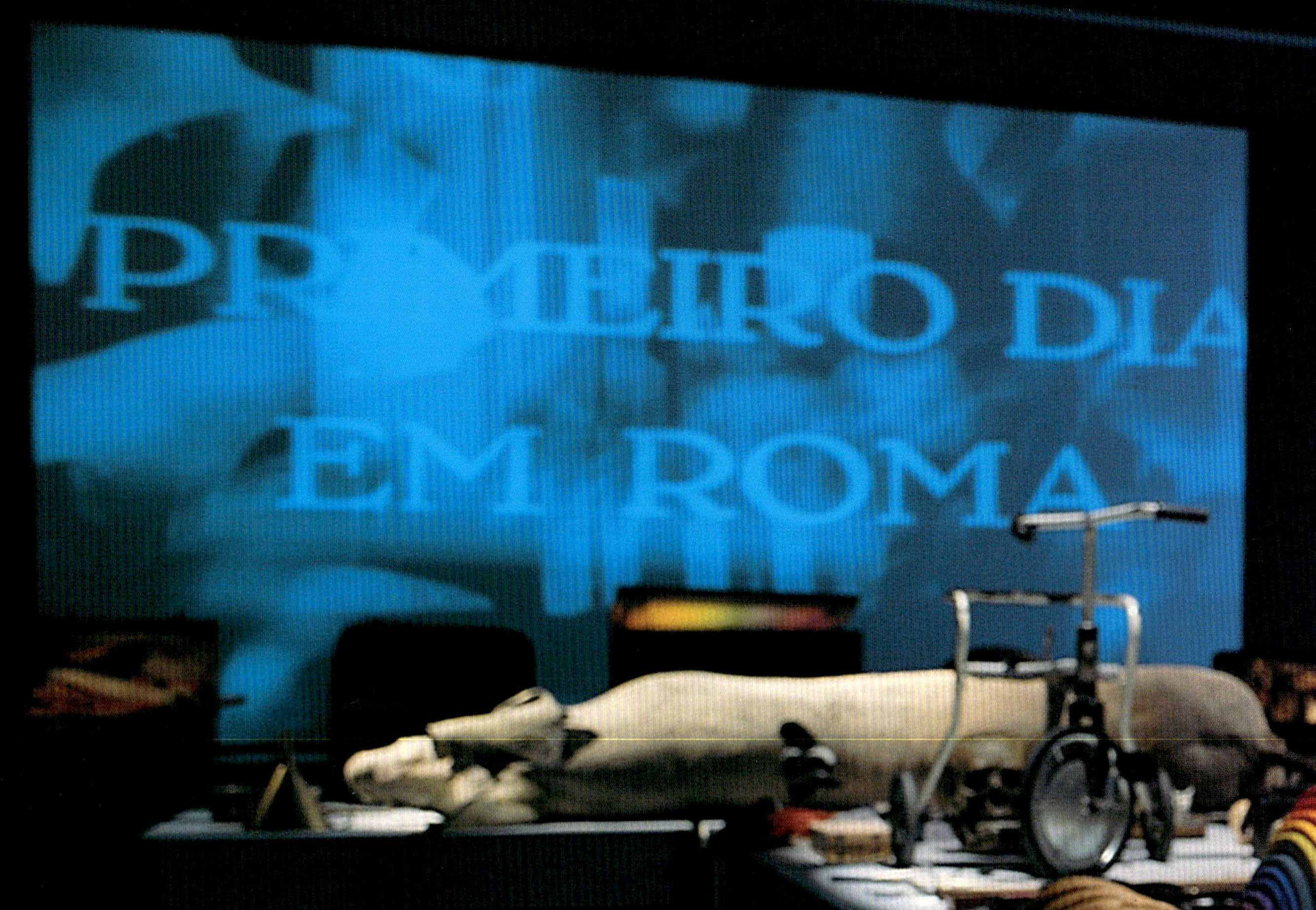

Published 2004 by Compton Verney House Trust on the occasion of the exhibition 'Luper at Compton Verney'
27 March – 31 October 2004

Initiated by Dr Susan Jenkins, Richard Gray and John Leslie
Exhibition organised by John Leslie,
assisted by Antonia Harrison and Ruth Inglefield

Catalogue edited by John Leslie and Alan Ward
Designed by Alan Ward @ www.axisgraphicdesign.co.uk

ISBN 0-9546545-4-4

Printed by Clifford Press, Coventry

Compton Verney
Warwickshire CV35 9HZ
tel + 44 (0) 1926 645500
cvht@comptonverney.org.uk
www.comptonverney.org.uk

Compton Verney is a registered charity, no. 1032478

Compton Verney House Trust was founded by Sir Peter Moores and is funded by the Peter Moores Foundation

PETER MOORES FOUNDATION

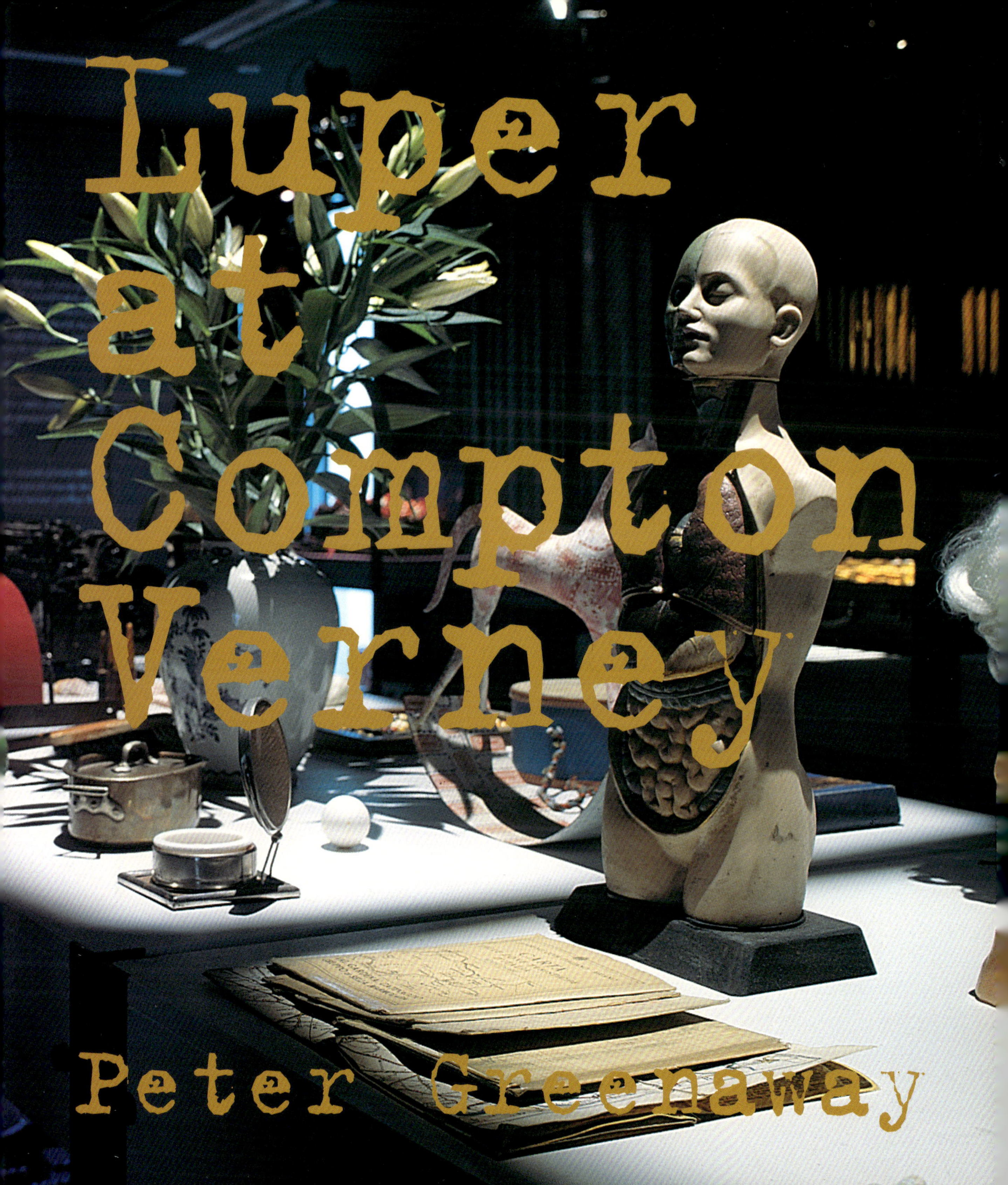
Luper
at
Compton
Verney
Peter Greenaway

Luper at Compton Verney
Introduction
by Peter Greenaway

SUITCASE 1 COAL. SUITCASE 2 TOYS SUITCASE 3 LUPER PHOTOS SUITCASE 4 LOVE LETTERS SUITCASE 5 & 6 CLOTHES SUITCASE 7 VAT

PHOTOGRAPHS SUITCASE 12 FROGS SUITCASE 13 FOOD DROP SUITCASE 14 DOLLARS SUITCASE 15 COINS SUITCASE 16 LUPER'S LOST FI

WALLPAPER SUITCASE 21 CLEANING FLUIDS SUITCASE 22 DENTAL TOOLS SUITCASE 23 CHERRIES SUITCASE 24 HONEY SUITCASE 25 NUM

KEYS SUITCASE 29 LIGHT-BULBS SUITCASE 30 PLACE-NAMES SUITCASE 31 BOOTS AND SHOES SUITCASE 32 ZOO ANIMALS ARK SUITCAS

RADIO EQUIPMENT SUITCASE 37 CLEAN LINEN SUITCASE 38 WATER SUITCASE 39 CODE SUITCASE 40 A SLEEPER SUITCASE 41 EROTIC

44 PRISON MOVIE FILM-CLIPS SUITCASE 45 MANUSCRIPTS FOR THE BABY OF STRASBOURG SUITCASE 46 HOLOCAUST GOLD SUITCASE 47 CH

51 SHOWER-HEADS SUITCASE 52 55 MEN ON HORSEBACK SUITCASE 53 CHINA DOGS SUITCASE 54 BRUSHES SUITCASE 55 DRAWINGS OF I

SUITCASE 59 INGRES PAINTINGS SUITCASE 60 BROKEN GLASS SUITCASE 61 MOITESSIER GOWNS SUITCASE 62 CRABCLAWS SUITCASE 63

MESSAGES SUITCASE 67 GREEN APPLES SUITCASE 68 PIG SUITCASE 69 SPENT MATCHES SUITCASE 70 SAUCEPANS SUITCASE 71 FLOWE

SPLINTERS SUITCASE 75 FIRE SUITCASE 76 LEAD SUITCASE 77 OBELISKS SUITCASE 78 ROMAN POSTCARDS SUITCASE 79 HOLY EARTH

83 MAPS SUITCASE 84 BOARD GAMES SUITCASE 85 INK & BLOOD SUITCASE 86 LUPER STORY MANUSCRIPTS SUITCASE 87 ICE SUITCASE 8

BOOK SUITCASE 92 LUPER'S LIFE SOME FAKE, APOCRYPHAL & UNAUTHENTICATED SUITCASES SUITCASE 93 LIVE SQUID SUITCASE 94 WH

It may be that the suitcase is an ideal metaphor for our times. As never before, people are on the move. Ask any North American where he or she was born, and, ten to one, they are not living or working there now. It is said that over 25,000 young people, each carrying a suitcase, arrive in Shanghai and Beijing every evening. And we know about the voluntary and involuntary movement of people in Eastern Europe since the Berlin Wall came down. And we are a material people as never before. Carry your world and your possessions with you. Just about as much as you can carry whilst walking. Not just a clean shirt and a new toothbrush and a change of underwear but all the other information of identity - memories, hopes, anxieties, guilt, foretaste of intention, ambition, wish-fulfillment. "I live out of a suitcase" is no longer necessarily the cry of a boastful or a sorrowful professional traveller. How many suitcases have you packed in your life? And what was in them?

RNOGRAPHY SUITCASE 8 FISH SUITCASE 9 PENCILS SUITCASE 10 HOLES SUITCASE 11 MOAB
ITCASE 17 ALCOHOL SUITCASE 18 PERFUME SUITCASE 19 PASSPORTS SUITCASE 20 BLOODIED
LETTERS SUITCASE 26 LUPER UNIFORMS SUITCASE 27 DOG BONES SUITCASE 28 LOCKS AND
EAS OF AMERICA SUITCASE 34 ANNA KARENINA NOVELS SUITCASE 35 CANDLES SUITCASE 36
NGS SUITCASE 42 92 OBJECTS TO REPRESENT THE WORLD SUITCASE 43 RAINBOWS SUITCASE
SUITCASE 48 DEAD ROSES SUITCASE 49 TRAINS SUITCASE 50 SEWING NEEDLES SUITCASE
UITCASE 56 MUSICAL INSTRUMENTS SUITCASE 57 SMOKED CIGARS SUITCASE 58 BODY-PARTS
S AND EGGS SUITCASE 64 YELLOW PAINT SUITCASE 65 TENNIS BALLS SUITCASE 66 BOTTLE
SUITCASE 72 RESTAURANT MENUS SUITCASE 73 92 ATOMIC ELEMENTS SUITCASE 74 VIOLIN
SE 80 GREEN FIGS SUITCASE 81 LIGHT SUITCASE 82 NOTES ON DROWNED CORPSES SUITCASE
RING TOOLS SUITCASE 89 TYPEWRITER SUITCASE 90 DOLLS SUITCASE 91 THE PHRENOLOGICAL
SUITCASE 95 HUMAN ASH

Until otherwise contradicted, Tulse Luper is associated with a life history of 92 suitcases, and since 92 is the atomic number of Uranium we can make that fact significant.

Born in 1911 in Newport Gwent, and possibly still alive, aged 92 last year, we know that Luper travelled the world. He was certainly in Moab, Utah where Uranium was officially "discovered' there in 1928. He was in Antwerp in 1939 when the Germans invaded Belgium. He was in Rome when the Americans arrived in 1944. He met Raoul Wallenberg in Budapest in 1945 and followed him to Moscow in the 1950s. He was at an East-West German checkpoint in 1963. And between times he was in Vaux, in Strasbourg and Dinard, on Sark, in Barcelona, on top of the Mole Antonelliana in Turin with Primo Levi, in Venice, and in Bolzano with a suitcase full of gold bars stolen from the Jews. He was in the Far East after 1965, in Hong Kong and Kyoto, and he was putting down his suitcase in Beijing in the early 1980s.

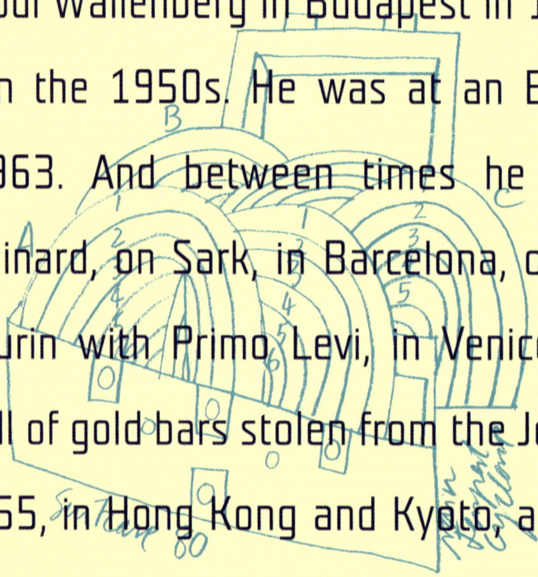

As an inveterate collector, collator and classifier, Luper packed and unpacked suitcases, left them in appropriate and inappropriate places, had them stolen, arranged to have them stolen, abandoned them or was persuaded to abandon them. Sometimes with, and sometimes without his permission, others, intimates and enemies, packed suitcases for him. And beware, there may be fakes and copies and more than a few unauthorised suitcases posing as Luper originals around the world.

We have assembled what we believe (or almost believe) is the definitive collection – certainly 92 of the suitcases associated with his name, and, as a start to their in-depth investigation, we have offered here at Compton Verney, a brief explanation, excuse or justification for each of them and their contents. Certainly these 92 suitcases are the basis for intensely examining Tulse Luper and his life, and sometimes his times, the times of Uranium from 1928 to 1989, covering the first chapter of that emotive element, from its "discovery", if you can ever "discover" Uranium, to the end of the Cold War. Luper might be called a Child of Uranium.

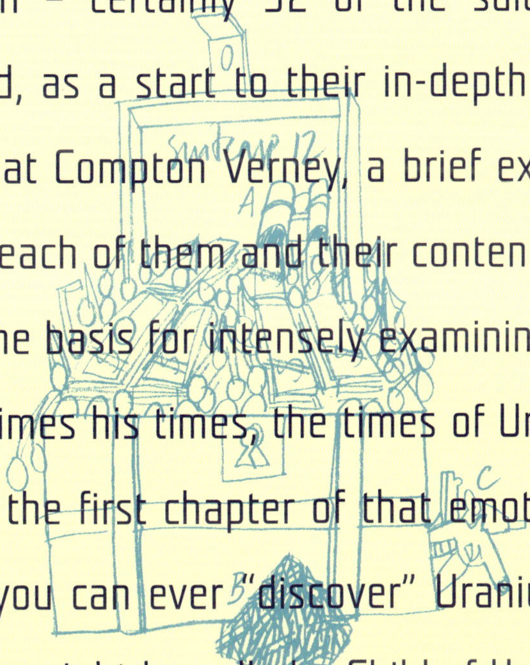

This intensive, if not to say obsessive, examination of Luper continues in many different ways, in an ambitious project called The Tulse Luper Suitcases, in feature films for the cinema and in programmes for television, on web sites, DVDs, in theatre and in opera presentations, in texts and books, and certainly in installations and exhibitions like this one at Compton Verney.

We are very grateful that the Compton Verney House Trust funded by the Peter Moores Foundation has graciously and generously permitted us encouragement and space to place this collection here at the newly refurbished Compton Verney House and Grounds, and has thoroughly supported our effort in every way. We thank all members of the Compton Verney House staff who have been most patient and sympathetic.

And we most warmly thank all those people of so many different disciplines who are associated and affiliated with the Kasander Company for helping to draw all the parts of this suitcase collection together and to provide for its exhibition.

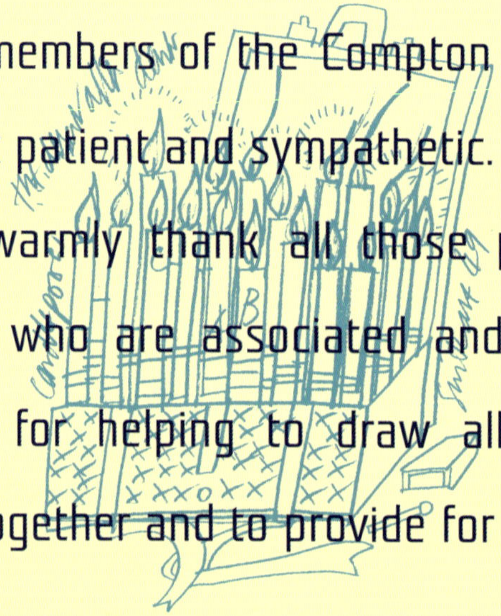

XMAS 1940!

As our Gallant and Beloved Prime Minister would say:—

"WE WILL DO OUR BEST!"

GOULBURN'S

2 to 18, OLD MILLGATE, MANCHESTER 4

(Not merged in any Syndicate or Trust.)

The Manchester G

No. 29,393 ★★ FRIDAY, DECEMBER 6, 1940

JOHN RYLANDS LIBRARY.—Public Afternoon Lecture WEDNESDAY NEXT, at 3 p.m. Guernsey: A sociological study." By Professor H. J. FLEURE, F.R.S.

SOCIETY OF FRIENDS.
At the
FRIENDS' MEETING-HOUSE, MOUNT STREET,
TO-DAY, 1.15 p.m.,
LUNCH-HOUR MEETING.
"QUAKERISM, WORSHIP, AND LIFE."
Speaker: HELEN B. BYLES FORD.
A cordial invitation is extended to all.

CITY OF SALFORD.

THE MAYORESS
(MRS. CROOKELL)
will be AT-HOME
at the
ART GALLERY, PEEL PARK,
on
WEDNESDAY, 11th DECEMBER, 1940,
from 2 p.m. to 4 p.m.

CLIFFORD TURNER FOR SLIPPERS.

Give your greetings in the nicest way. Give cheery, cosy, serviceable slippers from Clifford Turner's. Prices are low for such high quality and there's a wonderful selection. Come along right now.

CLIFFORD TURNER,
46, KING ST. (Opp. St. Ann's Passage), M/c 2.

BRITISH CELANESE, LIMITED.

7 PER CENT FIRST MORTGAGE DEBENTURE STOCK.
2 PER CENT MORTGAGE DEBENTURE STOCK.
Notice is hereby given, that the above-mentioned DEBENTURE STOCK REGISTERS will be CLOSED from the 16th to the 30th DECEMBER inclusive for preparation of the half-year's interest, payable 31st December, 1940.—By Order of the Board,
W. H. POXON, Secretary.
Registered Office: First Floor, 50-54, Union Street, Torquay, South Devon, 5th December, 1940.

JOHN I. THORNYCROFT & CO., LTD.

Notice is hereby given, that the SHARE TRANSFER BOOKS of the above Company will be CLOSED from Monday the 9th December, to Friday the 20th December, both days inclusive, for the preparation of dividend warrants.—By order of the Board.
A. H. MUSTO, Assistent Secretary.
Thornycroft House, Smith Square, Westminster, S.W. 1, December 4, 1940.

WILLIAM BLYTHE & CO., LTD.

Notice is hereby given, that the REGISTER of MEMBERS in respect of the PREFERENCE SHARES of the Company will be CLOSED from the 16th to 31st December, 1940, both days inclusive.—By order of the Board.
G. W. MIDDLETON, Secretary.

AIR-RAID PRECAUTIONS

BEFORE YOU CONSTRUCT YOUR
AIR-RAID SHELTER
CONSULT
THE LIMMER & TRINIDAD
LAKE ASPHALT CO., LTD.,
115, PRINCESS STREET, MANCHESTER 1.
Tel. CENtral 5125 (5 lines).

REINFORCED Concrete Sectional Indoor Sleeping Shelter, fitted with steel bunks, for four persons. On view at Conway's, Ltd., Plymouth Grove, Manchester. ARD. 2541.

REINFORCED CONCRETE UNDERGROUND SHELTERS. A. QUILIGOTTI & CO., Plymouth Grove, Manchester 13. ARD. 1791-2.

STIRRUP PUMPS, double handle, Home Office pattern, large stocks to clear, 21/. Manchester Trades Supply Co., Ltd., 89, City Rd., M/c 15.

HAULAGE, REMOVALS, &c.

RETURN LOADS.—Furniture Manufacturers require Carriers from London to Manchester. Apply LAMB, 101, Curtain Rd., London, E.C. 2.

HOWARDS REMOVAL SERVICE, Brooks's Bar. Long distance a speciality. Low rates. Excellent storerooms. Tel. Mos 1027.

MESSRS. EDWARD CURRAN & CO.

PERSONAL

TREATMENT FOR RHEUMATISM AT GASKELL'S, Oxford Road. A. R. Shelter.

MANCHESTER Merchant willing to Purchase any quantity Home Trade Cotton and Rayon Quotas. Write terms and quantities available. Address J 19, "M/c Guardian" 2.

WM. THOMPSON, Pawnbroker, 23, Oxford Rd., Manchester 1.
Cash Advanced up to £1,000 on valuable property of every description. Best prices given.
Tel. ARDwick 1511.

LARGE HOUSE in country near Glasgow. Safe area. Large gardens. Beautiful district. Modern, central heating, electric light. Owner and wife, no family, accept 2 children and nurse or two adult paying guests. No other guests. With sitting-room. Dine with owner. Six guineas per week each. Address G 166, "M/c Guardian" 2.

AIR RAID! Make sure that your valuables and documents are safe. PERFECT BOMB AND FIREPROOF SECURITY is offered at small cost by ST. JAMES'S SAFE DEPOSIT, 77, Oxford Street, Manchester 1 (opposite Gaumont Cinema). Telephone CENtral 4177.

HAYWARD'S GLASS & CHINA
LARGEST DISPLAY IN THE CITY
CHRISTMAS GIFTS.
THOUSANDS OF PIECES OF THE
FINEST CHINA AND CUT CRYSTAL
FREE OF TAX.

Dainty Morning Tea Sets from	6s. 6d.
Tea Sets in Great Variety from	10s. 6d.
Dinner Sets in Exclusive Designs	25s. 0d.

Special Show of
Royal Doulton and Susie Cooper Wares.
Open Saturday till five o'clock.
T. HAYWARD & CO., 64-66, Deansgate, M/c 3.

GRIME'S. SPECIAL COURSES.
UNIVERSITY ENTRANCE.
SCHOOL CERT.—H.S.C.—MATRIC.
PREVIOUS, RESPONSIONS, PRELIMS., LEGAL.
MANCHESTER TUTORIAL COLLEGE, 327, Oxford Rd.

PILOTS & OBSERVERS.—PRELIMINARY MATHS. and SCIENCE. ORAL, POSTAL. LOREBURN COLLEGE, 60-62, Spring Gdns., M/c 2.

GOLD 168/- PER OZ.
DIAMONDS, OLD GOLD, JEWELLERY, AND ANTIQUE SILVER PURCHASED FOR CASH.
SOVEREIGNS 39s. 3d.
OLLIVANT & BOTSFORD, LTD.
(Est. 1749),
12 & 14, ST. ANN ST., MANCHESTER.

NO MATTER how many waves of bombers—lovely, lustrous lasting waves are still yours when your hairdresser uses OTHERMO MACHINELESS PERMANENT WAVING. Safest and loveliest of all Permanents, without machinery or electricity—leaves you free to move to shelter—that's Othermo.

Kilgour French & Stanbury Ltd.,
TAILORS.
DOVER STREET, LONDON,
AT
MIDLAND HOTEL,
MANCHESTER,
MONDAY & TUESDAY, DEC. 9 & 10,
and ADELPHI HOTEL,
LIVERPOOL,
WEDNESDAY & THURSDAY, DEC. 11 and 12.
Showing full ranges of Suitings and Overcoatings.

RELIABLE Agents required by Firm Black Satteen specialists. O 152, "M/c Guard."

RHEUMATISM RAPIDLY RELIEVED BY CELUNOX—made from celery. Sufferers report amazing benefit. Mr. Lane writes: "All pains gone in two days, thanks to Celunox." Get a 1/9 or 3/6 bottle of Celunox (brand) tablets to-day from any Chemist. Prices include tax. If no benefit return empty case to makers, who refund money.

WORKS BROADCAST SYSTEMS for instructions and music in works and shelters. Complete from £26. Radio reception £5-£10 extra. Write for details HOLIDAY & HEMMERDINGER, LTD.,

WAR RISKS—SAFES. EXPLOSIVES, FIRE, & BURGLARY. 250 Safes, Milner's, Chatwoods, Chubbs. All Sizes. WITHY GROVE STORES, 35, WITHY GROVE, M/c 4.

ROBINSON'S REMOVAL SPECIALISTS KNOLLS HOUSE, MANCHESTER, Cent. 5564. Cricklewood, London, and Moseley, Birmingham. FINE FLEET of MODERN MOTOR-VANS Weekly London, S. Coast, Devon, Midlands, Wales, Yorks., Newcastle, Scotland, East Coast. Estimates free. SEVEN UNIQUE MODERN FURNITURE DEPOSITORIES.

STOCKPORT BEDDING COMPANY. All types of Bedding remade, WOOL or HAIR MATTRESSES converted into modern-type spring interior, from 42/- full size. Down Quilts re-covered. 23, Great Underbank, Stockport. Tel STO. 4665-6.

VISIT POPE & WARING'S SALEROOMS FOR MODERN SECOND-HAND FURNITURE. Low Reserves. 34, Booth Street, opp. Art Galleries.

LEGAL NOTICES

WAR CHARITIES ACT, 1940.

Notice is hereby given, that it is proposed to apply to the Lancashire County Council for the REGISTRATION under the above-mentioned Act of the DROYLSDEN HOSPITAL SUPPLY AND COMFORT FUND, the objects of which are shortly as follows:—
To provide comforts for local men serving in his Majesty's forces at home and abroad. To provide hospital supplies for the wounded and sick of H.M. forces and civilian population. To provide help for people rendered homeless, &c. due to enemy attack.
And the administrative centre of which is situated at 58, Market Street, Droylsden.
Any objections to the proposed registration should be sent in writing to the above-named Council within 14 days from the date of this notice.
Dated December 6, 1940.

THE COMPANIES ACT, 1929.—CONNOLLY KNOWLES & COMPANY, LTD.—Notice is hereby given, pursuant to section 238 of the Companies Act, 1929, that a MEETING of the CREDITORS of the above-named Company will be held at Midland Bank Chambers, Library Street, Wigan, on Thursday the 12th day of December, 1940, at eleven o'clock in the forenoon, for the purposes mentioned in sections 239 and 240 of the said Act.—Dated this 29th day of November, 1940.—By order of the Board.
A. S. KNOWLES, Director.

JOHN GREENWOOD MILLERS (1934), LTD. (in Voluntary Liquidation).—Notice is hereby given, that creditors of the above company are required on or before the 6th January, 1941, to send in their names and addresses and particulars of their debts or claims to the undersigned Walter Fred Harris, of 2, Billiter Avenue, London, E.C. 3, the liquidator of the said company, and if so required by notice in writing from the said liquidator to come in and prove their said debts or claims at such time and place as shall be specified in such notice or in default thereof they will be excluded from the benefit of any distribution made before such debts are proved.—Dated this 3rd day of December, 1940.
W. F. HARRIS, Liquidator.

IN the matter of THE GRAVINO COMPANY, LIMITED.—By order of the Stockport County Court, dated the second day of December, 1940, Mr. ARTHUR WRIGHT FIDLER, of 2, Shaw Road, Royton, near Oldham, Lancashire, has been appointed liquidator of the above-named Company with a Committee of Inspection.—Dated this fourth day of December, 1940.

IN the matter of NASMYTH, WILSON, and CO., LIMITED; and in the matter of the Companies Act, 1929.—Notice is hereby given that the Creditors of the above-named Company which is being voluntarily wound up are required on or before the 18th day of January, 1941, being the day for that purpose fixed by me, the undersigned, Albert Holden, of 8, The Sanctuary, in the City of Westminster, the liquidator of the said Company, to send their names and addresses and the particulars of their debts or claims and the names and addresses of their solicitors, if any, to me, and if so required by notice in writing from me are by their solicitors to come in and prove their said debts or claims at such time and place as shall be specified in such notice, or in default thereof they will be excluded from the benefit of any distribution made before such debts are proved.—Dated this 2nd day of December, 1940.
A. HOLDEN, 8, The Sanctuary, Westminster, London, S.W.

LILY ANN HOWARD, DECEASED.—Pursuant to the Trustee Act, 1925, notice is hereby given that all persons having any claims or demands upon or against the estate of LILY ANN HOWARD, late of 237, Clifton Drive South, St. Annes-on-the-Sea, in the County of Lancaster, spinster (who died on the 23rd day of August, 1940, and whose will was proved by Hugh Colley Irvine, the sole executor therein named, on the 5th day of November, 1940, in the Manchester District Registry of the Probate Division of his Majesty's High Court of Justice), are hereby required to send in the particulars of their debts or claims to the said executor at the offices of the undersigned, his solicitors, on or before the 6th day of March, 1941, and notice is hereby also given that after that day the said executor will proceed to distribute the assets of the said Lily Ann Howard deceased amongst the parties entitled thereto,

OPERA HOUSE. Evgs., 5 45, Sat., 2.
Barry K. BARNES, Diana CHURCHILL
ON APPROVAL
by Frederick Lonsdale.
Cathleen NESBITT, Roland CULVER.
NEXT TUESDAY, 5 45. Mats. Wed., Thurs., Sat., 2.
VIC OLIVER,
SARAH CHURCHILL,
in
TO-NIGHT AT 5 45.
Joyce Carey, Inga Andersen.
Commencing Tuesday, 24th December, at 5 30.
Subs. Twice Daily at 2 & 5 30, includ. XMAS DAY.
TOMMY TRINDER, FAY COMPTON,
NAUGHTON AND GOLD,
IN EMILE LITTLER'S ALL-COMEDY PANTOMIME
CINDERELLA.

PALACE THEATRE. 3 30 and 5 45.
THIS AND NEXT WEEK
GARRISON THEATRE.
Actual London Palladium Production with
JACK (Blue Pencil) WARNER,
JOAN WINTERS,
GARRISON THEATRE BAND.

MANCHESTER HIPPODROME,
3-30 Ardwick 5-45.
3-30 Green. 5-45.
REGINALD FOORT and his Mighty Theatre Organ.
Murray and Mooney and Star Acts.
10 to 8 p.m. ARDwick 4101-2.
COMMENCING MONDAY NEXT,
6-0 PERFORMANCES COMMENCE AT 8-0

SALES BY PRIVATE CONTRACT

Engines, Machinery, Tools, &c.

A Capital Selection of Engines, Boilers, and Pumps, Machine Tools, Electrical, Colliery, & Contractors' Plant always in stock. Thos. Mitchell & Sons, Ltd., Bolton.

AN Excellent Selection of Boilers, Engines, Pumps, Tanks, Air Compressors, and Contractors' Plant always in stock. CHRIS HOLDEN, LTD., Blackburn.

AVAILABLE for Hire, immediately, Several Broom-Wade Diesel Engined Air Compressors, 110 cubic ft.; machines in first-class condition. Enquiries to ORMEROD & SHIELDS, Tulketh Road, Preston.

BLEACHING, DYEING, and FINISHING MACHINERY Reconditioned and Guaranteed: over 200 Calenders, Mangles, Drying Cylinders, Stenters, Dye Jigs, Raising Machines, Hydro-Extractors. Can be seen erected at WM. BATES, SON, & CO., Sowerby Bridge.

DAVIS PIPE CUTTING-OFF MACHINE, 4in., power feed. F. J. EDWARDS, LTD., 359, Euston Road, London, N.W. 1.

DIESEL GENERATING PLANT, by Tangye; 250 volts, 24-28 amps, complete with fuel and water-cooling tanks; may be seen working; offers wanted. Apply WHITHAM'S GARAGE, King Street, Oldham.

FOR SALE, Vertical BOILER, 8ft. 6in. x 3ft. 6in. x 100lb. w.p. ALLEN KNIGHT & SON (BOILERS), LTD., Huddersfield.

FOR SALE, KWICKSTEAM Vertical BOILER, 10ft. x 4ft. x 100 b. w.p. ALLEN KNIGHT & SON (BOILERS), LTD., Huddersfield.

FOR SALE, 60 TONS Large W.I. SHAFTS; full particulars and sketches. Apply COX and DANKS, LTD., Frederick Road, Salford 6.

FOR SALE, Modern 30ft. x 8ft. x 100lb. w.p. LANCASHIRE BOILER with extended front end, by good maker. ALLEN KNIGHT & SON (BOILERS), LTD., Huddersfield.

FOR SALE, 10,000 BALL RACES;
POLISHING BARREL;
RANSOME PAN MIXER,
REAMERS.
SEBCO, LTD., Willenhall Road, Wolverhampton.

GAS ENGINE, 16 h.p., suitable for town supply. F. J. EDWARDS, LTD., 359, Euston Road, London, N.W. 1.

GREENHALGH & CO., LTD., Atherton. 'Phone 26. Mill Gearing, Pipes, over 5,000 Pulleys in Stock.

GRAINING MACHINE, by Geo. Mann; zinc-lined wood shaking table, 4ft. x 3ft. 4in.; belt-driven, weight 10 cwt. F. J. EDWARDS, LTD., 359, Euston Road, London, N.W. 1.

Wanted

LIMEWASHING and PAINT SPRAYING MACHINE, in good working condition; state price and where seen. Donegal Tweed Company, Ltd., Fleet St., Liverpool.

WANTED, Ring Doubling Frame, 2 3in. rings, suitable for making fancy yarns. Address J 53, "M/c Guardian" 2.

WANTED, 60-70-k.w. 110-volt D.C. Compound-wound Generator direct coupled on combination base to approx. 105 h.p. 400 r.p.m. forced lubricated Steam Engine; steam pressure 120-150 lbs.; complete with condensing equipment and auxiliaries. State full particulars and price to the Darwen Paper Mill Co.,

CO
HOULDSW
TO-DAY
THE H
FR.
STRING QUA
CLARINET QU
TICKETS 1s. 6

Continuous from 12 noon.
GARY CO
"THE
Times:
(Sat. exc.) Hug
VILLAIN STILL P
Continuous 12 till 9.
Repeating her "
"WAT
Screened a
Popula
Continuous from 12 30.
To-day: JACK H
"UND
Screened
Also WARNER
"EARTH BOUND

SALES BY
Motor

WANTED, all ... ticularly A... h.p. long chassis ... model saloons, 2 ... paid for low mile ... and ZONIS, 186- ... 'Phone: Broughto

£10 to £1,00 ... please state ... strictest confide ... dealing. J. Kirk ... Manchester. Tel

Motor Van

FOR SALE, For ... J 1

FOR SALE, ... Hydraulic T

TOM C
Used C
1938-39-40 M
Obtair
10-12, Pe
TELEPHONE:

W

92 SUITCASES

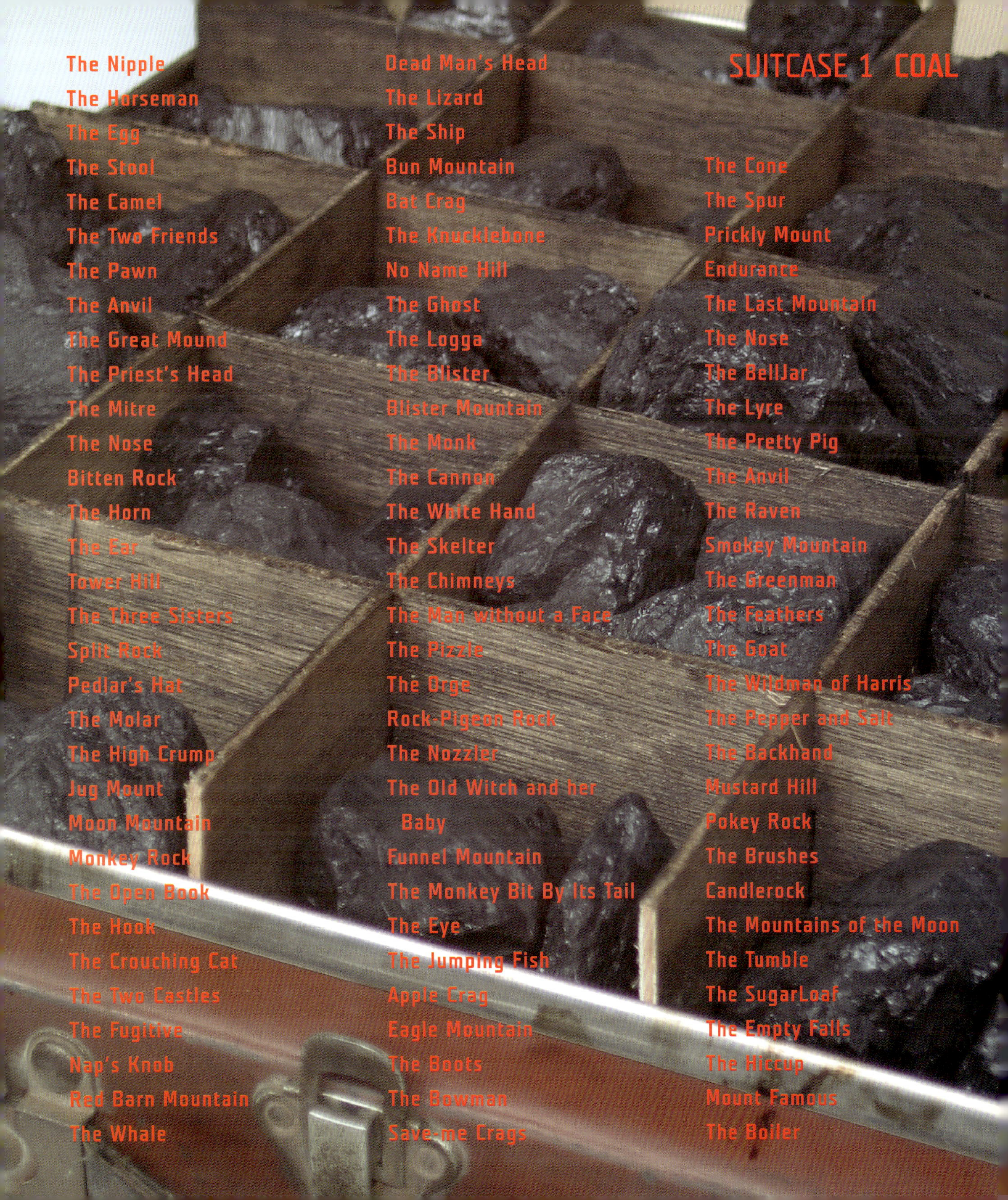

SUITCASE 1 COAL

The Nipple
The Horseman
The Egg
The Stool
The Camel
The Two Friends
The Pawn
The Anvil
The Great Mound
The Priest's Head
The Mitre
The Nose
Bitten Rock
The Horn
The Ear
Tower Hill
The Three Sisters
Split Rock
Pedlar's Hat
The Molar
The High Crump
Jug Mount
Moon Mountain
Monkey Rock
The Open Book
The Hook
The Crouching Cat
The Two Castles
The Fugitive
Nap's Knob
Red Barn Mountain
The Whale

Dead Man's Head
The Lizard
The Ship
Bun Mountain
Bat Crag
The Knucklebone
No Name Hill
The Ghost
The Logga
The Blister
Blister Mountain
The Monk
The Cannon
The White Hand
The Skelter
The Chimneys
The Man without a Face
The Pizzle
The Orge
Rock-Pigeon Rock
The Nozzler
The Old Witch and her Baby
Funnel Mountain
The Monkey Bit By Its Tail
The Eye
The Jumping Fish
Apple Crag
Eagle Mountain
The Boots
The Bowman
Save-me Crags

The Cone
The Spur
Prickly Mount
Endurance
The Last Mountain
The Nose
The BellJar
The Lyre
The Pretty Pig
The Anvil
The Raven
Smokey Mountain
The Greenman
The Feathers
The Goat
The Wildman of Harris
The Pepper and Salt
The Backhand
Mustard Hill
Pokey Rock
The Brushes
Candlerock
The Mountains of the Moon
The Tumble
The SugarLoaf
The Empty Falls
The Hiccup
Mount Famous
The Boiler

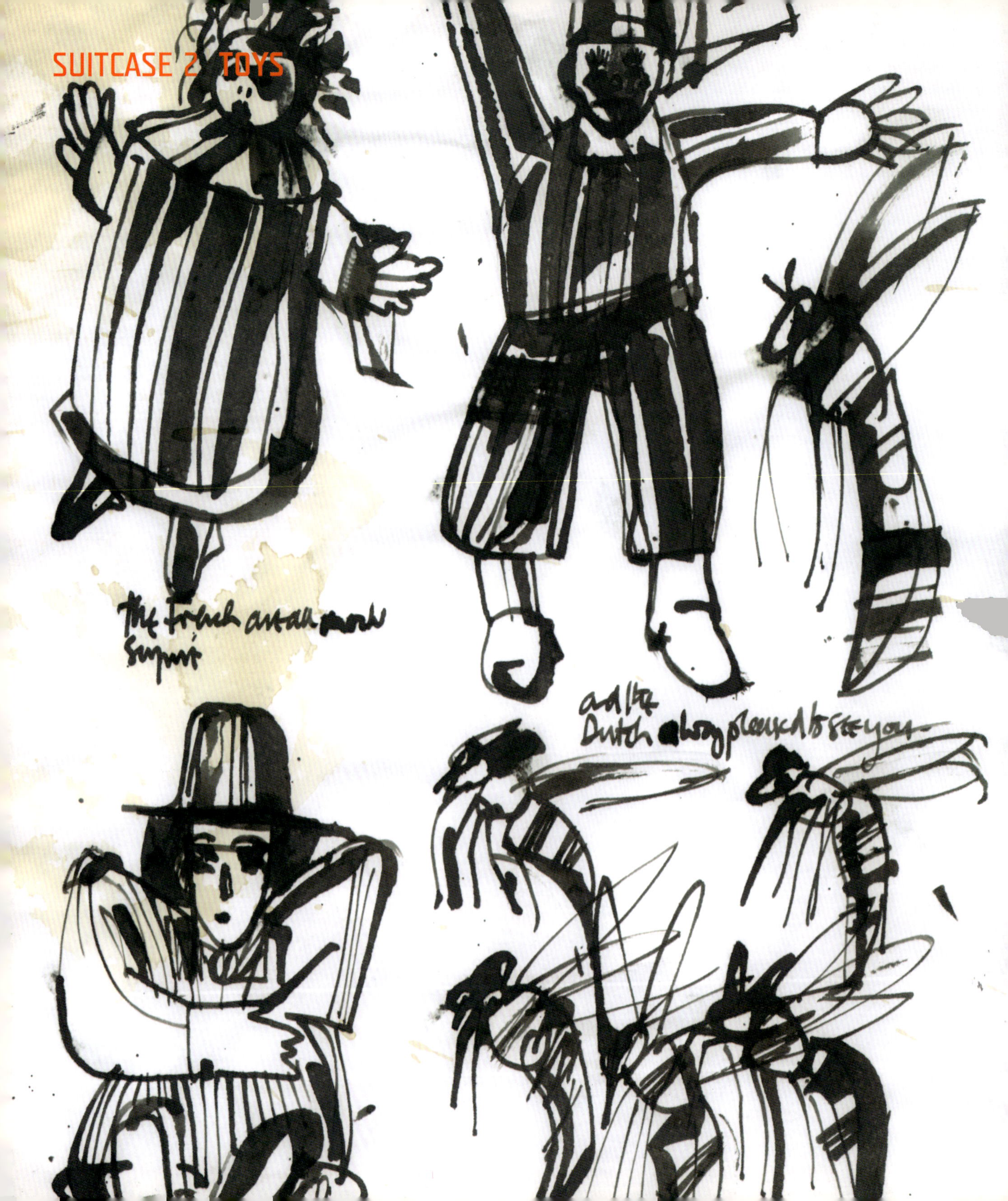
the French are all mock surprise
and the Dutch always pleased to see you

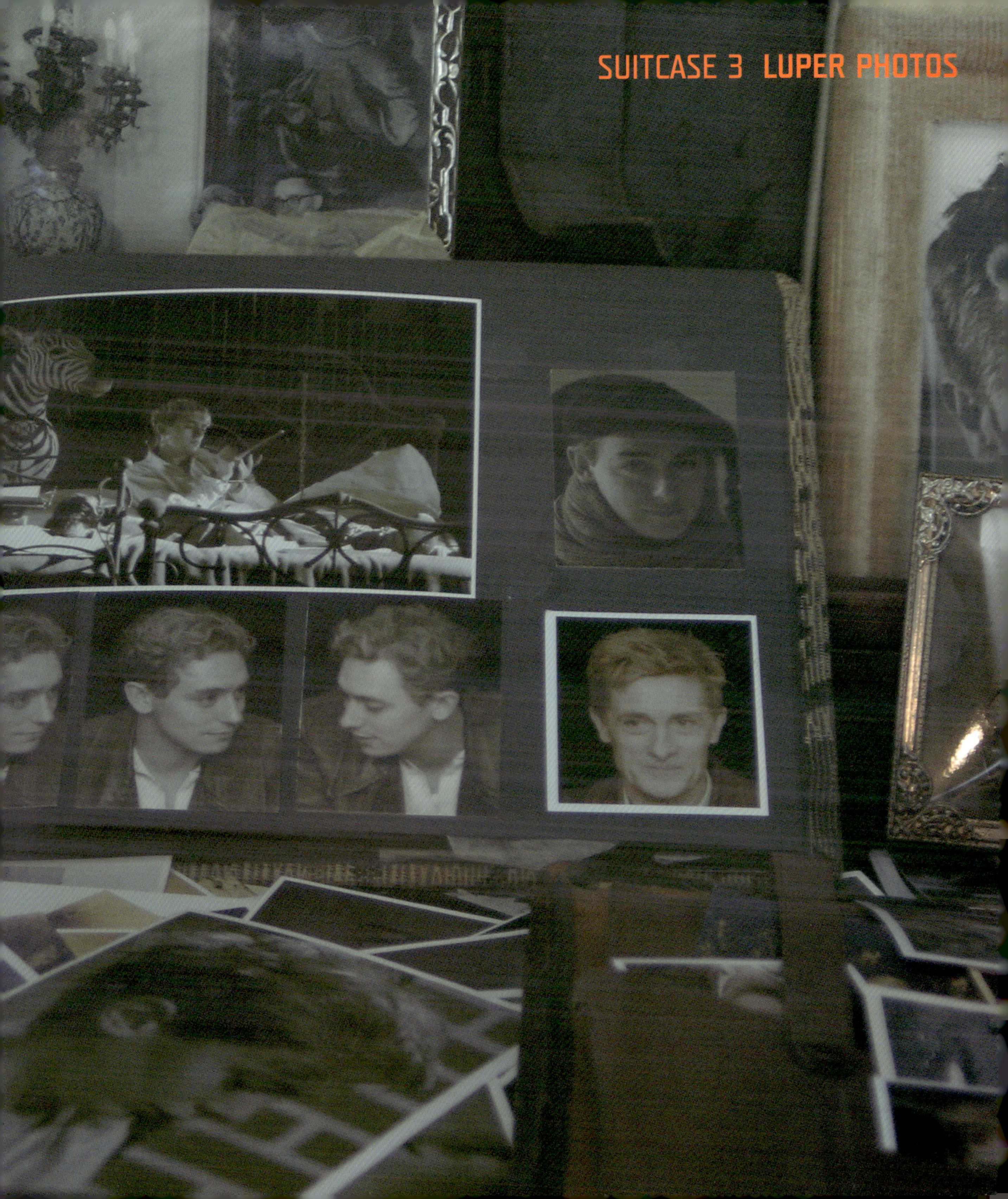

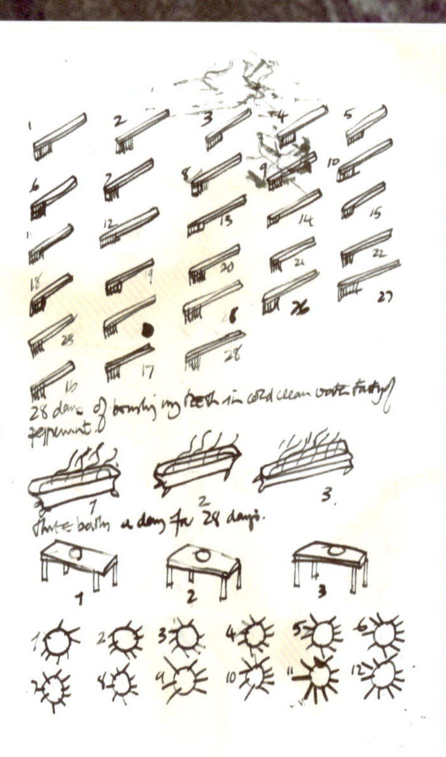
28 days of brushing my teeth in cold clean water tasting of peppermint.
three baths a day for 28 days.

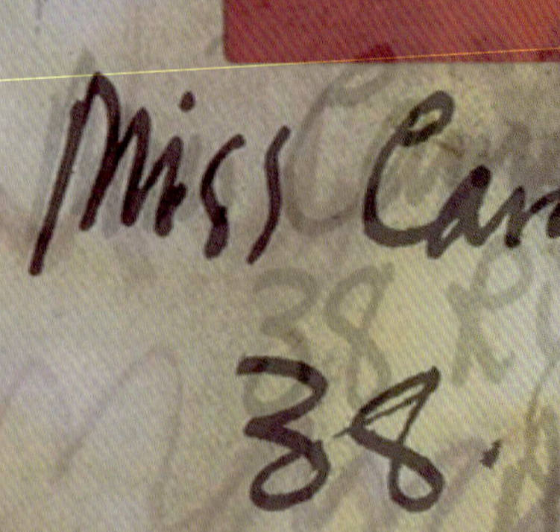

ne Ashdown
igh Road.
rport.
outh Wales-
U.K.

Dear Carrie
I dream constantly and I dream curiously not of
[illegible], vans, [illegible] and the cold, but of you and
summer and clear skies. Most of the [illegible] is
covered with such small [illegible] the familiar
[illegible] the [illegible] [illegible] [illegible]
and over again, our lives are on the edge [illegible]
waiting all the time for the worst to happen, not the
best and certainly not 'here' in familiar. Even the
ground under your feet and the landscape before your
eye can change overnight. Today a forest, tomorrow
a mud bath. Today birds, tomorrow silence. I knew
at home where I [illegible], here I know nothing. The only
fixed point in my universe is you. Can I show you
[illegible] in the bakery, about to [illegible] lunch, your
hands are sticky with flour and icing sugar, your hair
falling out of your scarf [illegible] in the window
[illegible] the [illegible], the shop-door above the
closed, the shutter pulled down and everyone home to
lunch. Home to lunch — God how strange that sounds
[illegible] [illegible] [illegible], [illegible] is food. When I next
home. Time-rain and [illegible] bugs(?).

RAIN. RAIN. RAIN. RAIN. RAIN.

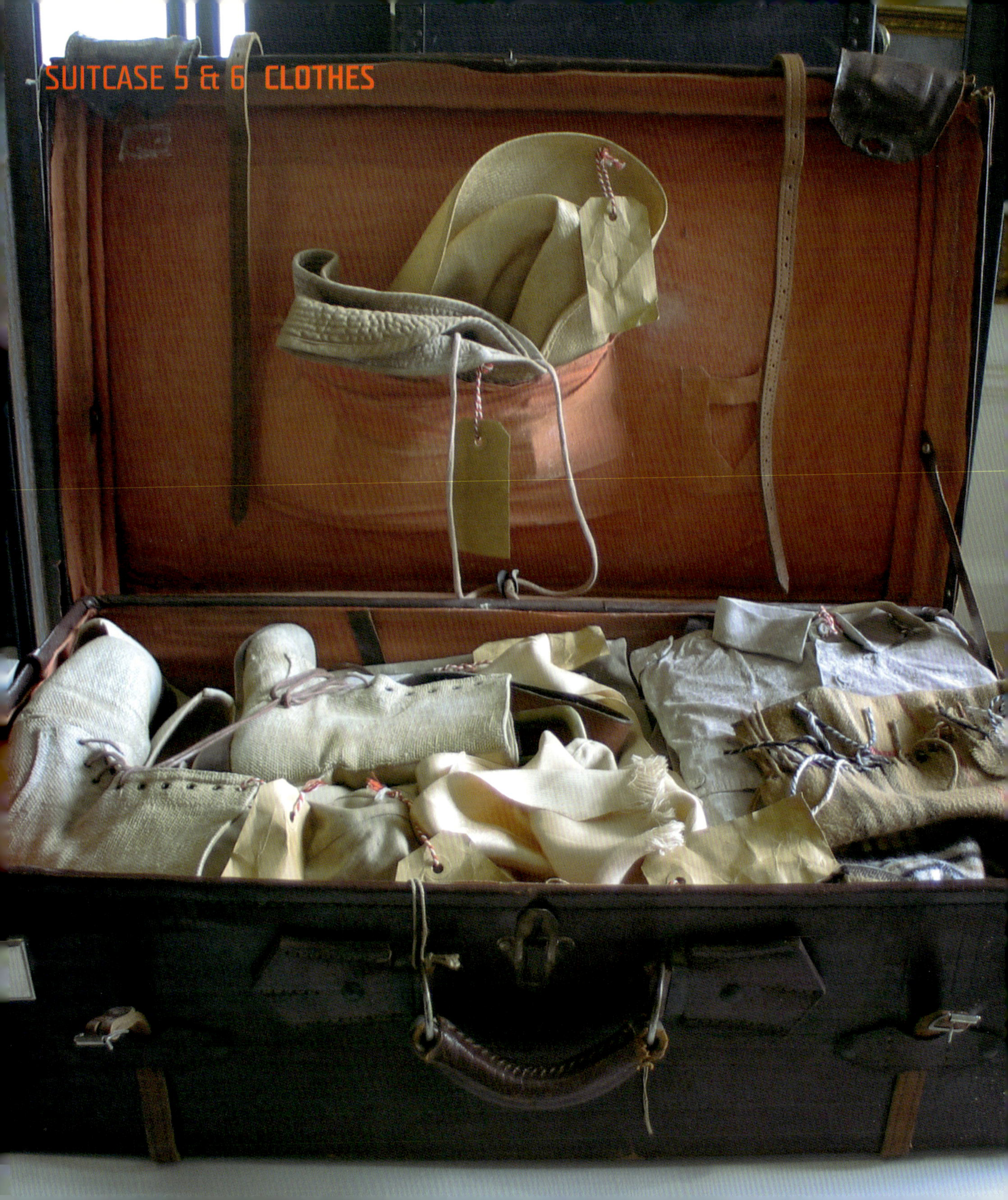

SUITCASE 5 & 6 CLOTHES

SUITCASE 7 VATICAN PORNOGRAPHY

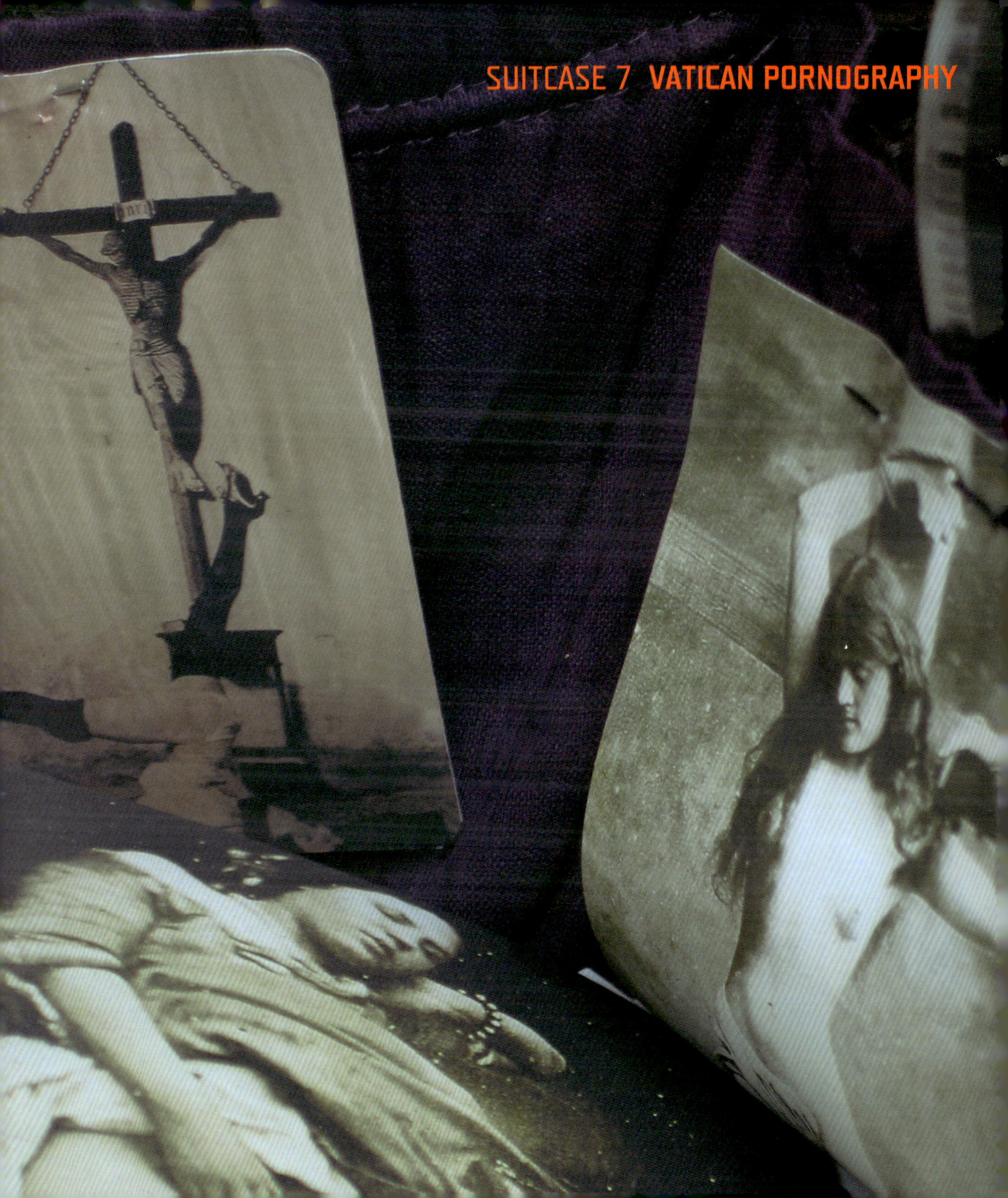

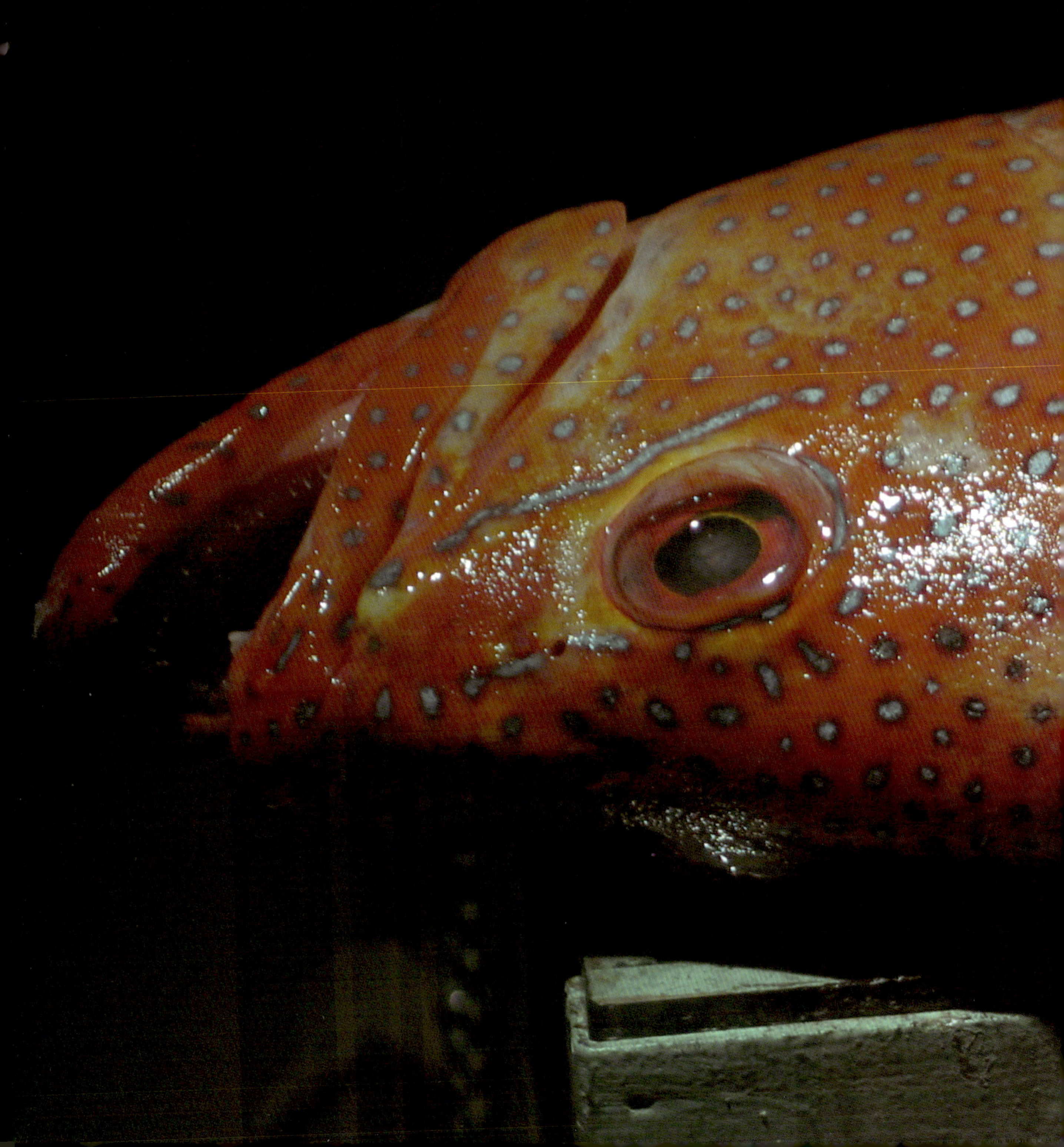

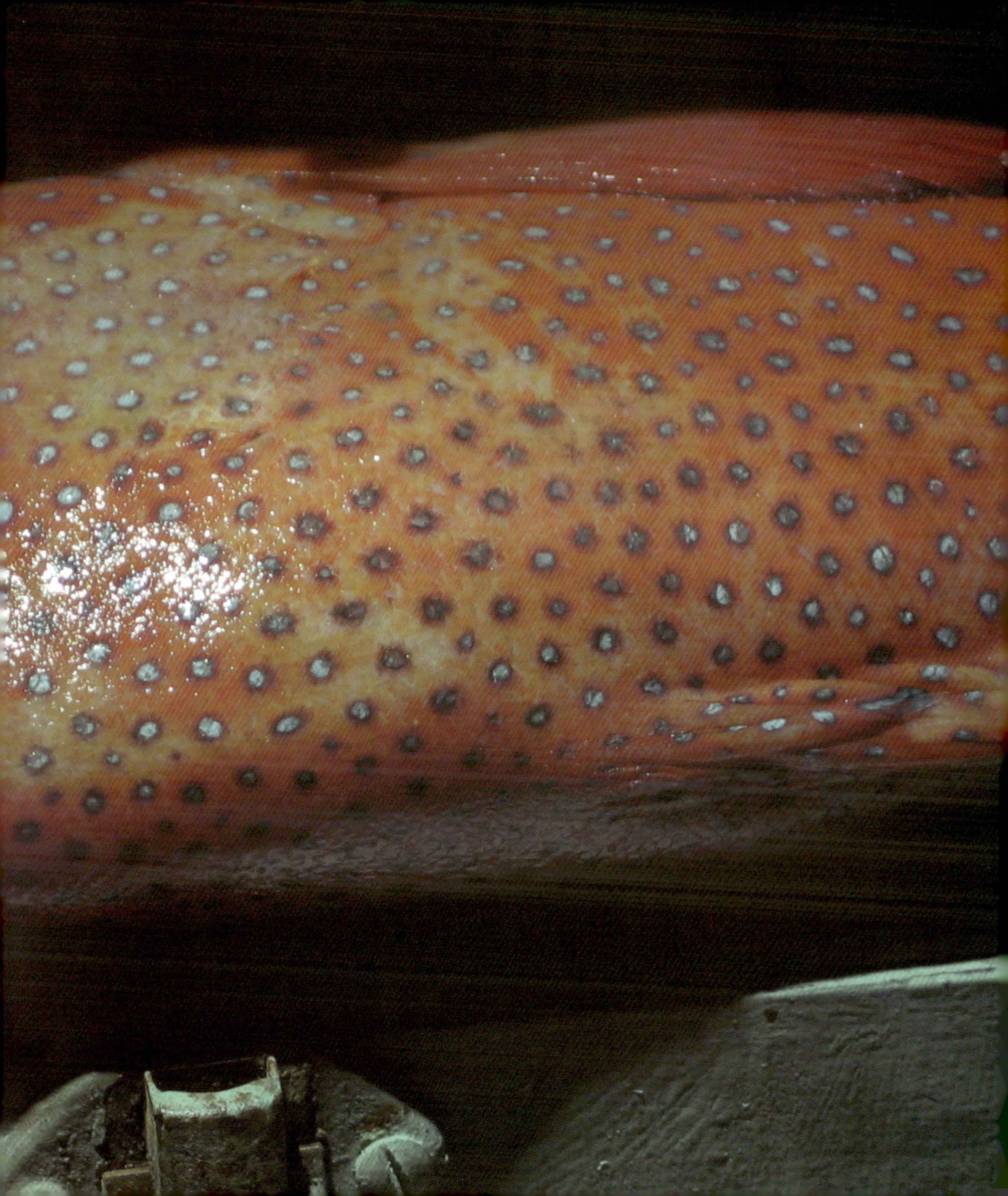

SUITCASE 9 PENCILS

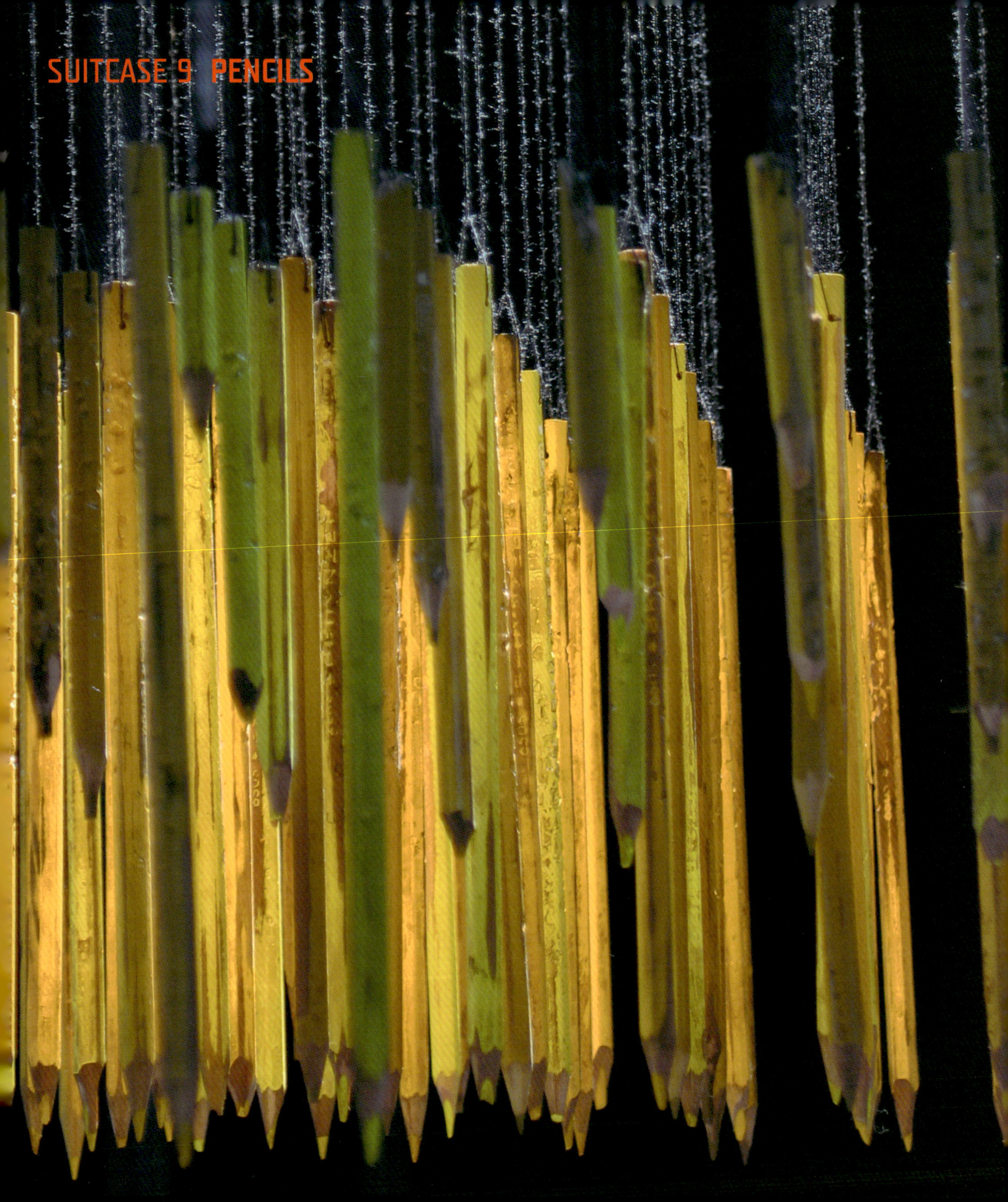

SUITCASE 10 HOLES

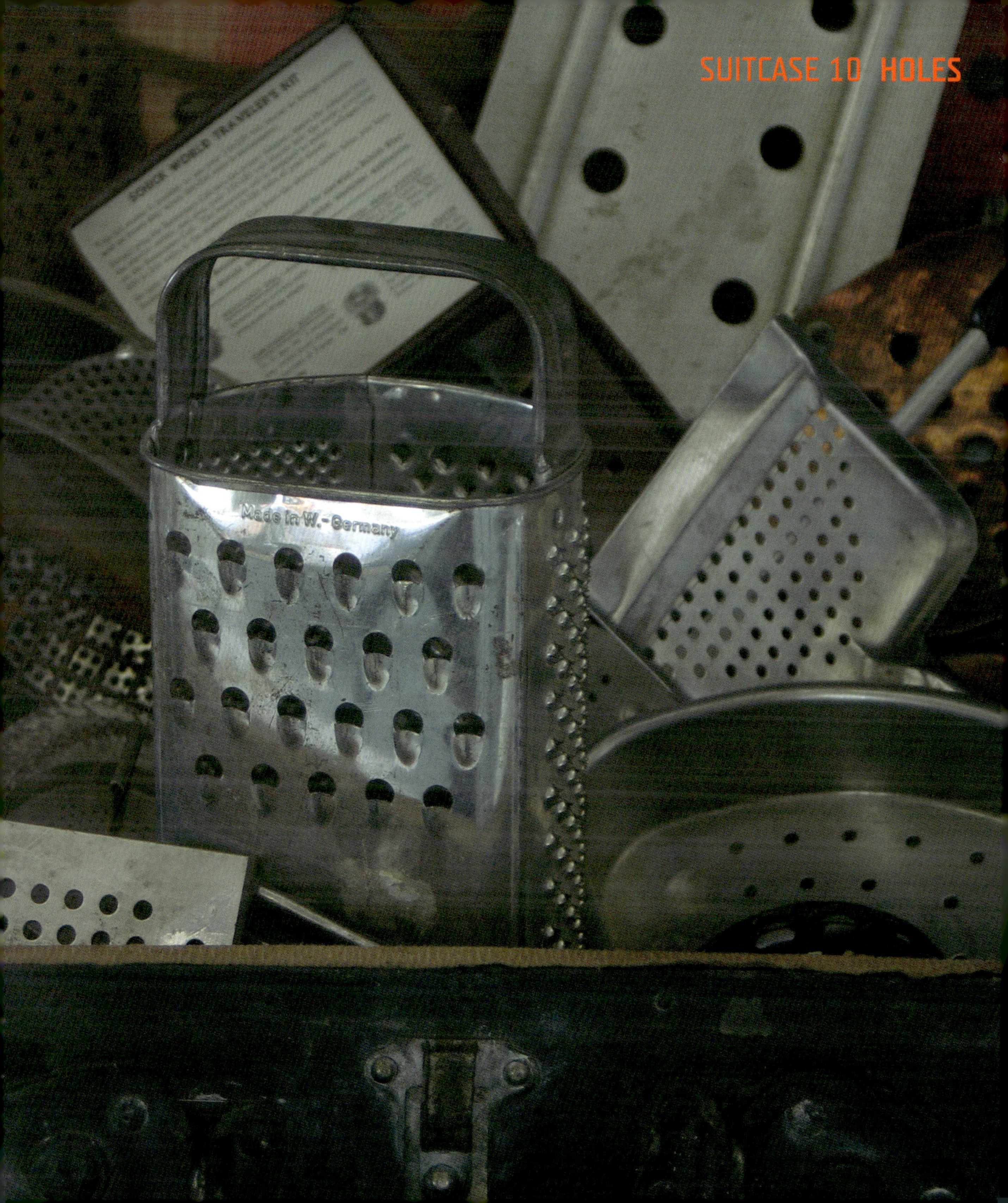

SUITCASE 11 MOAB PHOTOGRAPHS

Roger Boarman	Biting babies
Abe Loose	Pie-throwing
Kretchen Fisher	Being drunk, lewd and swearing in church
Achery Foster	Goosing a pregnant woman
Babyface Max	Horse-stealer
Magrebber	Filthy talk
Ricco	For being Italian and curling his moustache like Jesse James
Red End	Robbing banks
Honeyboy	Digging up the dead and doing dirty things to them
Mooney Pecker	Simple rape
Dude James	Stealing wood
Finchey	Shitting on the church roof at night
Andriessen. M	Peeing in the Samson well
Topolli	Buying cheap and selling expensive
Barber Fleet	Spying and being generally furtive
Mackerel	Kidnapping boys
Blind Eye Simon	Drumming at night
P. Gutteridge	Robbing
Passover Myrtle	Milking cows she had no business to
Elmer Fossey	Embezzeling
Pigs Trotter	Laughing and bullying when he ought not to
Valkerie	Stealing wheels
Amazon	Being cheap on Sundays
Apple Jacques	Compound rape

Slattery	Squinting to please the devil
Purple Maisie	Spitting on the sidewalk in front of the minister's house
Salmon Eye	Robbing
Noel Floraty	Revealing himself
Steely Gripe	Spitting in church
Duo Parker	Staring at pregnant women
Glotto Sparks	Stealing figs
Reno Fox	Fouling the minister's bed
The Orangeman	Making a nuisance on a Sunday
Pipette Wipers	Kicking the minister's dog
Danish Peters	Hayrick arson
Albie Spica	Shooting his wife's lover
Ulster Irish	Tampering with the gas
Filthy Simon Jr	Illegal phone listening
Becky Sharpe	Social climbing whoring
Arcansaw	Eavesdropping at the drugstore
Chips Buloo	Stealing cabbages
Stops Manson	Driving over the limit
Blox	Stealing a lame horse
Mahoney	Stealing a pickup truck with a baby inside
Chris Hooker	Cooking smells past midnight
Magenta Smyth	Compound adultery leading to disturbing the peace
Tipper Clements	Changing road signs without permission
Stourley Krackos	Pretending he was an architect
Taxi Palmer	Defacing shop fronts
Tiger Barman	Trying to commit suicide on private property (50)

Tripper	Siphoning petrol from the mayor's car
Topol Zooley	Rape with menaces
Jo Maddox	First degree murder
Pierce Roe	Humiliation of women
Mallow Edge	Repeated domestic disturbance with menaces
Newman Port	Writing 'Fake' on the Colorado locomotive
Pally Roe	Emptying the swimming-pool out of spite
J R Neville	Drawing for profit without license
R Madgett	Falsifying accidental death by drowning
Fleeman Host	Falsifying name and address for gain
Marcia Speke	Wasting police time with stories of Moon landing
Byman Palmer	Spitting blood on the minister's carpet
Open Bluey	Abusing his third wife because she wore lipstick
Scratchey Bell	Burning bibles
Candle Roe	Shamming to win favour
Scotch Gomen	Being obscene in front of matrons of honour
Ivor Van Os	Blinding a horse with a fish-hook
Baskette Manny	Hiding sexual identity
Gopher Stops	Shooting the telephone wires
Alice Topper	Drunk in possession of a loaded shotgun
Beamer Fils	Hitting his wife at a bible class
Hoary Titmus	Drugs
Joanus Bibbs	Falsifying age to join the army
Noah Jannsen	Wearing female clothing in public
Atmos Fleece	Wounding his brother with a knife
Macey Vine	Being afriad of the dark

Jethro Tongues	Wife-swapping
Matthew Crabb	Child abuse and non-payment of stamp duty
Boy Springer	Stealing laundry
Tabith Golight	Fixing a train derailment
Donaldson G	Conspiring to make rain on harvest Festival Sunday
Jude Collins	Taking bribes
Thomas True	Embezzlement
Praline Bright	Being po-faced on a jury
Giomap Boss	Stealing wicks
Vampy Mole	Injuring a teacher with a forked stick
Brandon Parker	Smashing an Eastman camera
Single Froth	Writing obscenities for publication
Simon Bisop	Laundering Mexican money
Gus Brandon	Avoiding army recruitment
Billy Conlon	Truancy
Stephen Parks	Pretending too much too many times
Dancer Roe	Calling the minister foreign names
Posse Thomas	Scaring children in the dark with screams
Stepson Olive	Devil-worship
Owly Green	Rape of an eighty-year old woman
Fludd Streeter	Travelling beyond state boundary on remand
Whale Streeter	Bossineying
Tears Malone	Falsifying evidence to obtain preferment
Mart True	Bullying

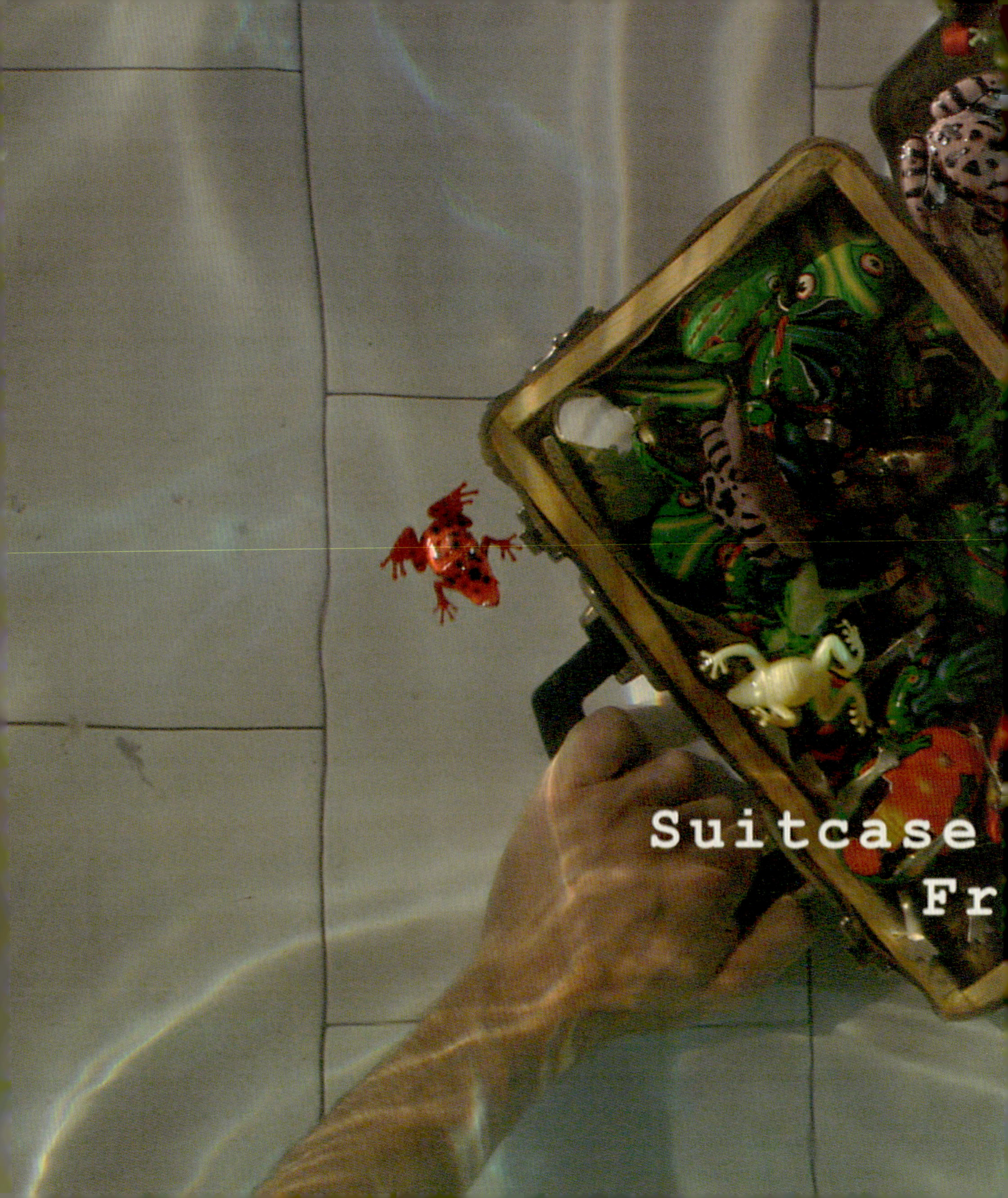
Suitcase
Fr

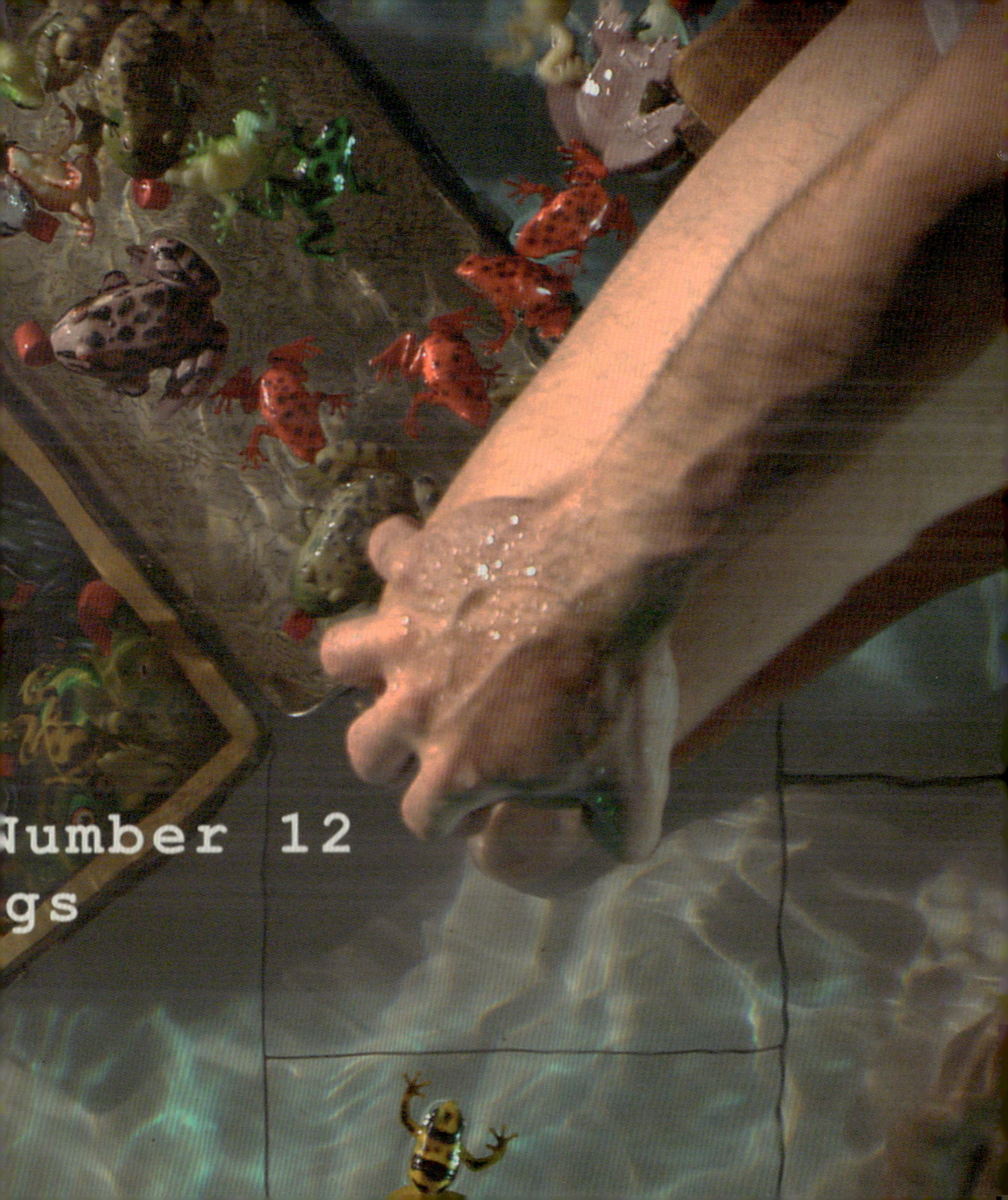

Number 12
gs

" We are hungry "

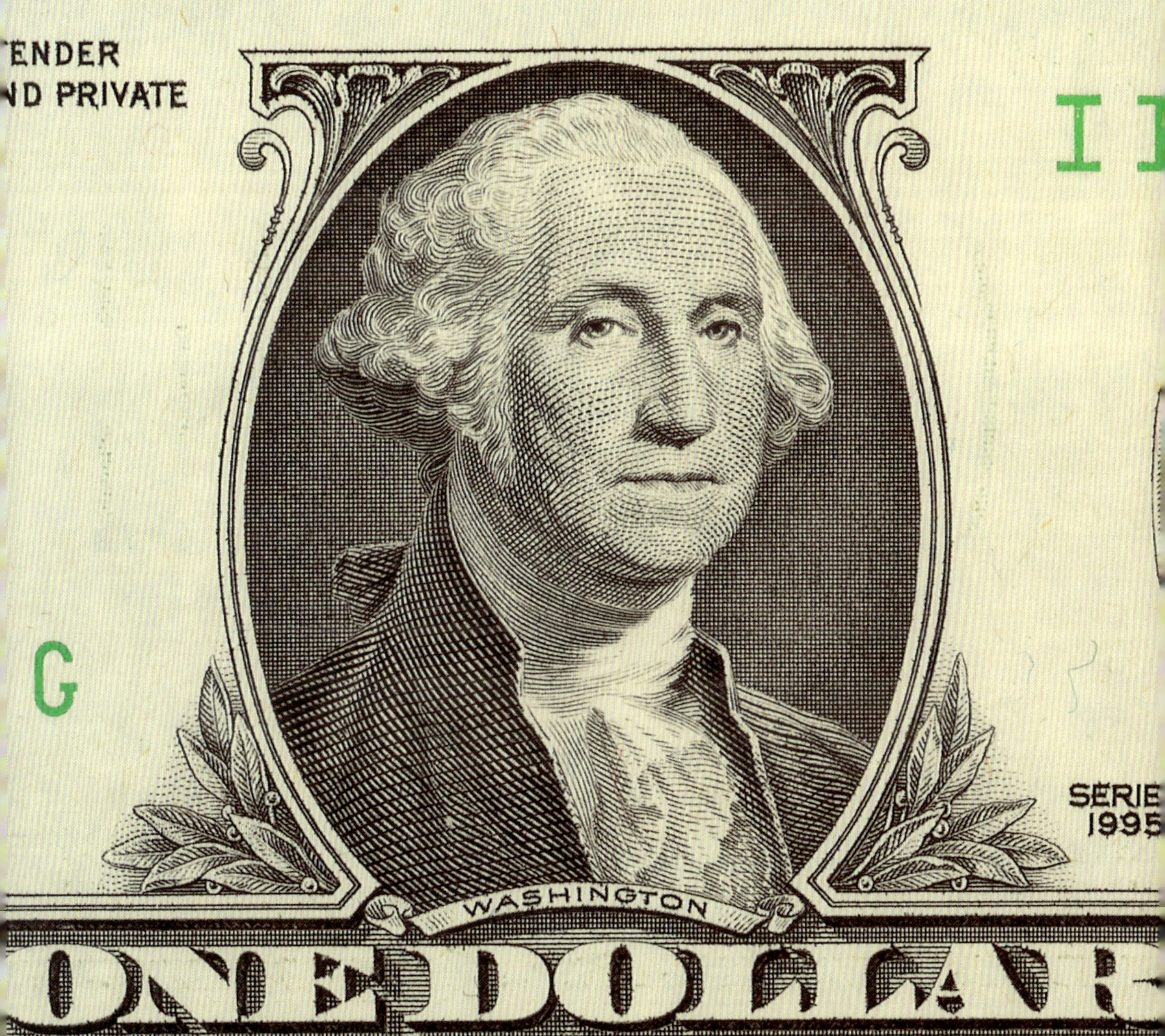
ENDER
ND PRIVATE
G
SERIE
1995
WASHINGTON

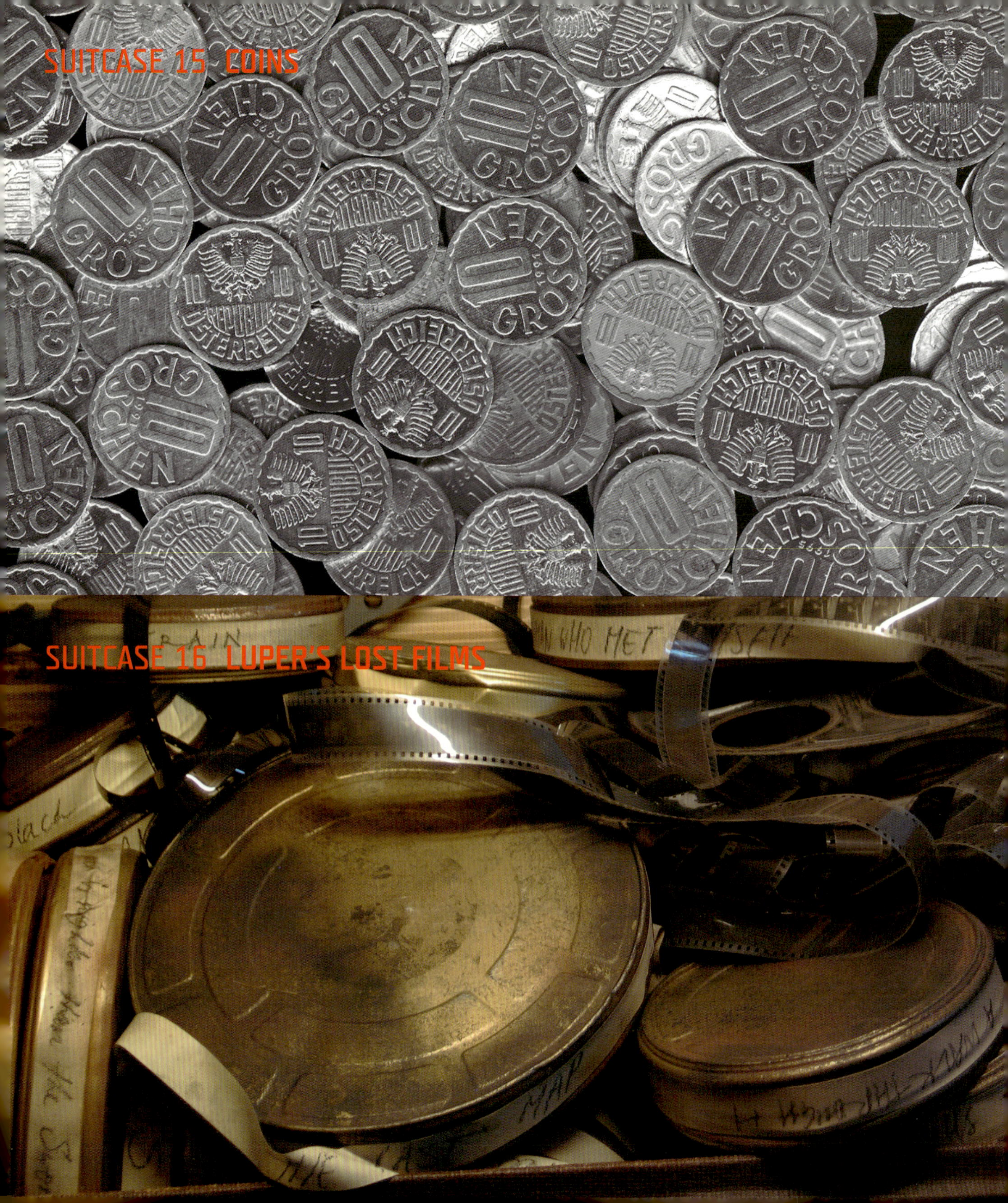

SUITCASE 15 COINS

SUITCASE 16 LUPER'S LOST FILMS

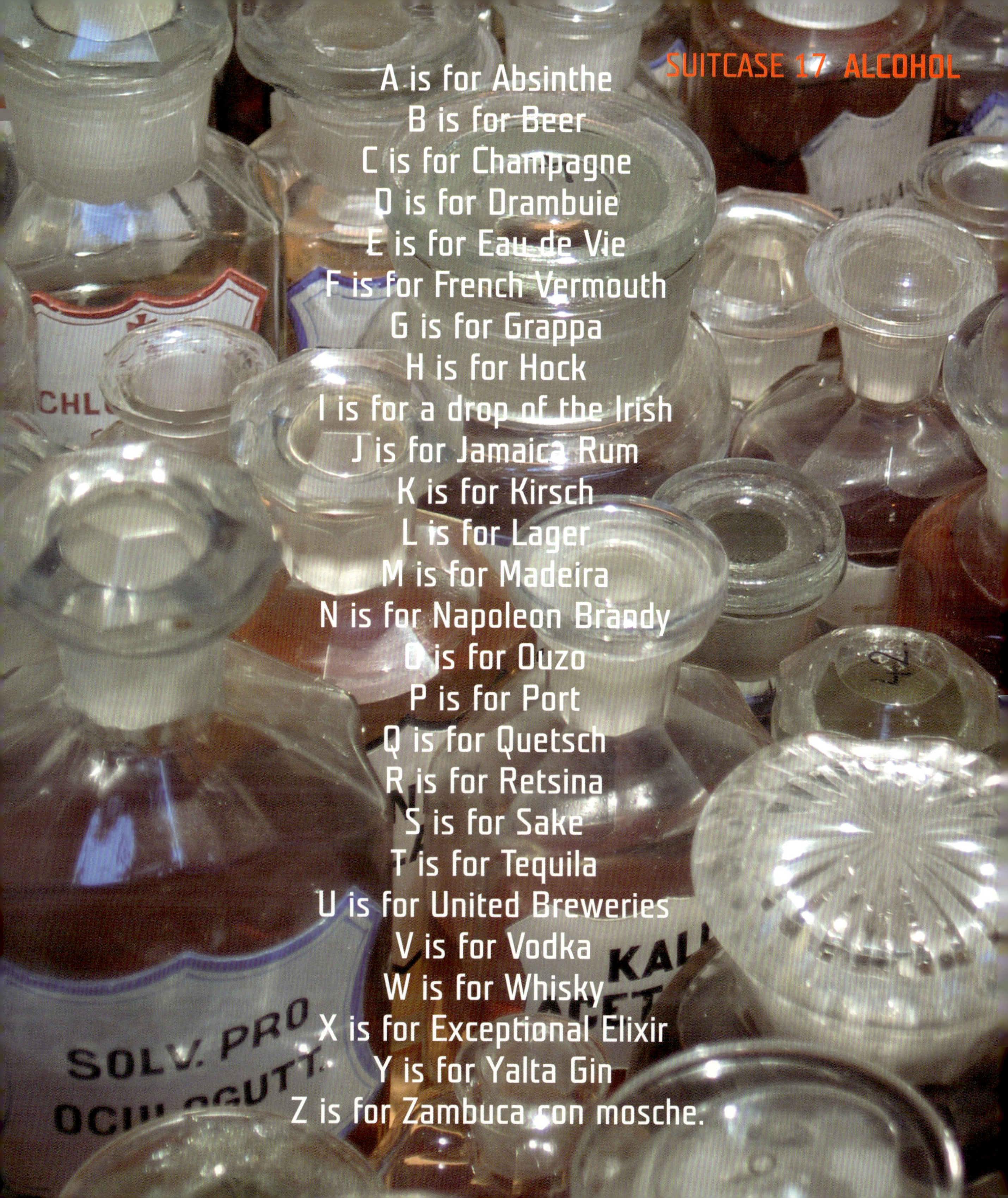

A is for Absinthe
B is for Beer
C is for Champagne
D is for Drambuie
E is for Eau-de Vie
F is for French Vermouth
G is for Grappa
H is for Hock
I is for a drop of the Irish
J is for Jamaica Rum
K is for Kirsch
L is for Lager
M is for Madeira
N is for Napoleon Brandy
O is for Ouzo
P is for Port
Q is for Quetsch
R is for Retsina
S is for Sake
T is for Tequila
U is for United Breweries
V is for Vodka
W is for Whisky
X is for Exceptional Elixir
Y is for Yalta Gin
Z is for Zambuca con mosche.

SUITCASE 18 PERFUME

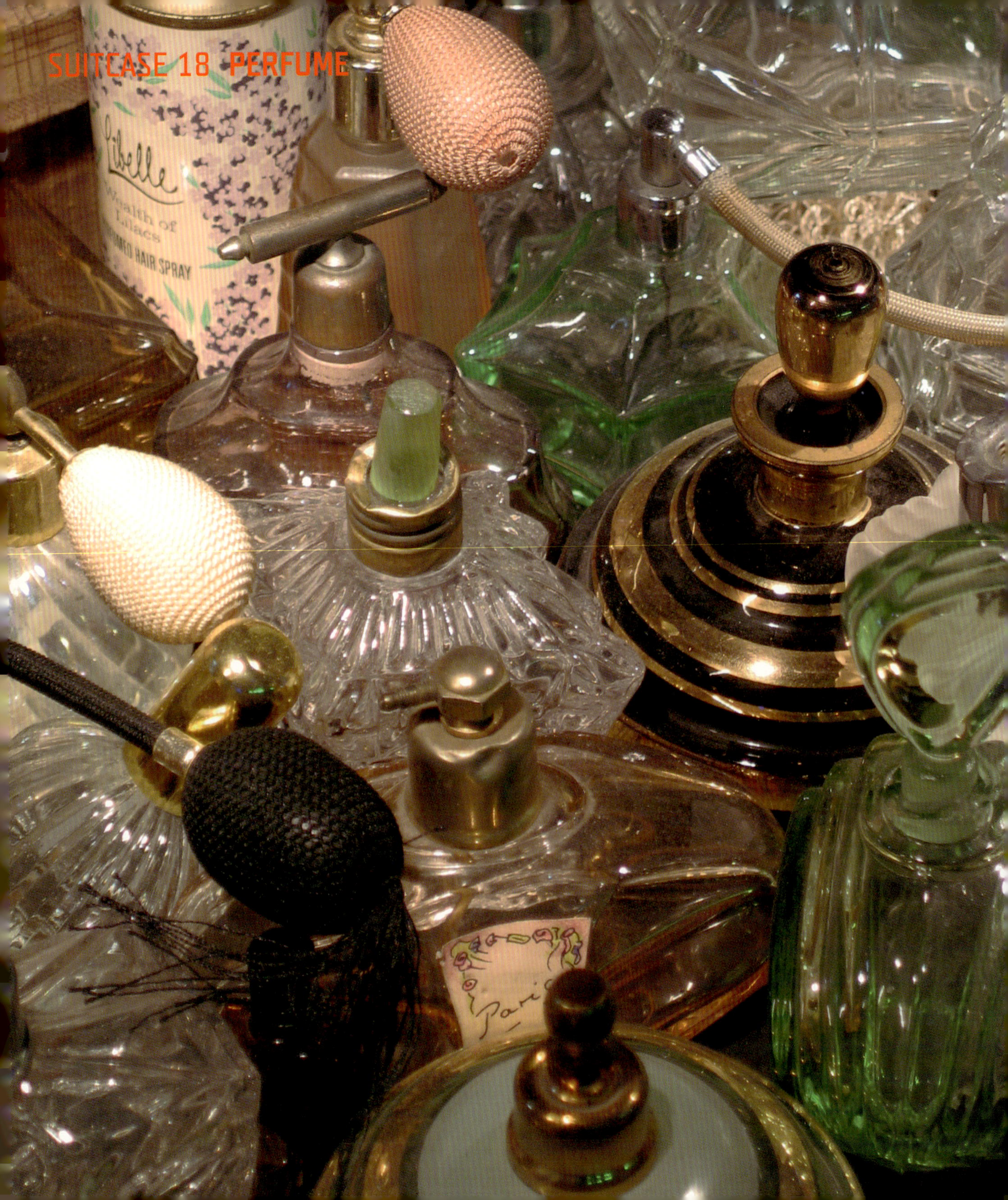

SUITCASE 19 PASSPORTS

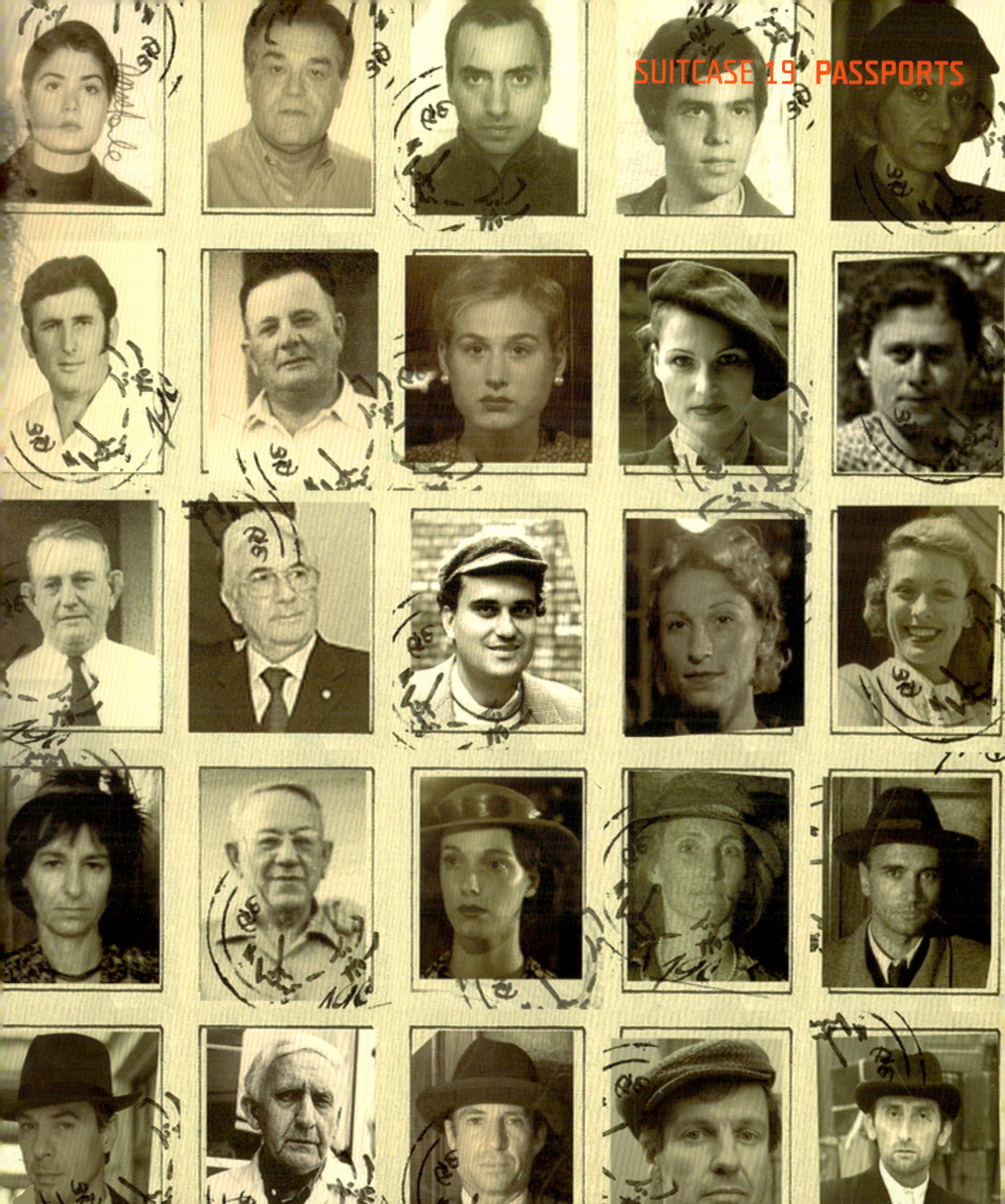

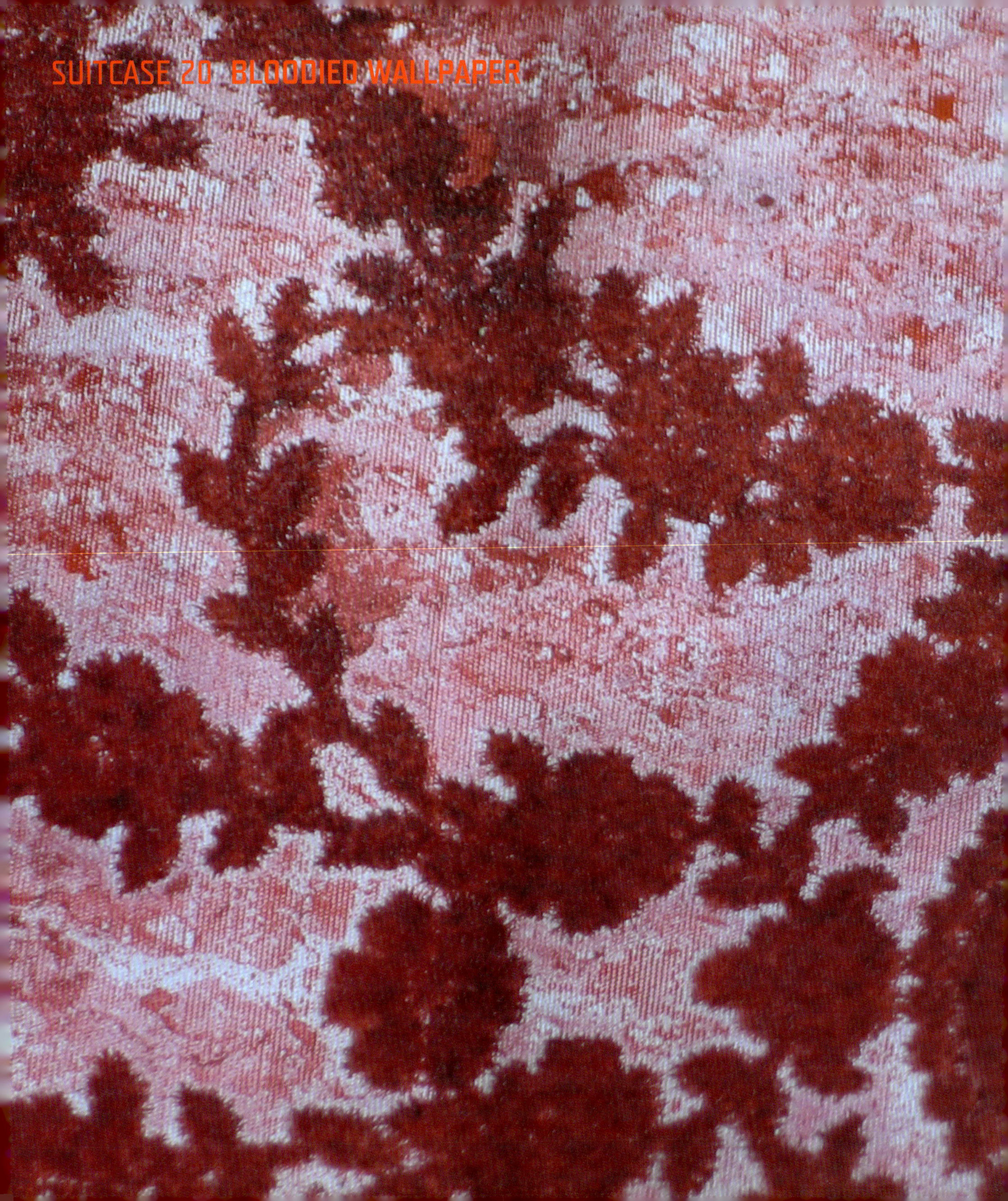

SUITCASE 20 BLOODIED WALLPAPER

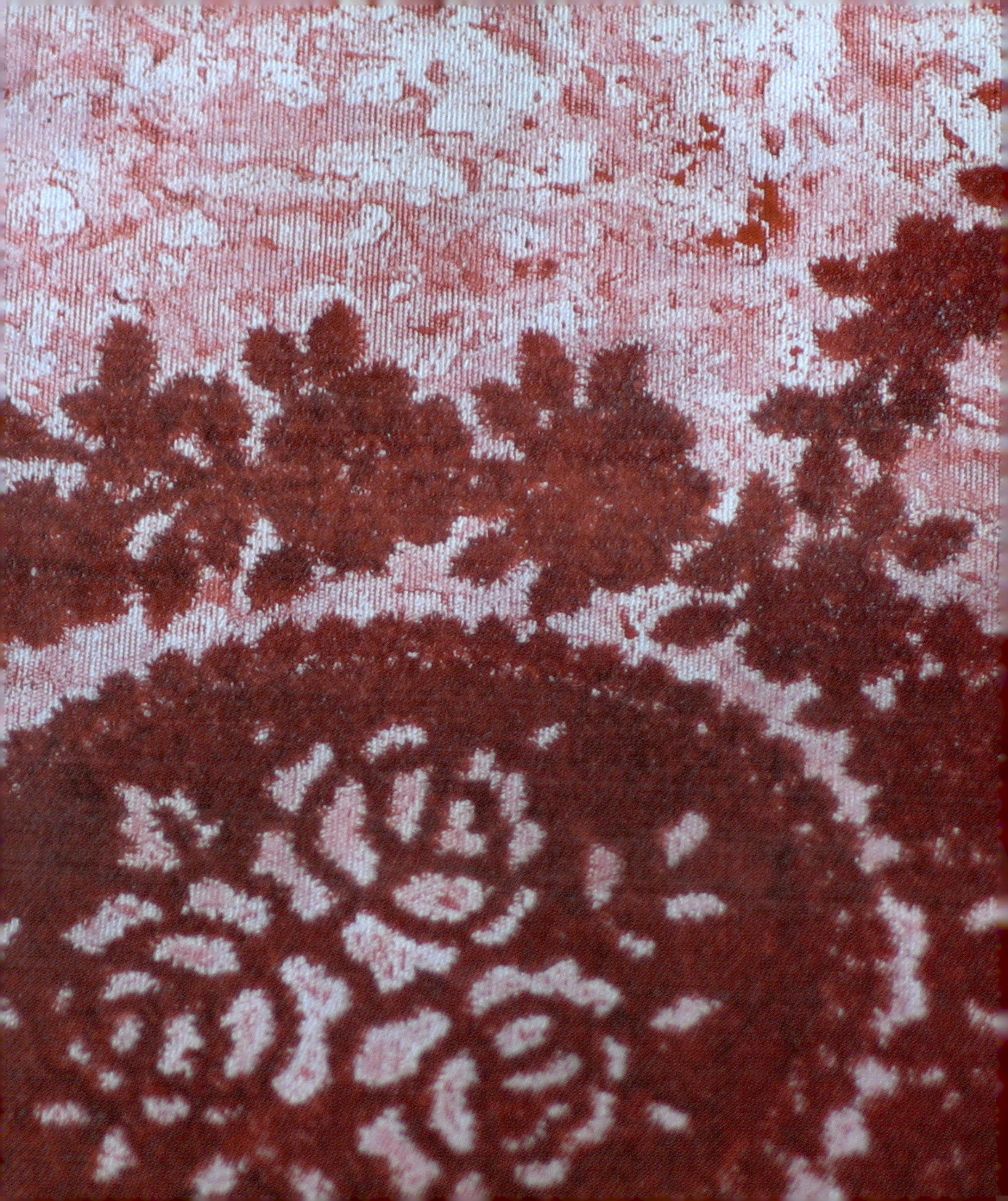

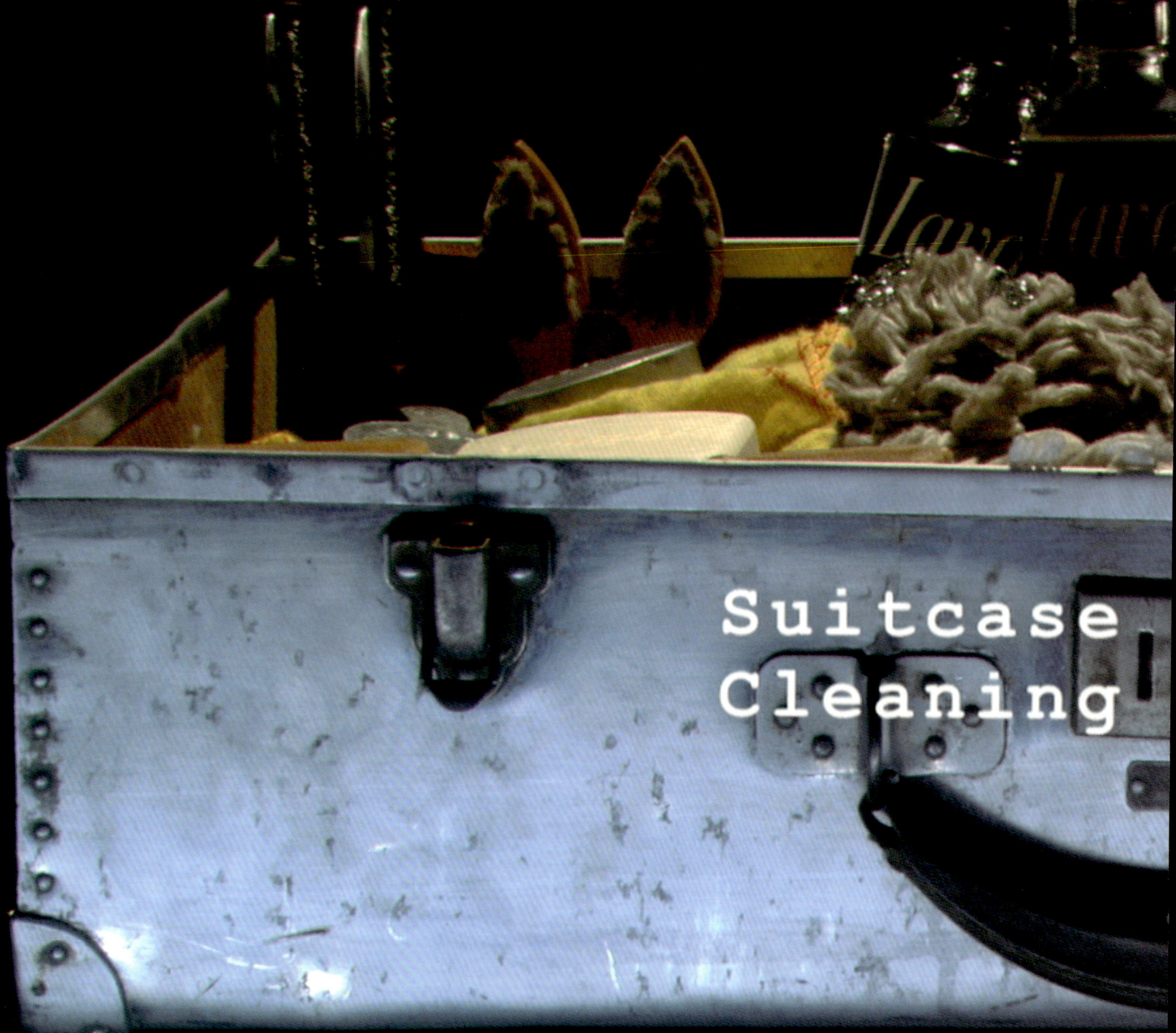
Suitcase
Cleaning

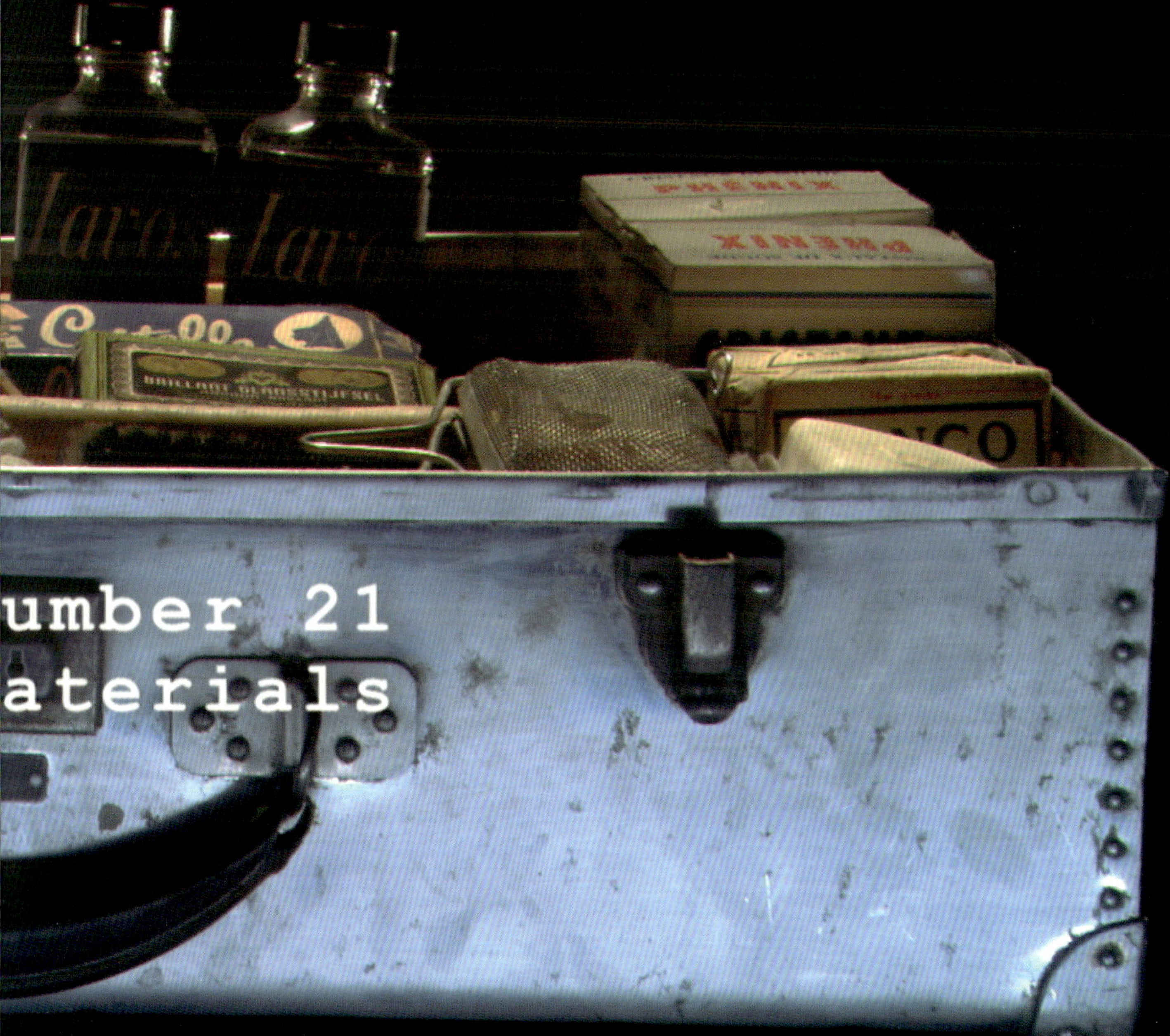
umber 21
aterials

Painless Dentistry.

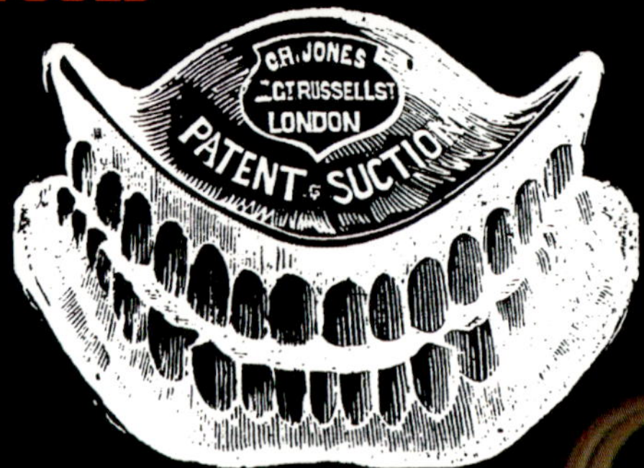

ARTIFICIAL TEETH.

Mr. G. H. JONES, Surgeon Dentist,

57 GREAT RUSSELL STREET, LONDON, W.C.,

(Immediately opposite the British Museum),

Has obtained

HER MAJESTY'S ROYAL LETTERS PATENT

For his improved method of adapting

Artificial Teeth by Atmospheric Pressure.

Note.—Improved Prize Medal Teeth (London and Paris) are adapted in the most difficult and delicate cases, on a perfectly painless system, extraction of loose teeth or stumps being unnecessary, and by recent scientific discoveries and improvements in mechanical dentistry detection is rendered utterly impossible, both by close adjustment of the artificial teeth to the gums and their life-like appearance. By this patented invention complete mastication, extreme lightness, combined with strength and durability, are insured; useless bulk being obviated, articulation is rendered clear and distinct. In the administration of Nitrous Oxide Gas, Mr. G. H. Jones has introduced an entirely new process.

TESTIMONIAL.

My Dear Sir,—Allow me to express my sincere thanks for the skill and attention displayed in the construction of my Artificial Teeth, which renders my mastication and articulation excellent. I am glad to hear that you have obtained Her Majesty's Royal Letters Patent, to protect what I consider the perfection of Painless Dentistry. In recognition of your valuable services you are at liberty to use my name.

S. G. HUTCHINS,
By appointment Surgeon Dentist to the Queen.

To G. H. JONES, Esq.

PAMPHLET GRATIS AND POST-FREE.

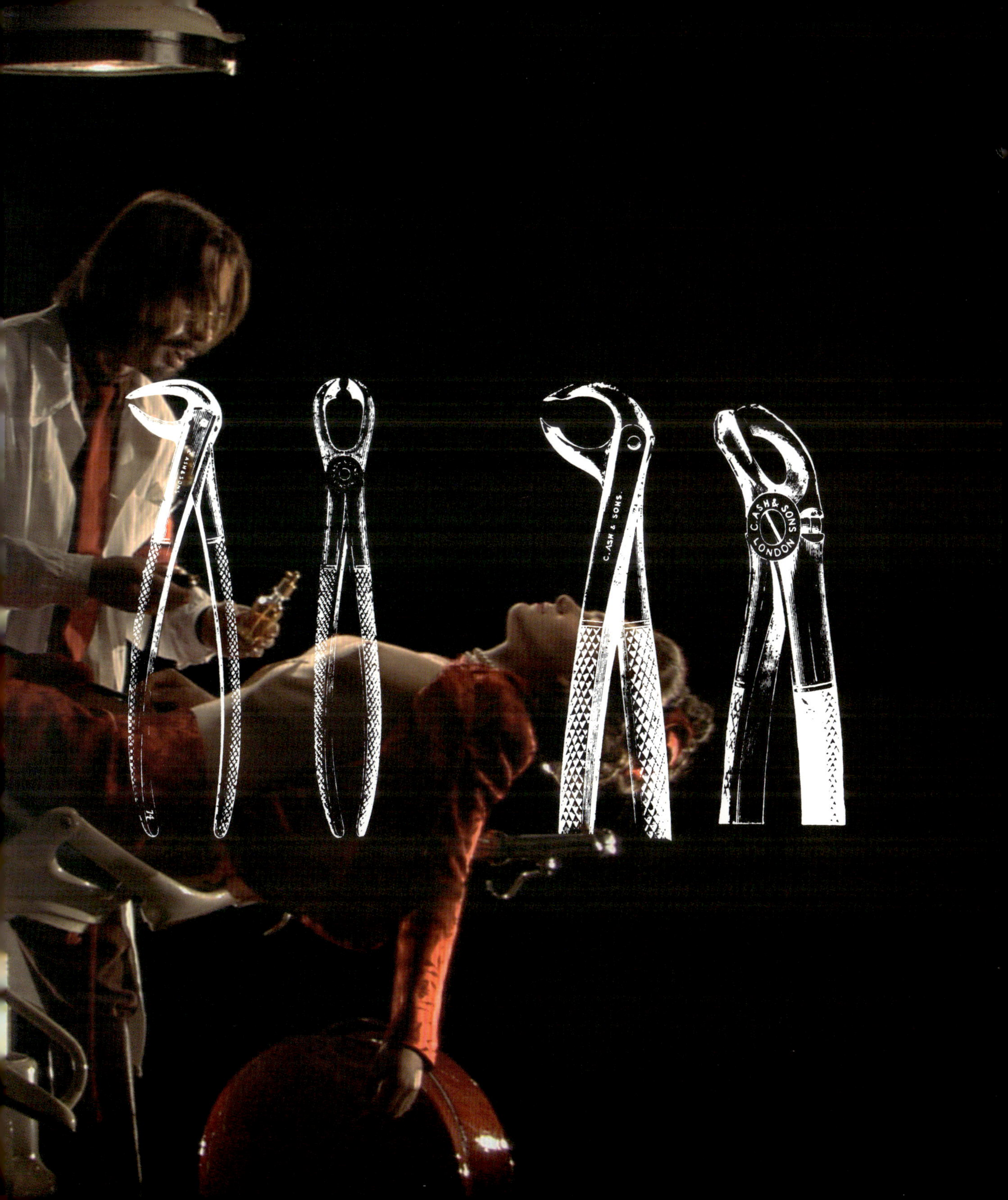
C. ASH & SONS.
C. ASH & SONS
LONDON

SUITCASE 23 **CHERRIES**

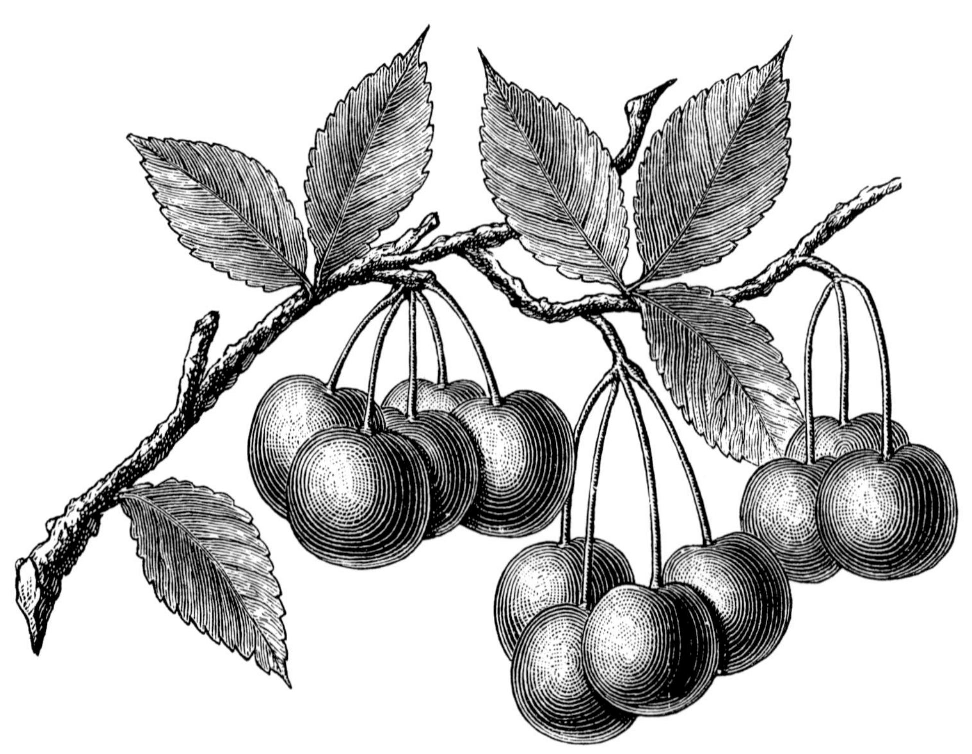

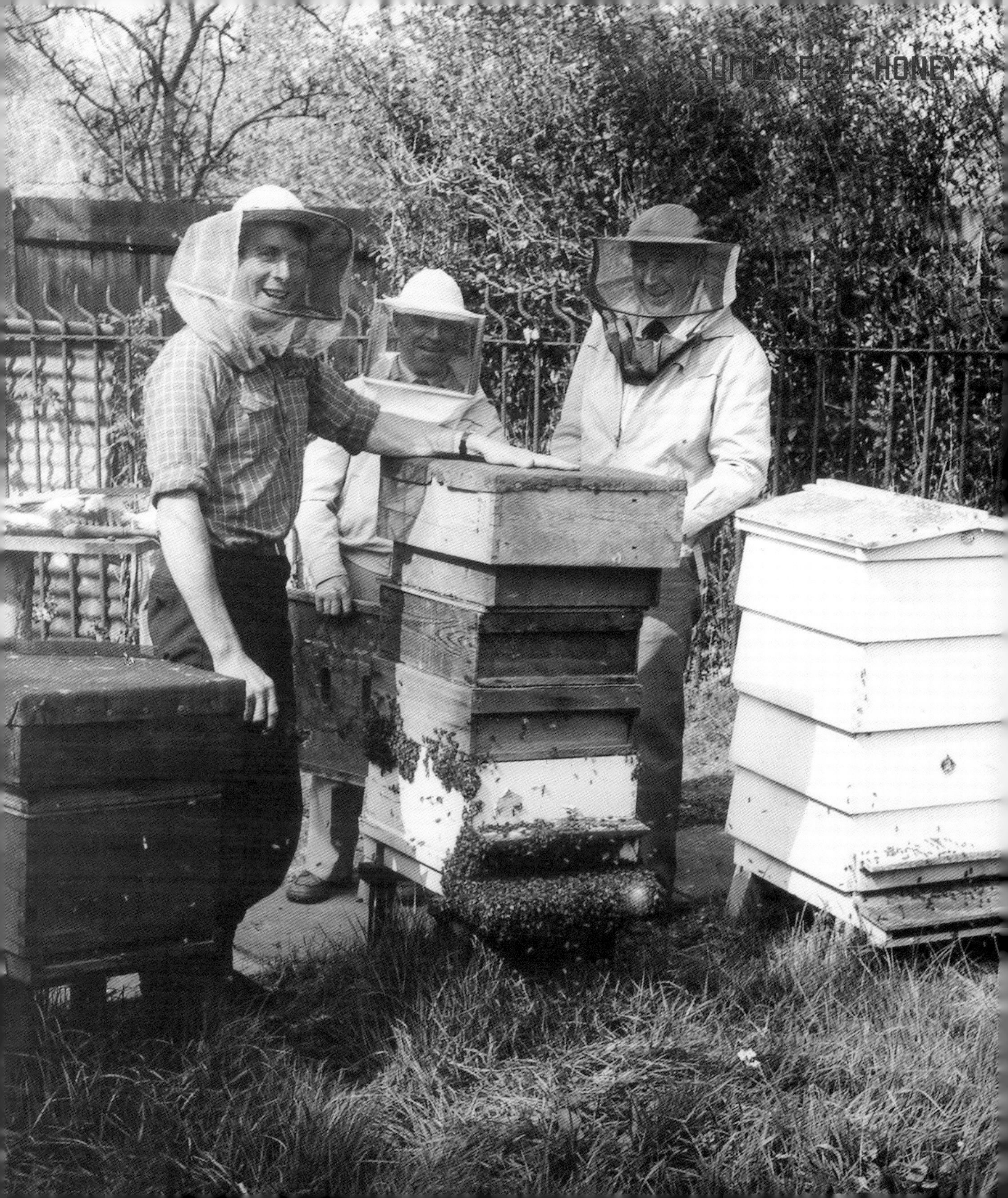

SUITCASE 25 NUMBERS & LETTERS

teacher teacher teacher

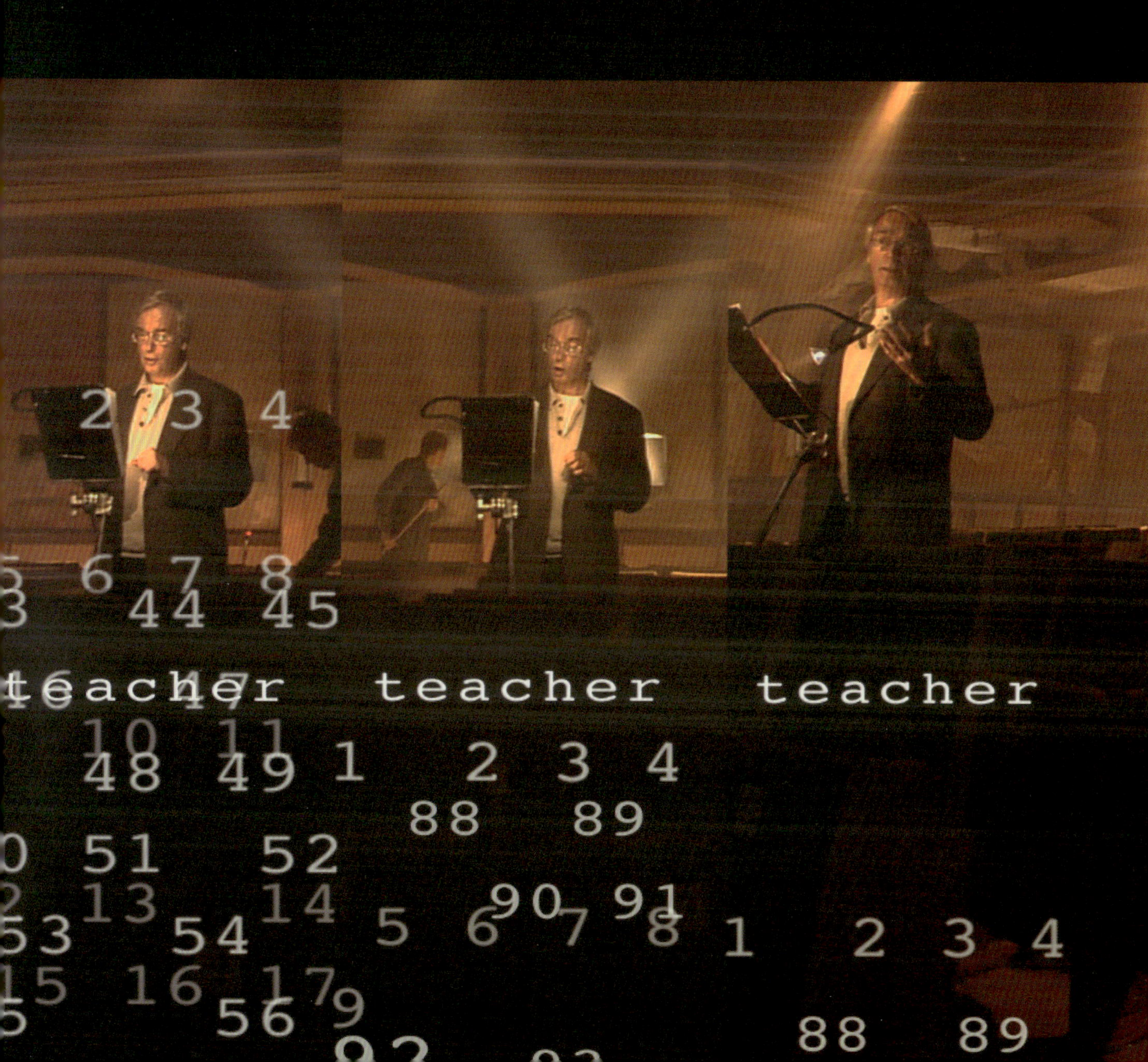
2 3 4
6 7 8
44 45
teacher teacher teacher
10 11
48 49 1 2 3 4
88 89
51 52
13 14 90 91
53 54 5 6 7 8 1 2 3 4
15 16 17 9
56
88 89

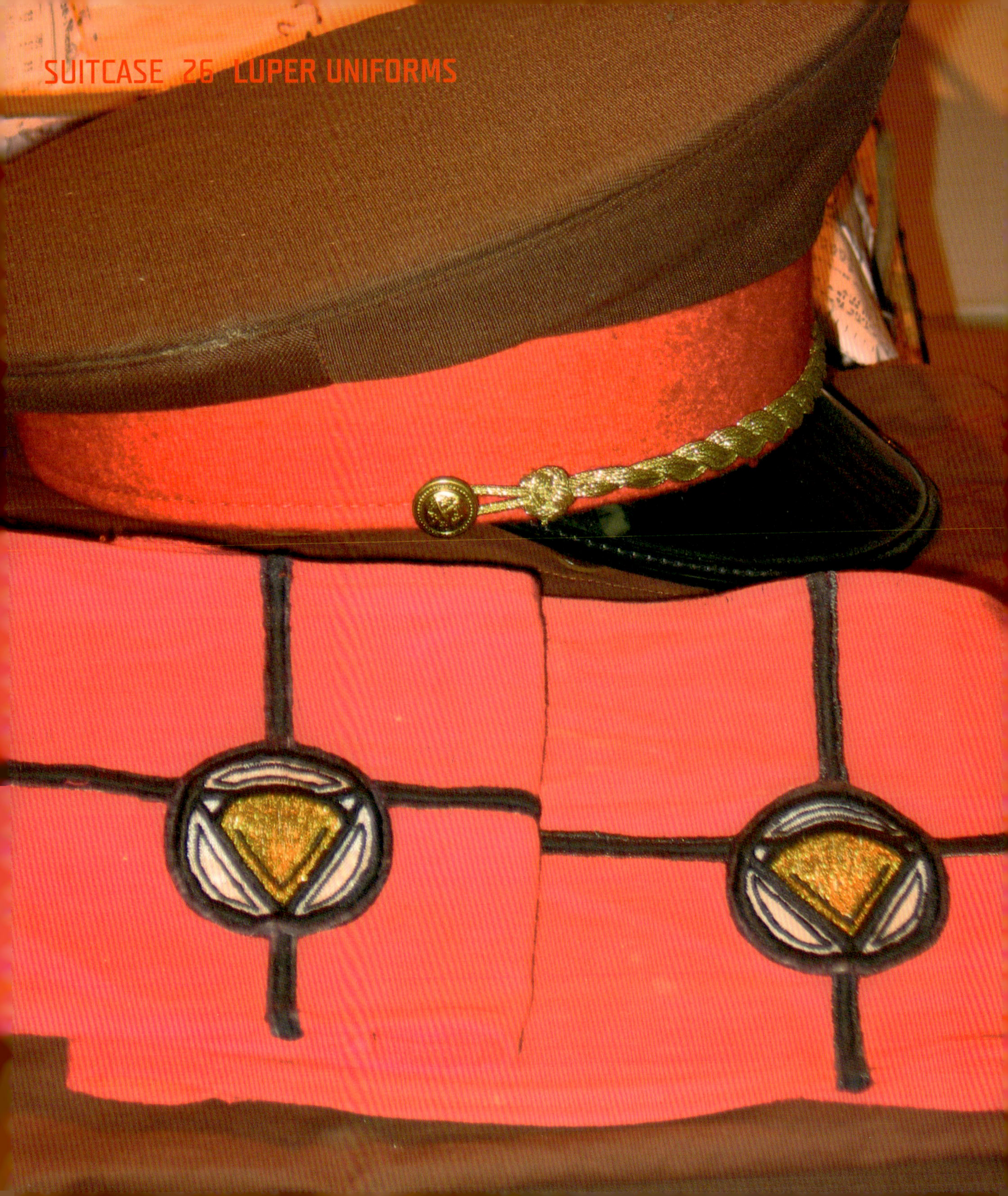

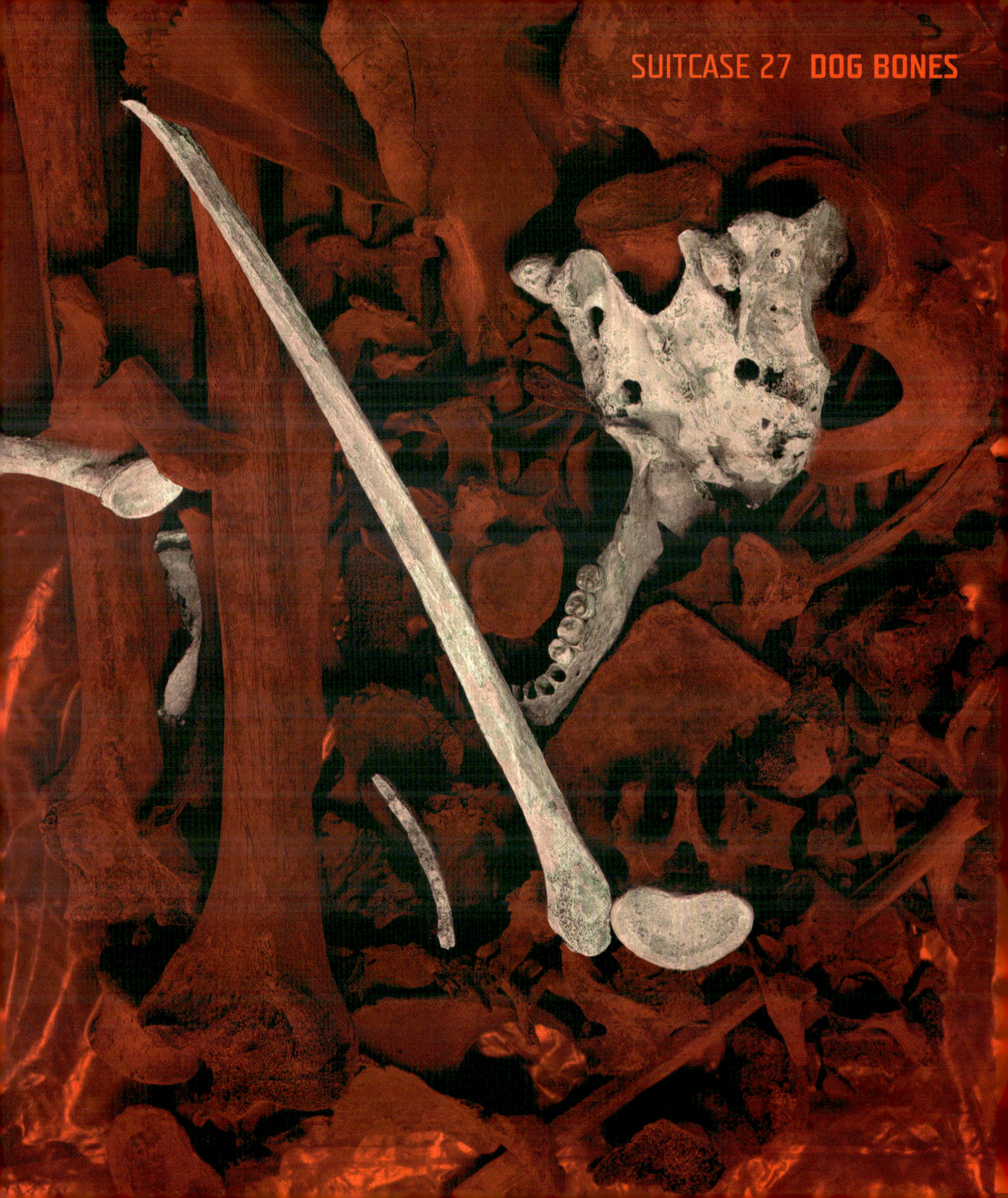
SUITCASE 27 DOG BONES

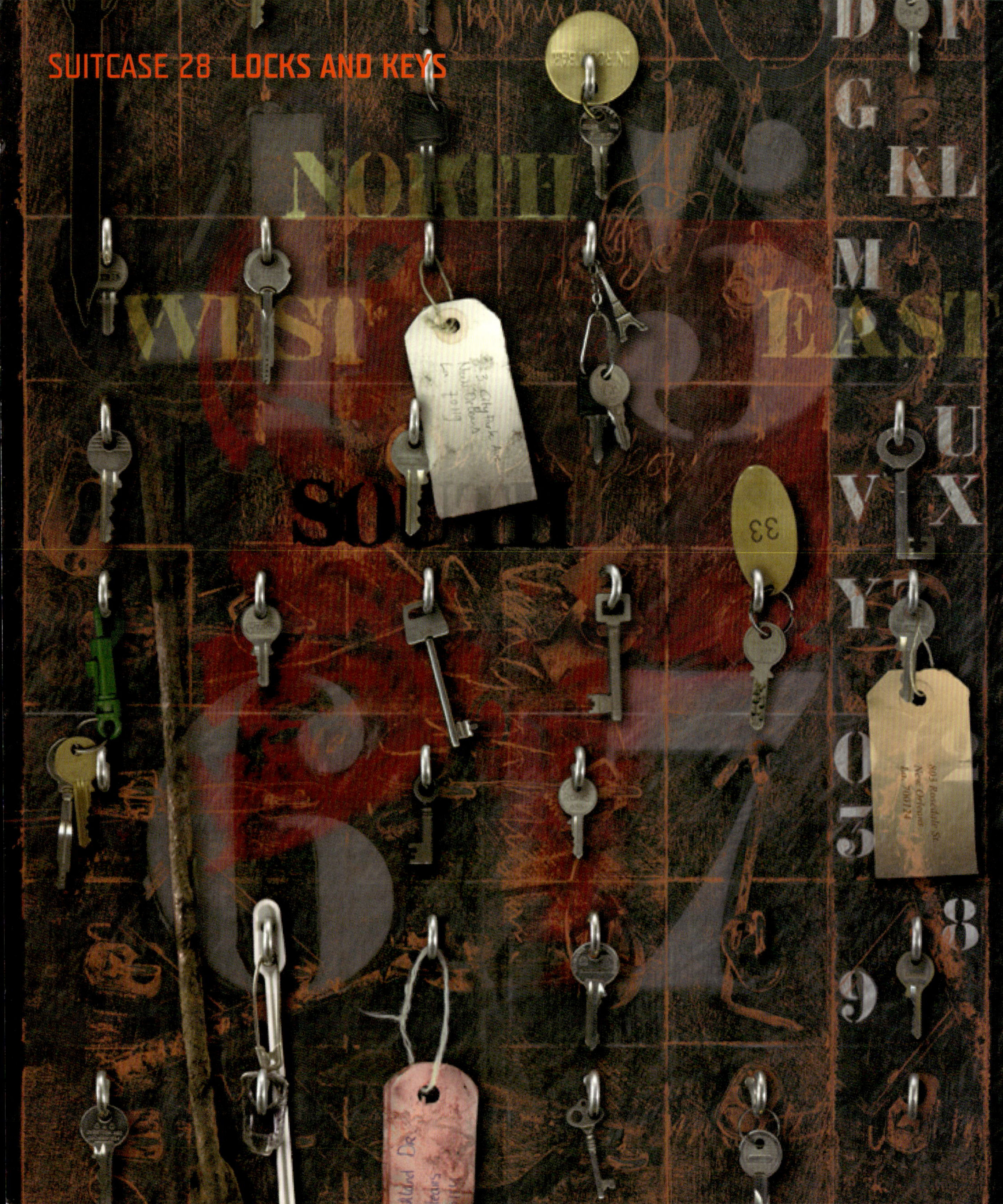
NORTH
WEST
EAST
SOUTH
33

SUITCASE 29 LIGHT-BULBS

SUITCASE 30 PLACE-NAMES

ROMA STAZIONE TERMINI
PARIS
LYON
GENOA
RAPALLO
LA SPEZIA
PISA
FIRENZE
GHENT
AMERTENDEN
MAASTRICHT
IDENHOVEN
VAN DEIMENLAND
MENILMONTANT
L'EPEE VERDE
FONTENAY
GUSTAVIA
EIFFELO
BUSTARDA FILO
PICARDO POSTO
L'ESCARGOT DE ARC-EN-CIEL
COLOMBE-LES-DEUX-EGLISES
POMPONIO AUGUSTUS
VAUX LE VICOMTE
BEAUREGARD-EN-MER
SANTA PHILOMENA
ROMARIGRAD
LEISENDROGRAD
BADEN MARIENBADEN
CARCASSONE
MACARADOTTE
APRES-ROUGE
MARMONTIERE
APENSTOCKHAUSEN
VALENCIENNES FILS
FANJEAUX
BLUE STAG BAY
SAARBRUCKEN
MIREAUPOIX
CREVECOEUR
REGIS AUGUSTINO
EPEN SANDS
AGRIGENTO
CAFFERELLI
AEGYPTO RUSTINA

LAMPEDUSA
CIMAROSA
SANTA POMPONIO
CASTELLO DEL MONTE
ASSASSINO
CASTRICASTROS
LASTERINO
POTTAGER CHINS
ABBAN-ANGENERE
FERRARIO
BOLESTERLAAN
SANTA SANDRIA
PESTERENDER
LAESTORI
HARPENSTADIA
GAETANELLI
BENEVENTURA
RIPOSTE
PARAY-LE-MONDIAL
GROGAROSTORA
KNOCKALL MAISTER
BOCKERESTER
MUCKLEBURY STEPS
MINKSARIA
POLOCKI

CARLSBURGEN
LEIDENFRAG
ESTERHAZY MENARES
BORISTAVARI
THEYDON BOYES
MEYDEN DEN LARGO
SANTA BARBARINO
ARIES
POSTONBERRY EDGE
ST CLOUD EN MER
AUGSBERGENFELDT
COMPTON ANSTY
OLIVIANO
ST SEBASTIANO DEL
BORGO
PRATOLINO SPATS
STUNFASTNET
ARCANTINI
RIPPOROLLO
DISS STAFFORD DISS
ELEPHANTOSOPHIA
INKERING
DIDEROT STAYS
ZASTERAYS
BOCHERLIN

SUITCASE 31: BOOTS AND SHOES

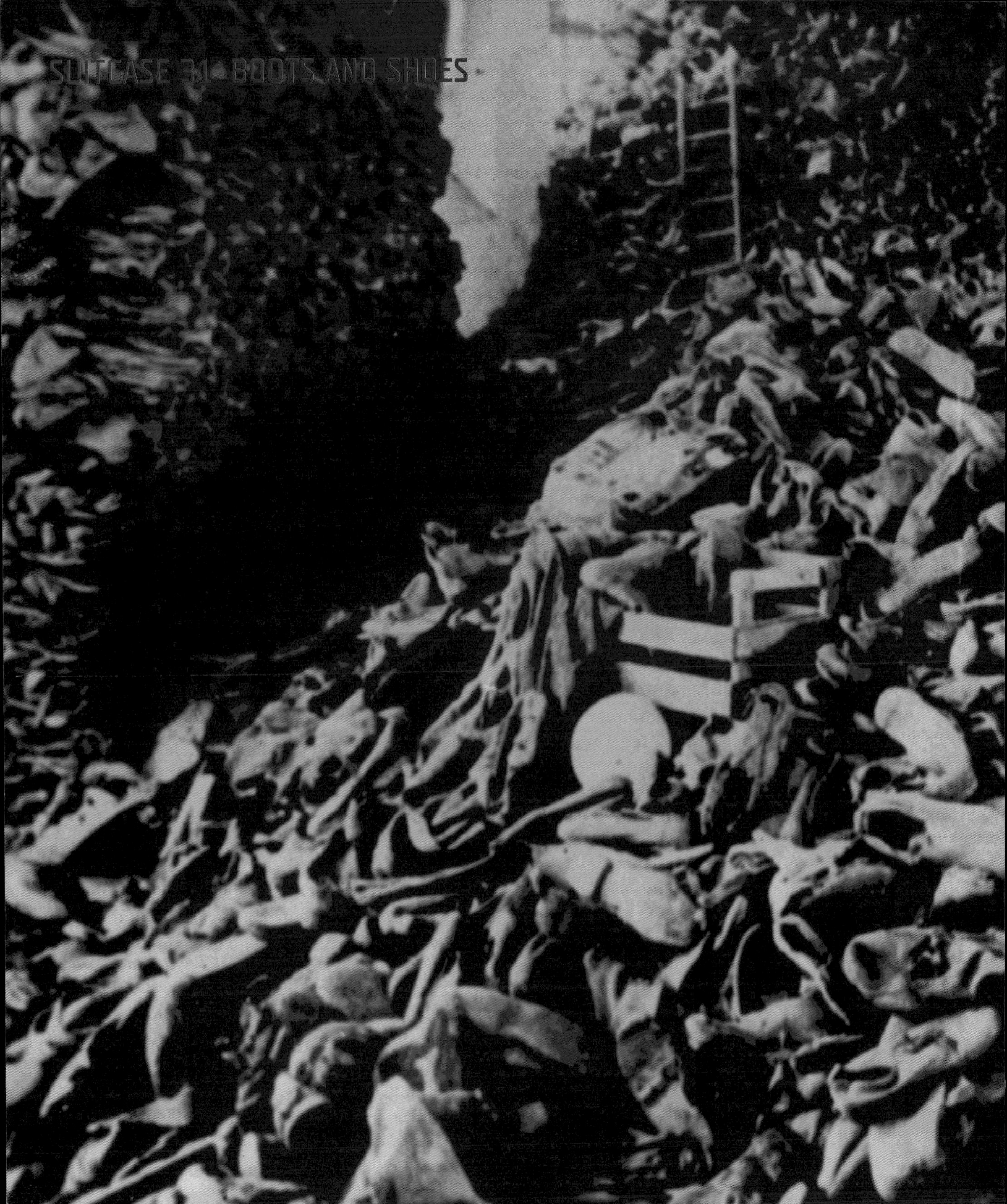

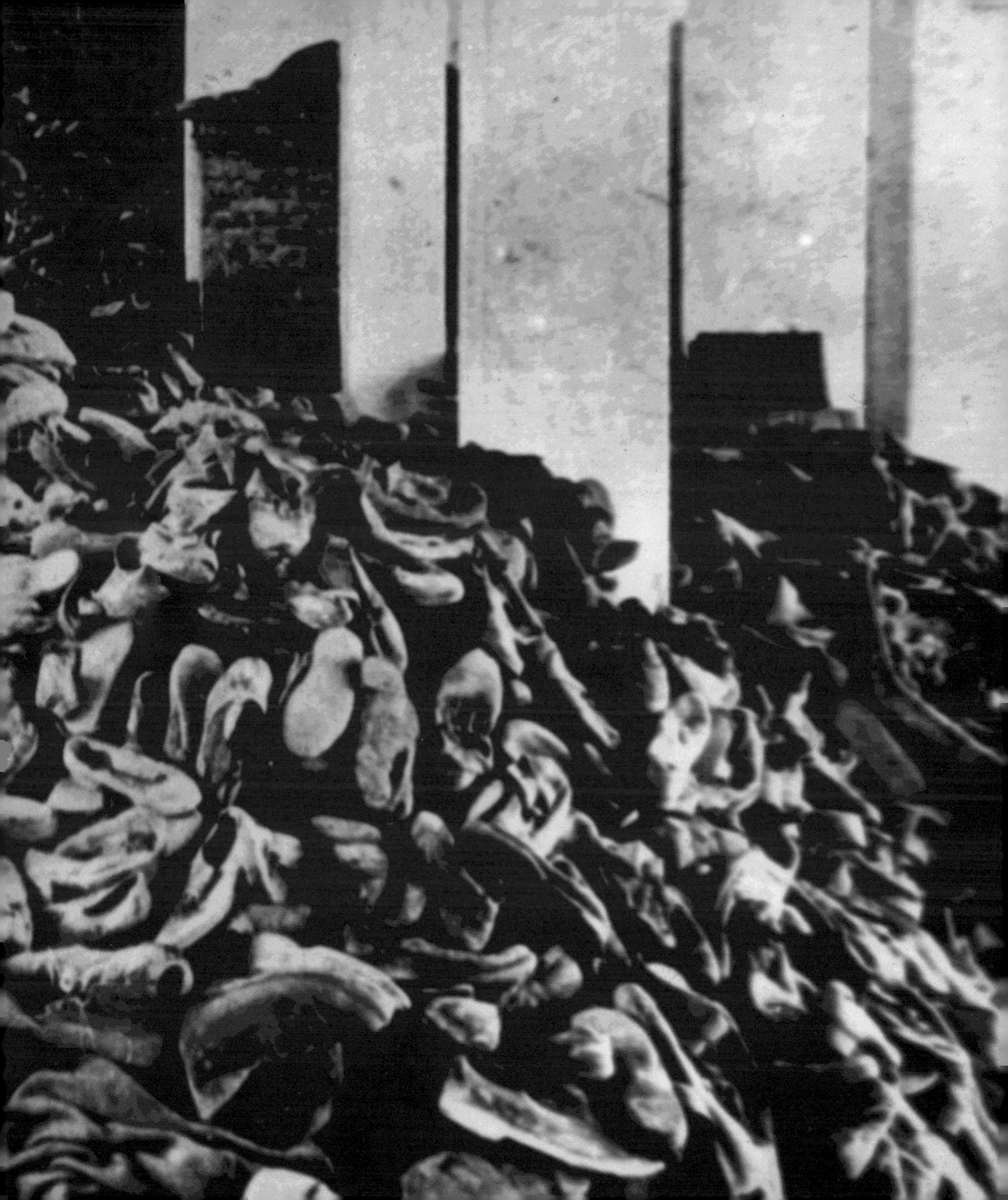

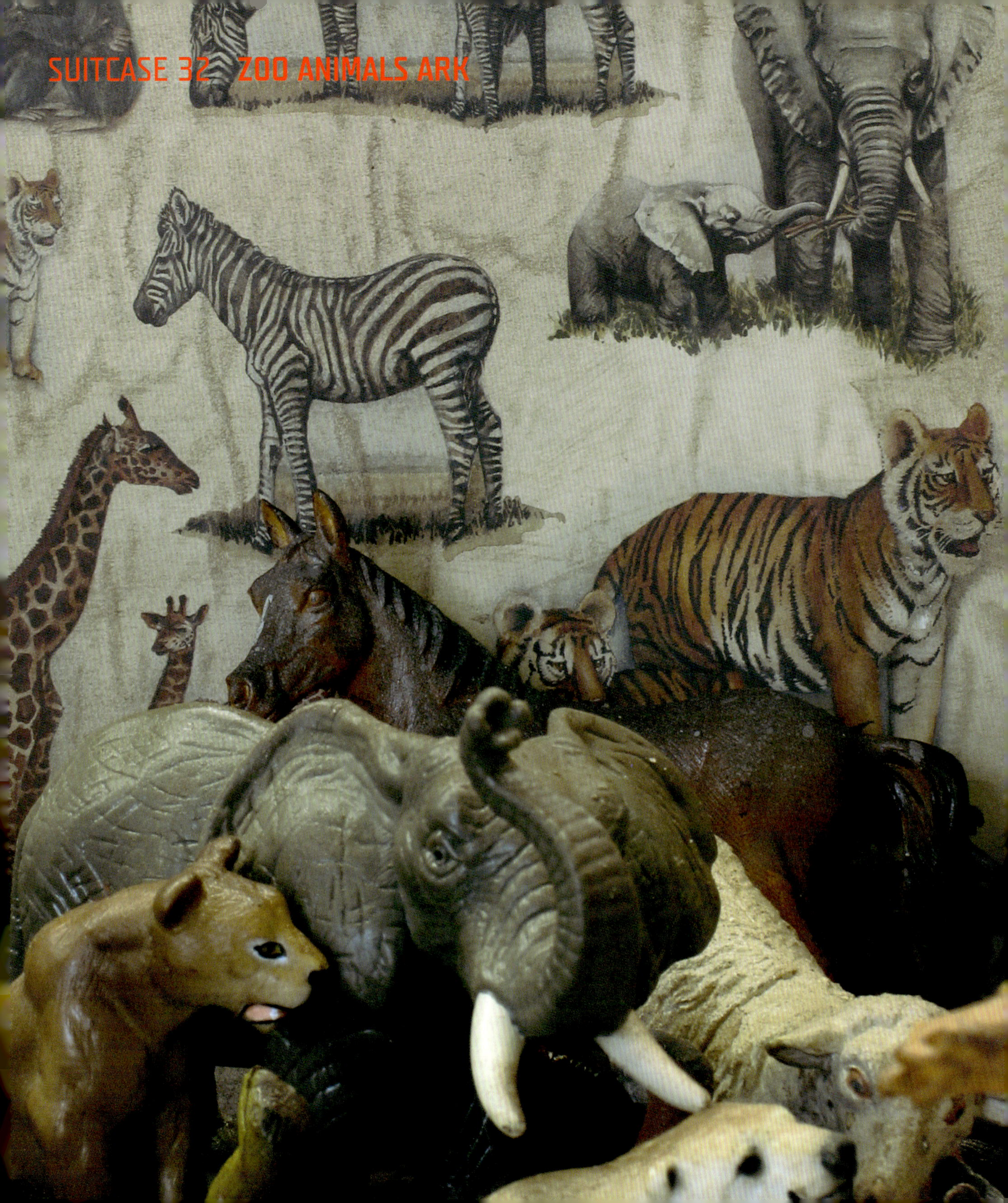

SUITCASE 32 ZOO ANIMALS ARK

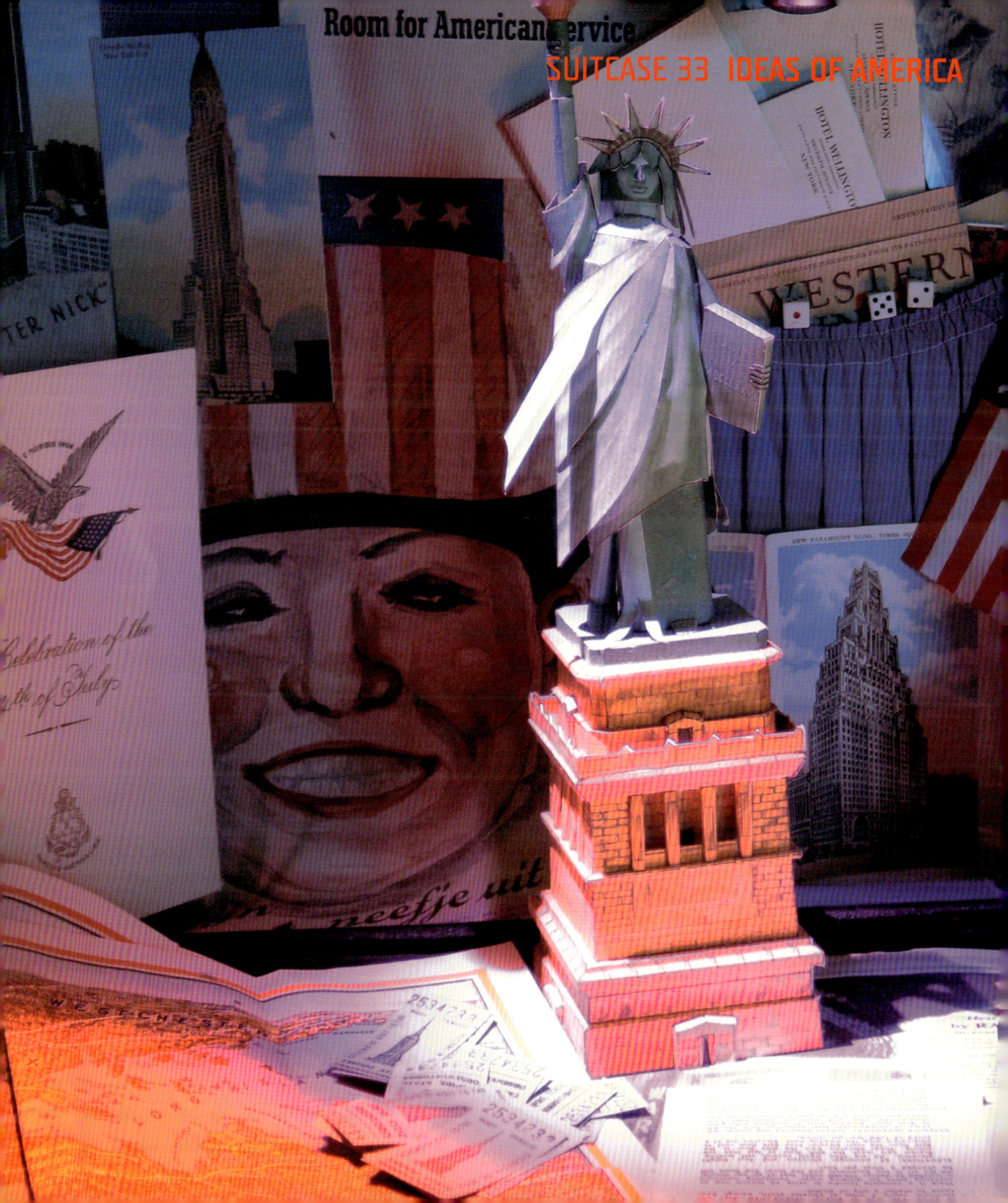

SUITCASE 33 IDEAS OF AMERICA

SUITCASE 34 **ANNA KARENINA NOVELS**

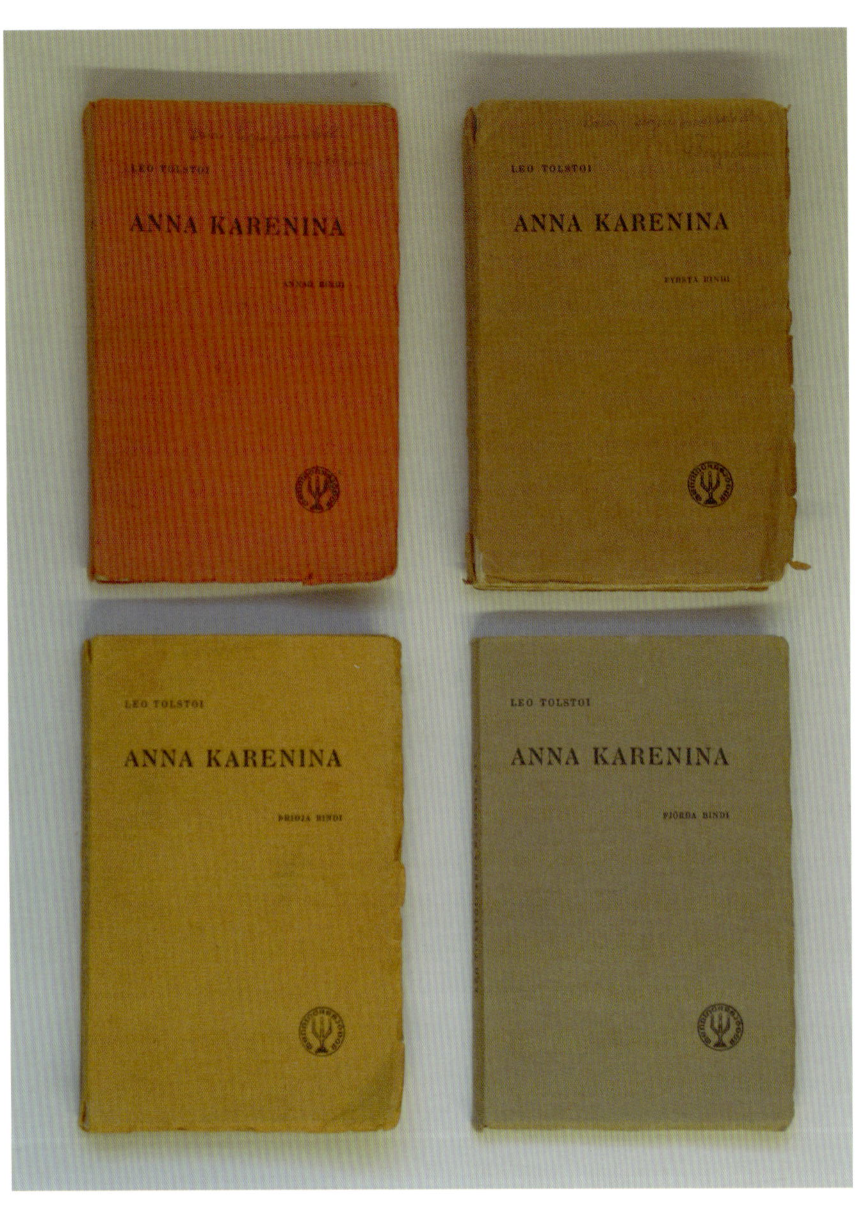

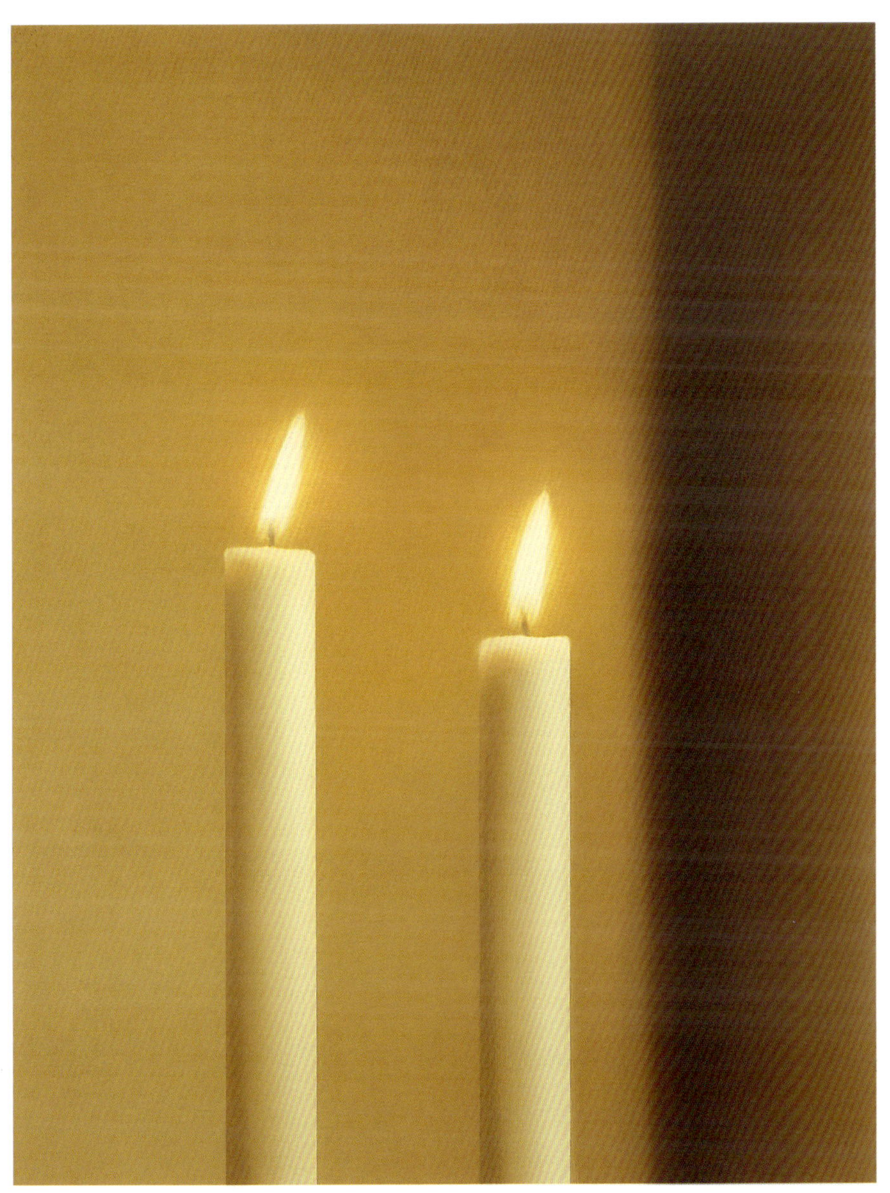

SUITCASE 36 RADIO EQUIPMENT

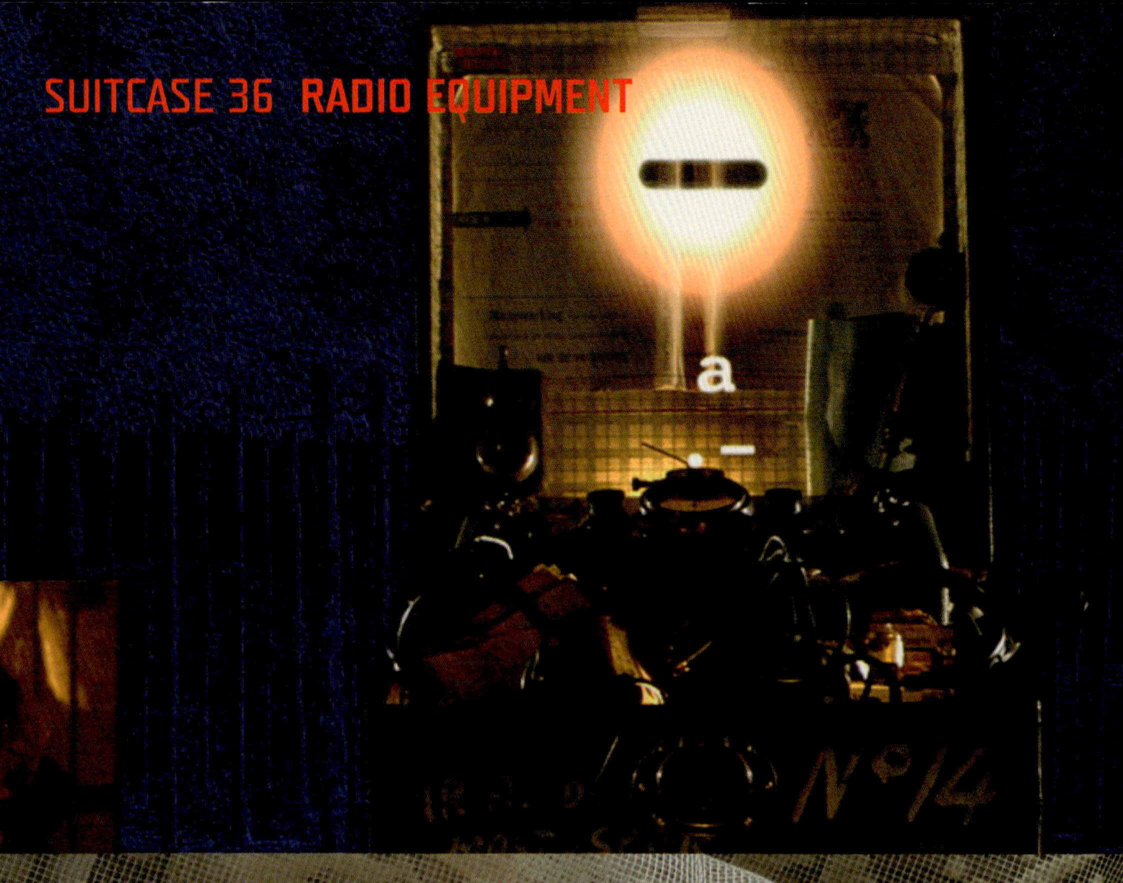

SUITCASE 37 CLEAN LINEN

LUPER

Is a list such a simple thing? Take the most obvious one - a laundry list. Two pairs of sheets, four pillow-cases - two plain, two edged in lace, two shirts, two blouses - two white, two off-white. Four vests, four underpants, a white broiderie anglais petticoat.

... a camisole, two pairs of knickers, sixteen pairs of white stockings, a garter-belt, a white damask table-cloth, twelve matching damask napkins ... You see. A whole household is revealed.

All in one colour. Domestic relationships are uncovered. Class, wealth, tensions, extravagances - perhaps a history - even happiness. The imagination of the reader is excited. And the lists can be re-ordered, the catalogues updated. The inventories can embrace everything. Yet all these objects with their histories and associations can be packed in one suitcase.

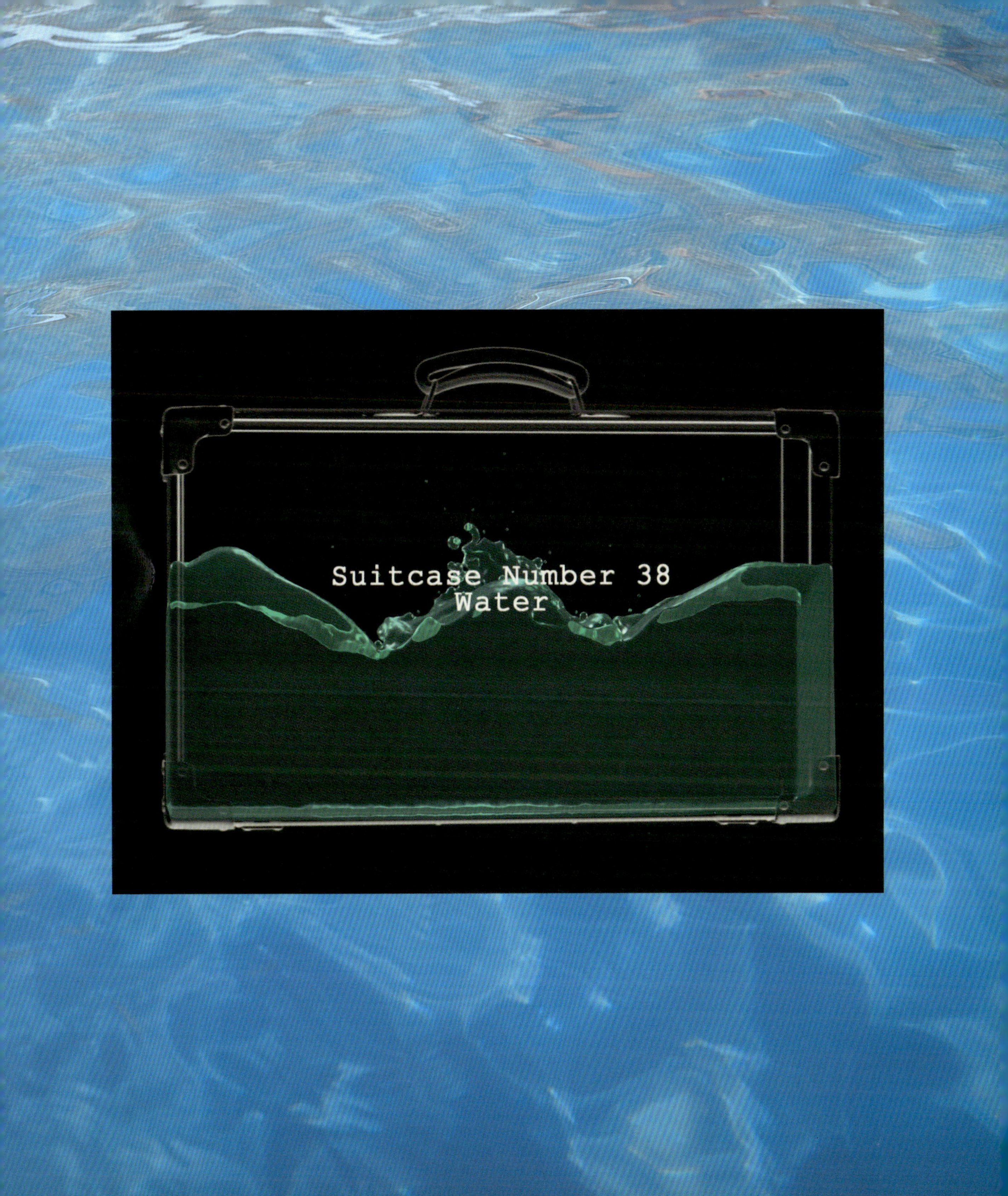
Suitcase Number 38
Water

ge ehndee sehbeeohteaehge
reentea steauff when the
ehuteyeyeful, soh gareeen e
eehnge ehndee beeareohwn

Suitcase Co

wohuldee neveare eveare

ehndee undeeeareseauarea
wohohdees lohohk soh beee
ndee yellohw ehndee ohar
ehndee seaareeyemsohn, eh
eareme
we de

Number 39

eah eh
deeohn't we? Ehndee Eye
nk ehn

de

esy eh
th the
well,
mehnne
beear
aree u
hyeng
ohare
enseah
beee, even eyef yohuare e

SUITCASE 40 A SLEEPER

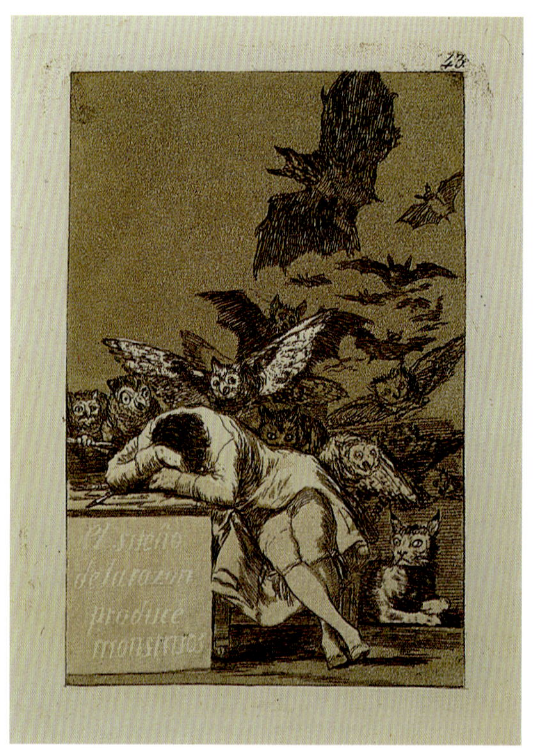

SUITCASE 41 EROTIC ENGRAVINGS

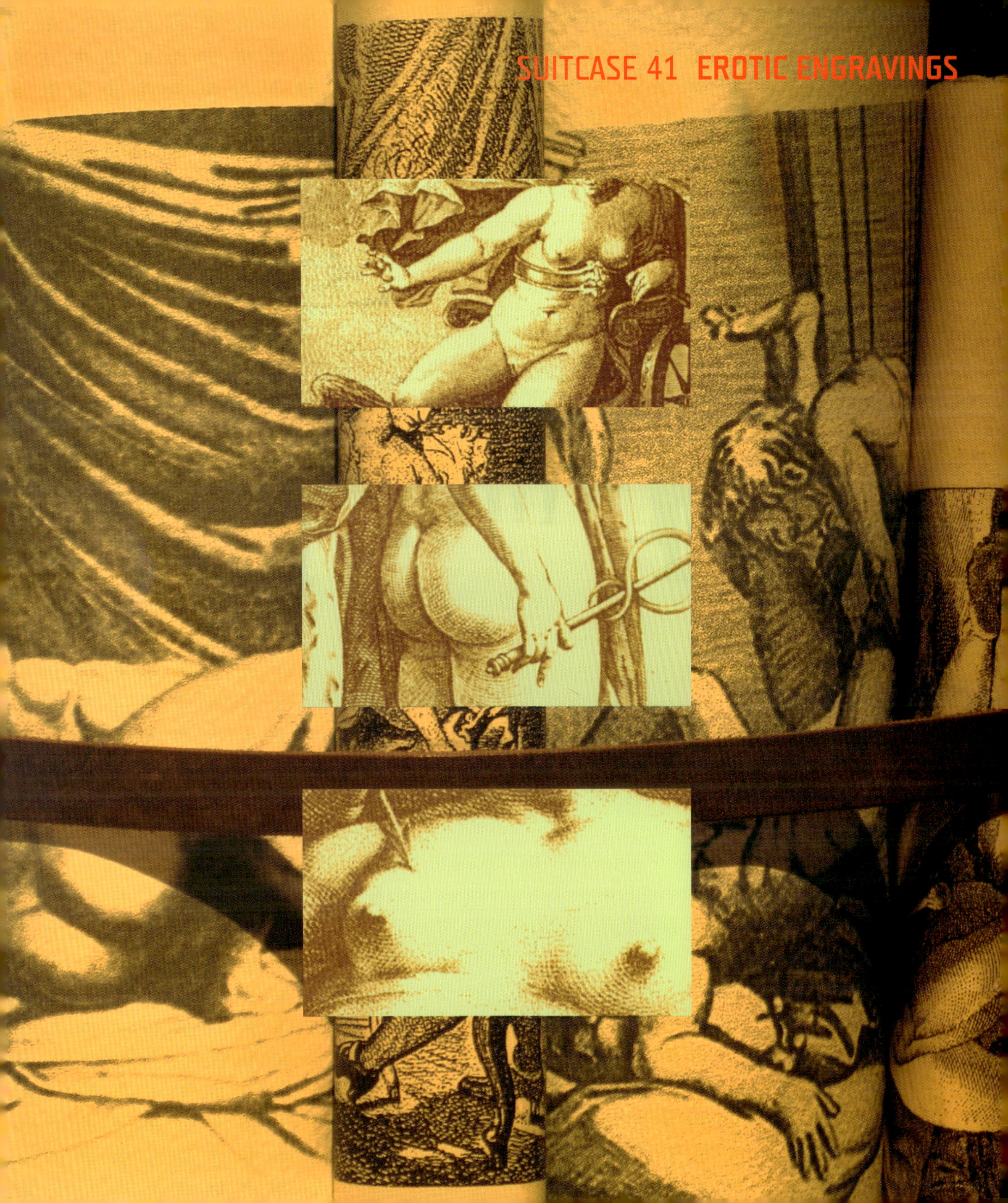

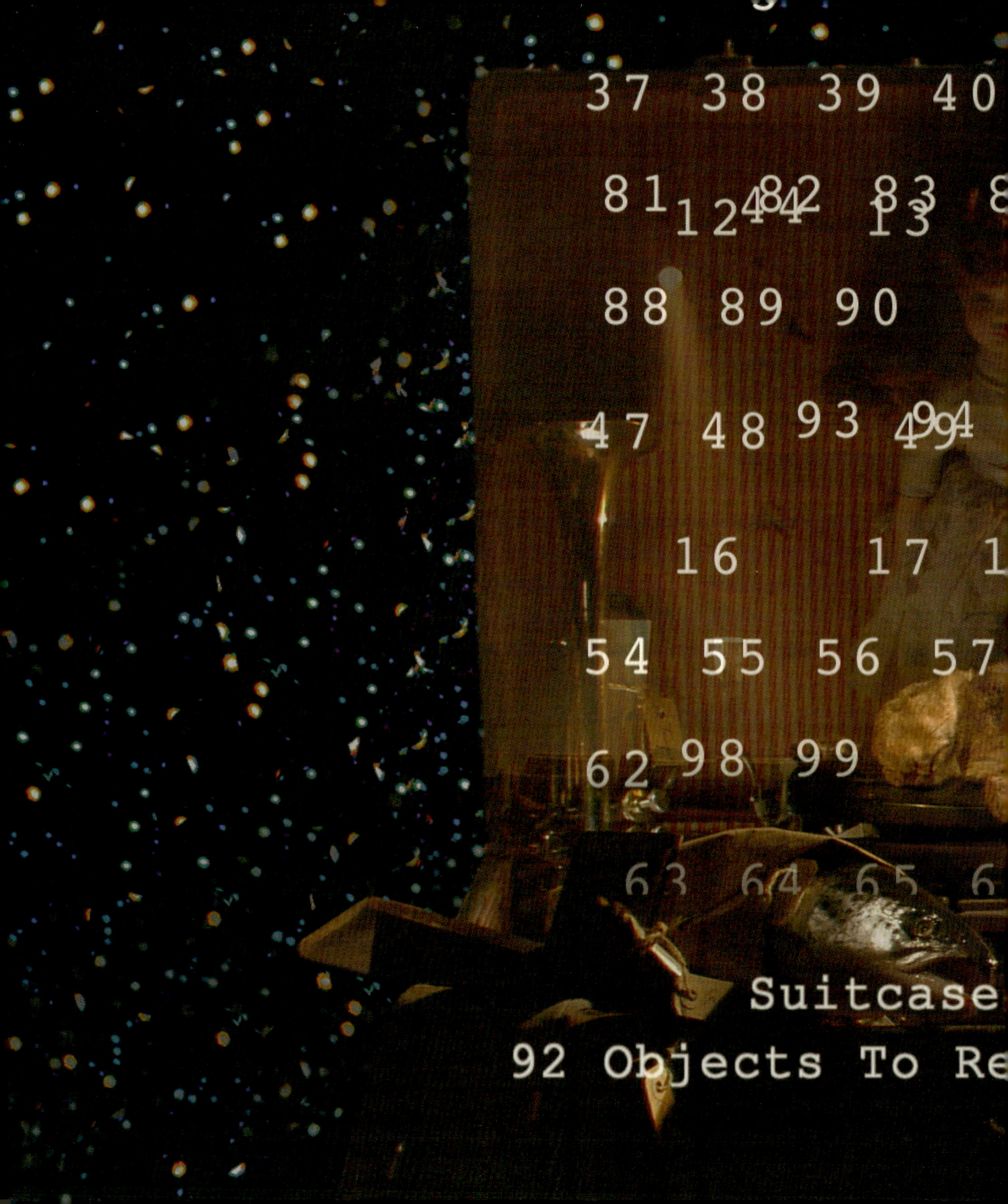

37 38 39 40

81 82 83 8
12 44 13

88 89 90

47 48 93 94 49

16 17 1

54 55 56 57

62 98 99

63 64 65 6

Suitcase

92 Objects To Re

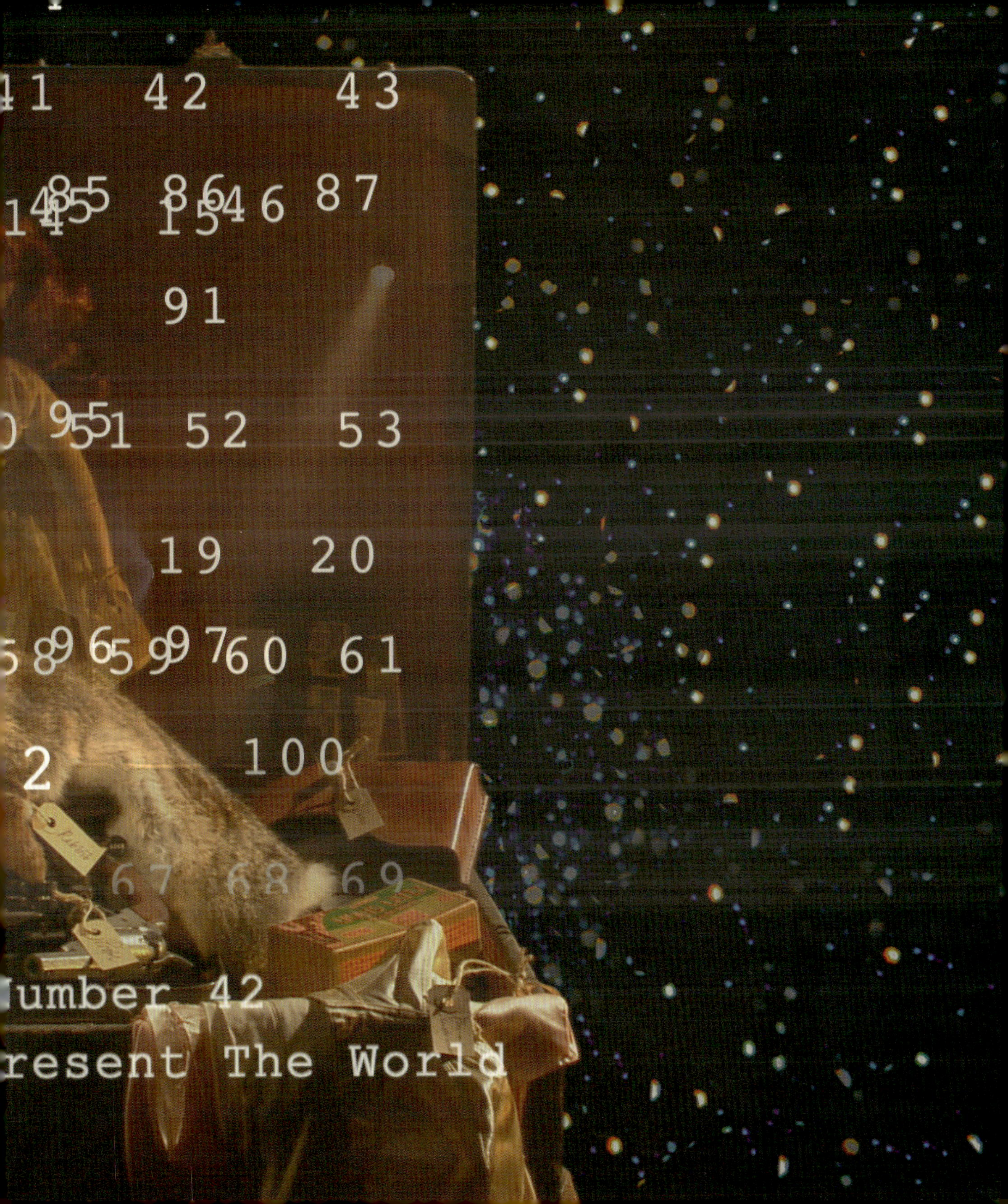

41 42 43

85 86 87

14 15 46

91

95 1 52 53

19 20

5 8 96 59 97 60 61

2 100

67 68 69

umber 42

resent The World

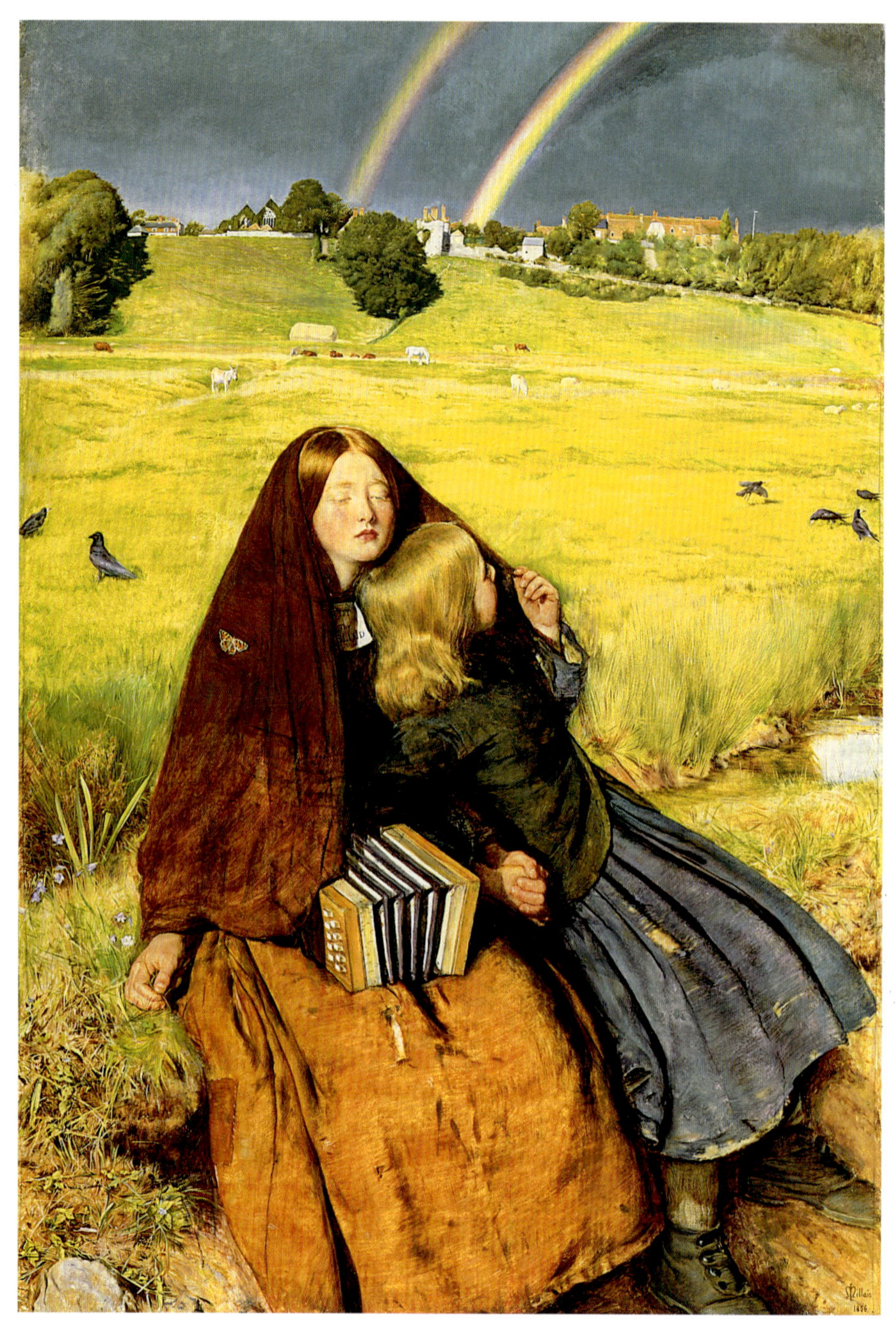

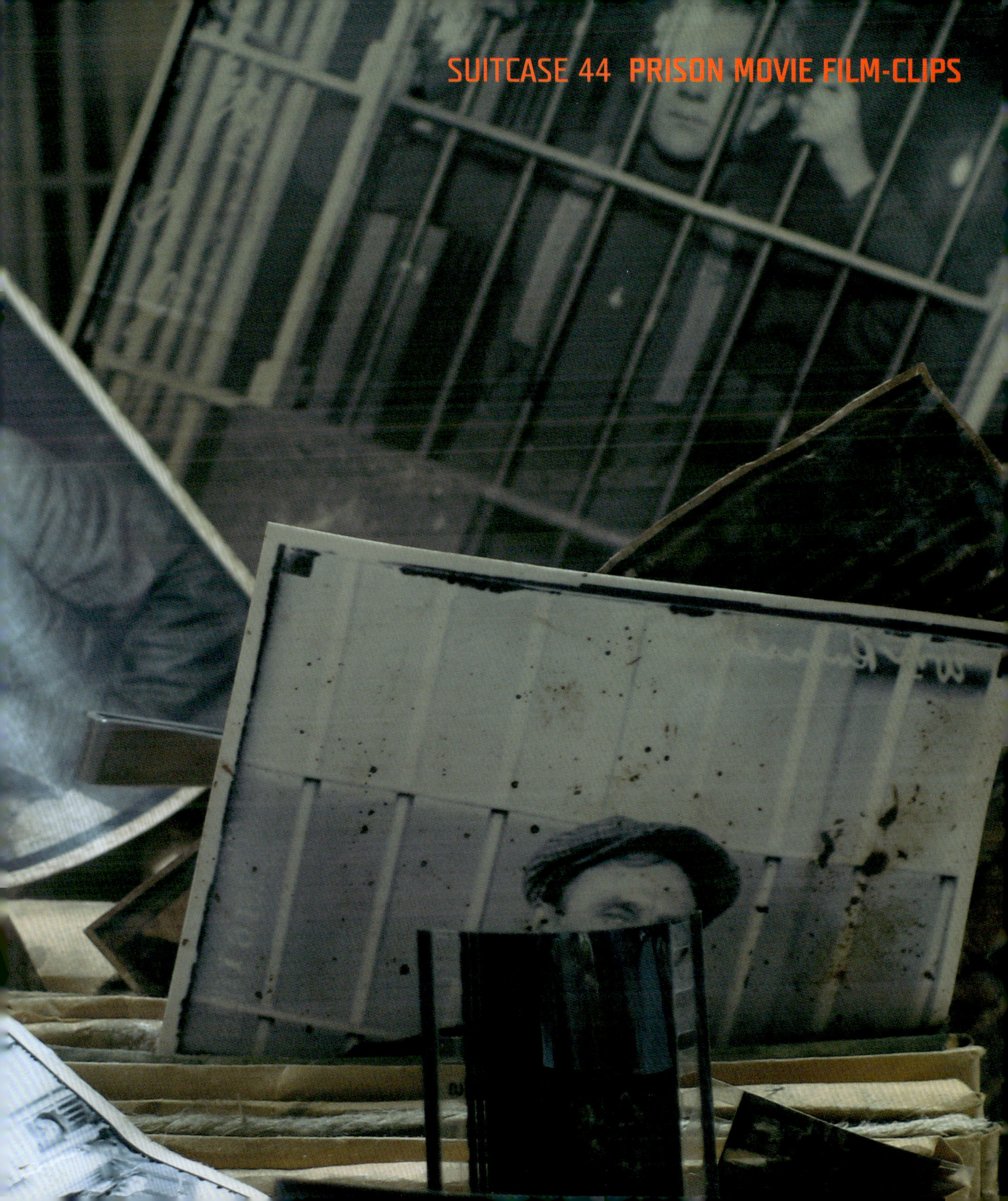

SUITCASE 44 **PRISON MOVIE FILM-CLIPS**

SUITCASE 45 **MANUSCRIPTS FOR THE BABY OF STRASBOURG**

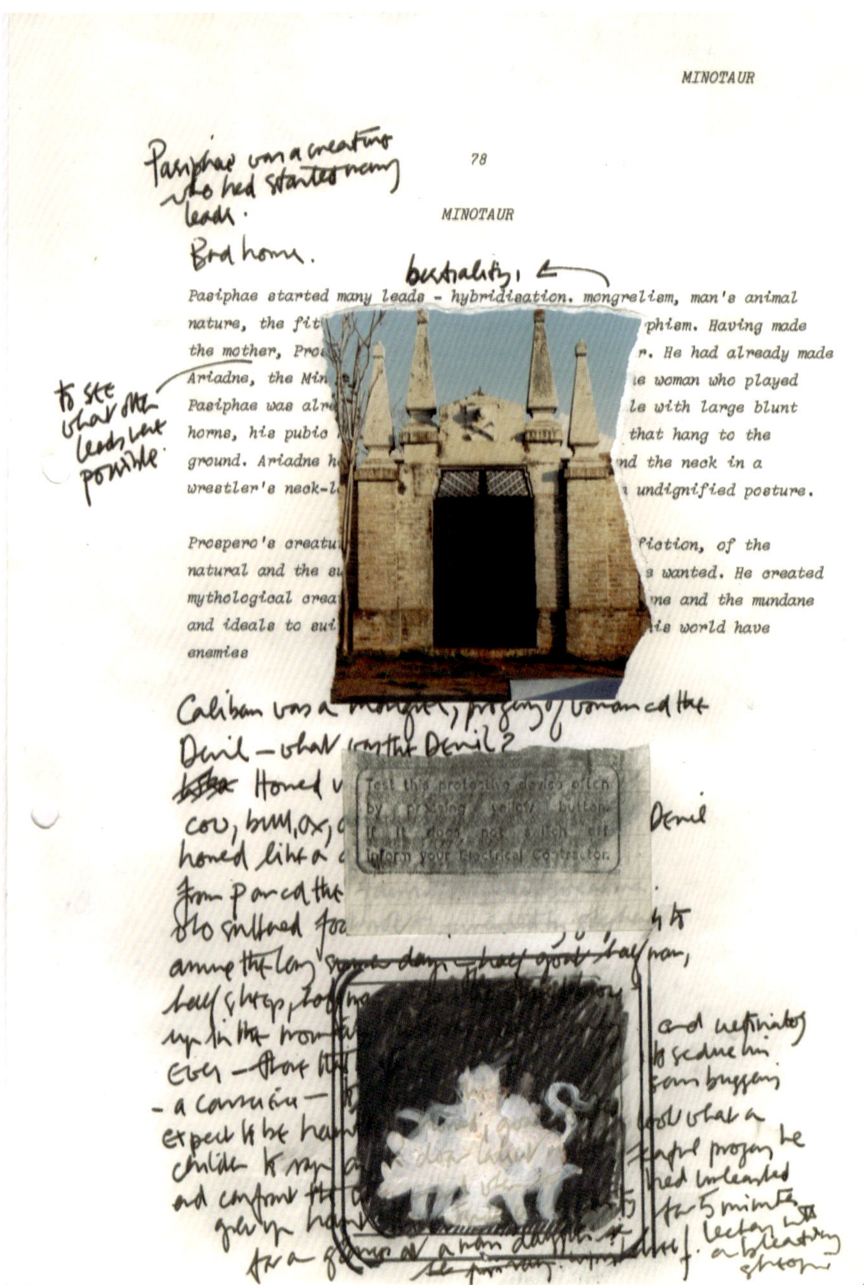

MINOTAUR

78

MINOTAUR

Pasiphae started many leads - hybridisation, mongrelism, man's animal nature, the fit phism. Having made the mother, Pro r. He had already made Ariadne, the Min e woman who played Pasiphae was alr le with large blunt horns, his pubic that hang to the ground. Ariadne h nd the neck in a wrestler's neck-l undignified posture.

Prospero's creatu fiction, of the natural and the s wanted. He created mythological crea ne and the mundane and ideals to su is world have enemies

Test this protective device often by pressing yellow button. If it does not switch off inform your Electrical Contractor.

SUITCASE 46 HOLOCAUST GOLD

1 LAST APPLE 2 BLONDI 3 PROPERTY OF THE BBC 4 BUTTER CRUCIFIX GOLD 5 THE SCHERHERAZADE COMMANDANT 6 THE COAT OF YELLOW STARS 7 THE BISCUIT TIN 8 THE NAKED JOCKEY 9 THE BURNT ELEPHANT 10 PETER THE GREAT 11 THE COLOSSEUM JEWS 12 THE VIOLIN SUITCASE 13 THE SAUSAGEMAN 14 THE GOOSEGIRL 15 DANAE 16 LOVE OF DENTISTRY 17 THE LEFT-BIASED STEERING-WHEEL 18 THE HAYSTACK STORY 19 THE RING COLLECTOR 20 HOT WATER VALUABLES 21 THE GOLDEN WEATHERCOCK 22 TWELVE DAYS OF CHRISTMAS 23 THE GOLD PISTOL 24 PHOTOGRAPHIC EVIDENCE 25 IN THREES 26 THE CANADIAN ENVELOPES 27 CALLISTO MAGDALENE 28 THE RING CYCLE 29 MIDAS 30 GLOVED IN THE BATH 31 THE DOLLSHOUSE BOOTY 32 THE CIGAR-BOX 33 THE GOLDEN FLEECE 34 THE PUSHER 35 THE RAILWAY LINE 36 HH TO POSTERITY 37 THE THREE BEARS 38 THE SPECTACLES 39 THE WATCH CHILDREN 40 GROSZ ENTHUSIASM 41 THE TOOTHBRUSH 42 PAPER-CLIPS 43 THE RABBI CONSPIRACY 44 LILAC SOAP 45 PRE-COLUMBIAN DEATH 46 A FAMILY HERITAGE 47 BURNT HANDS 48 EUTHANASIA 49 THE ITALIAN LETTER WRITERS 50 JACKDAW GOLD 51 GOLDEN BOOKSHOP 52 MAGRITTE'S BUSINESSMAN 53 PASSPORTS TO VESPUCCIO, HADEN AND EREWHON 54 BIRD JEWELLERY 55 BODY PARTS 56 MUNICH RAILWAY STATION 57 THE PORK WAITER 58 THE SWALLOWED RING 59 GOEBBEL'S DIARY 60 THE GOLDEN GARDENERS 61 THE TROOP TRAIN 62 FRANK'S FRIENDS 63 RUSSIAN HOT RINGS 64 TWELVE GOLDEN KILOMETRES 65 GIVING AWAY GOLD 66 THE INITIAL B 67 AMERSFORT ICE 68 THE TENNIS MATCH 69 THE GOLDEN BULLET 70 THE THREE SISTERS 71 I AM DEAD 72 THE U-BEND 73 RINGS ON A KNIFE 74 GOLDEN HEELS 75 THE TRAM DECISION 76 BREAKING GLASS 77 THE GOLDEN FILM 78 STORKS 79 TRAIN GOLD 80 CRYSTAL COLLECTION 81 THE BLUE ROOM 82 THE HEAPS AND PILES MAN 83 SCARECROW 84 NAVEL GOLD 85 TREE GOLD 86 THE GOLDEN PEN 87 SANTA CLAUS 88 THE RUNOVER GOLD 89 THE HAIRDRESSER 90 FINGER GREASE 91 THE SEMPSTRESS 92 HARPSCH'S STORY

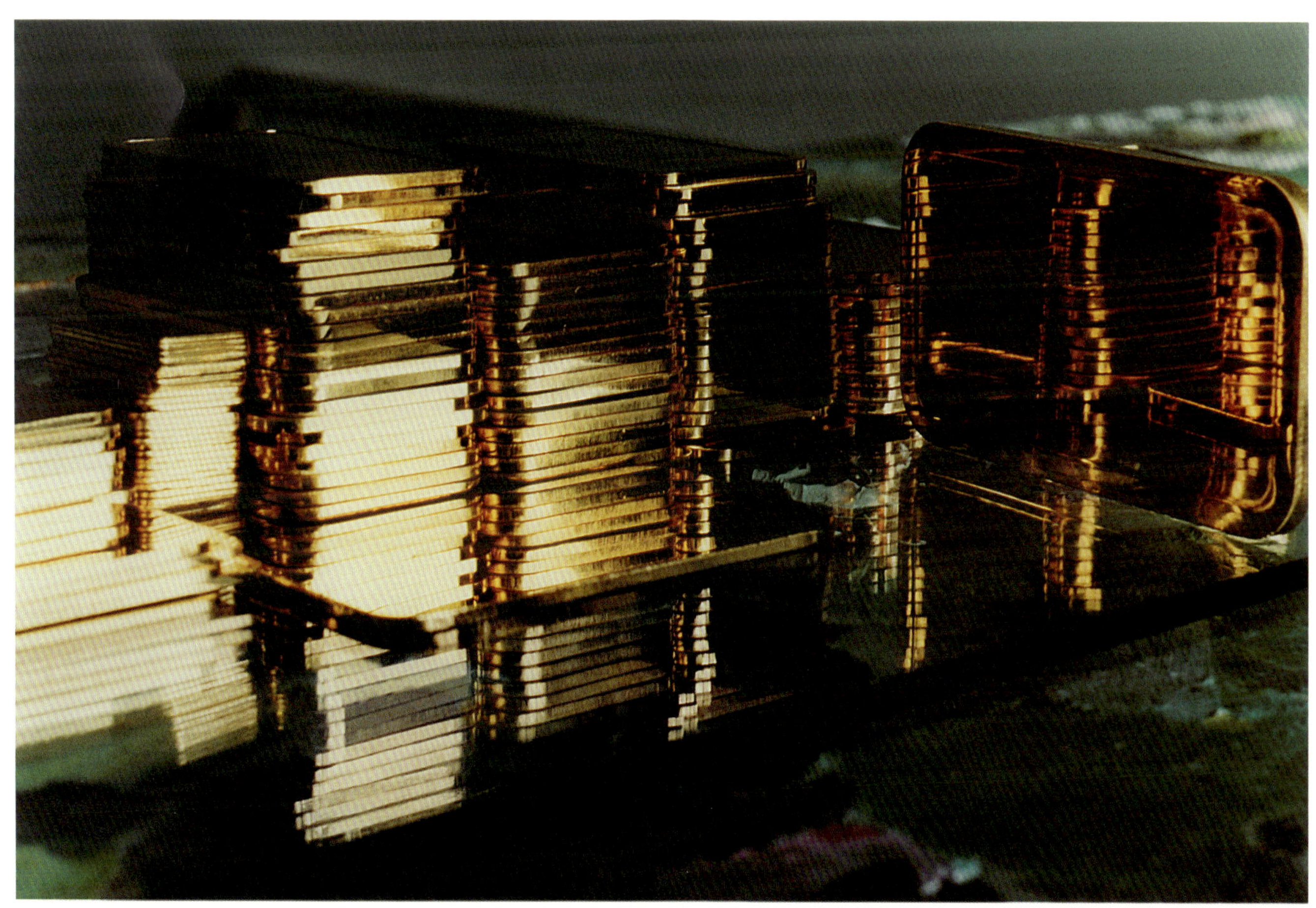

SUITCASE 47 CHILDREN

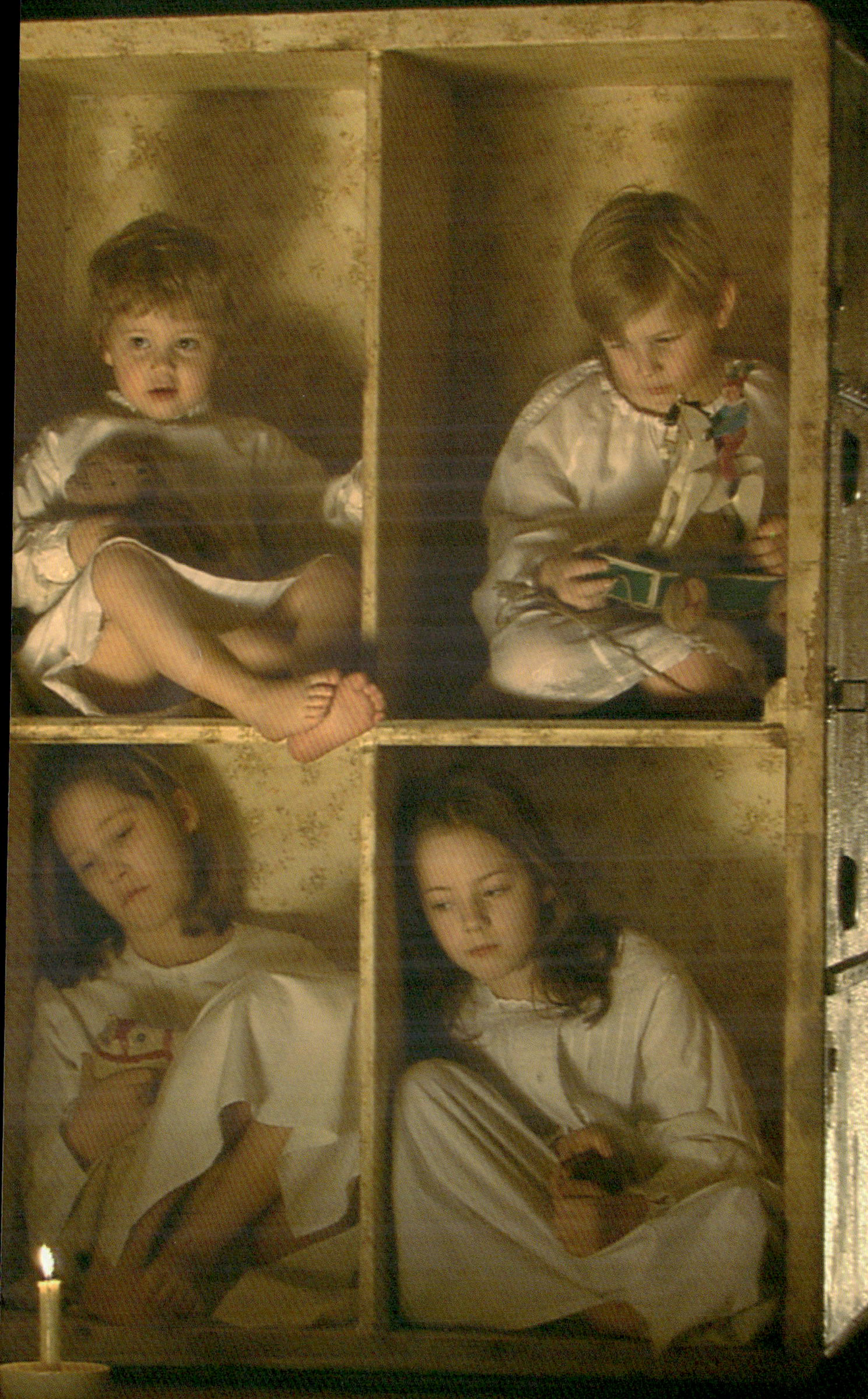

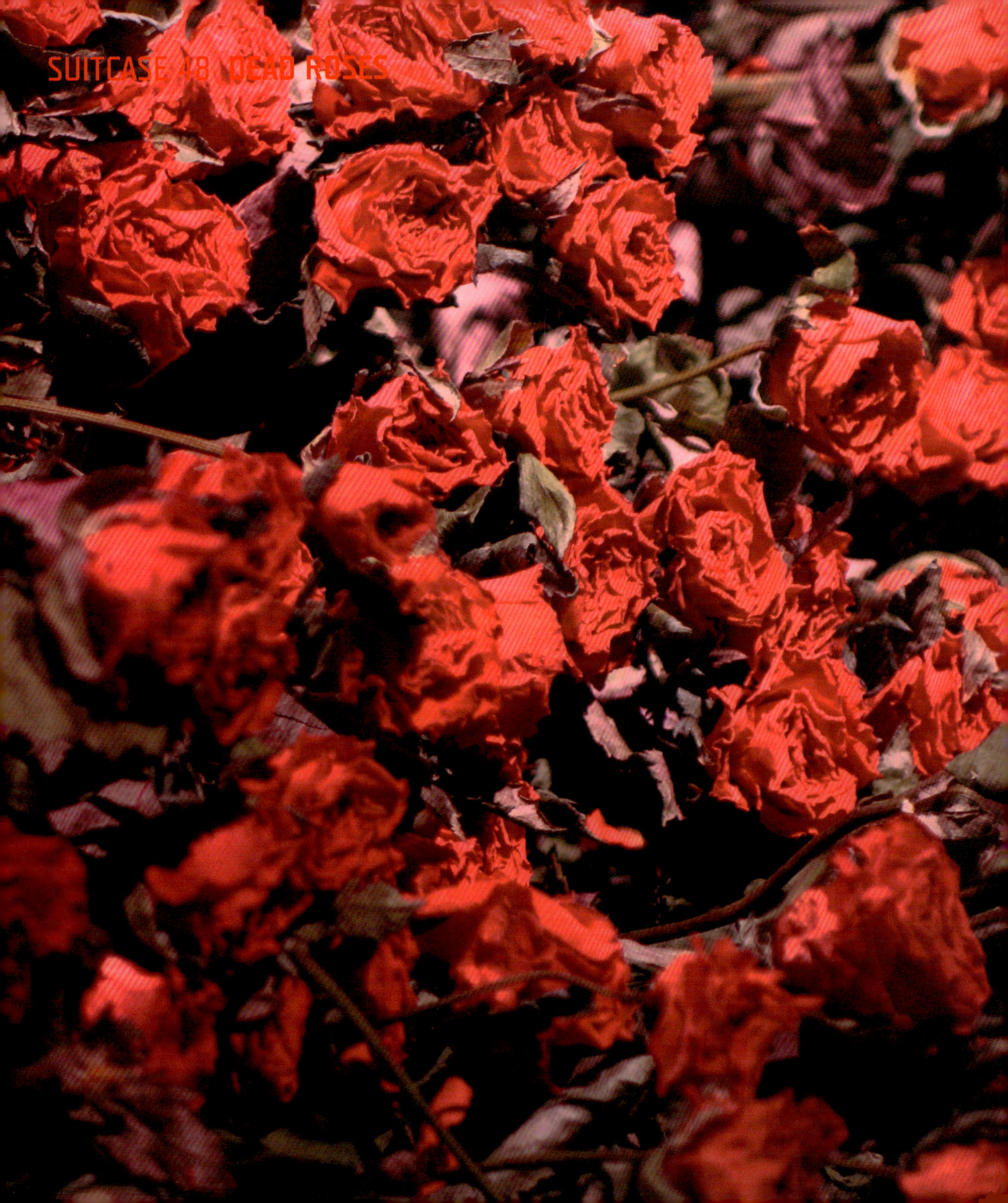
SUITCASE 48 DEAD ROSES

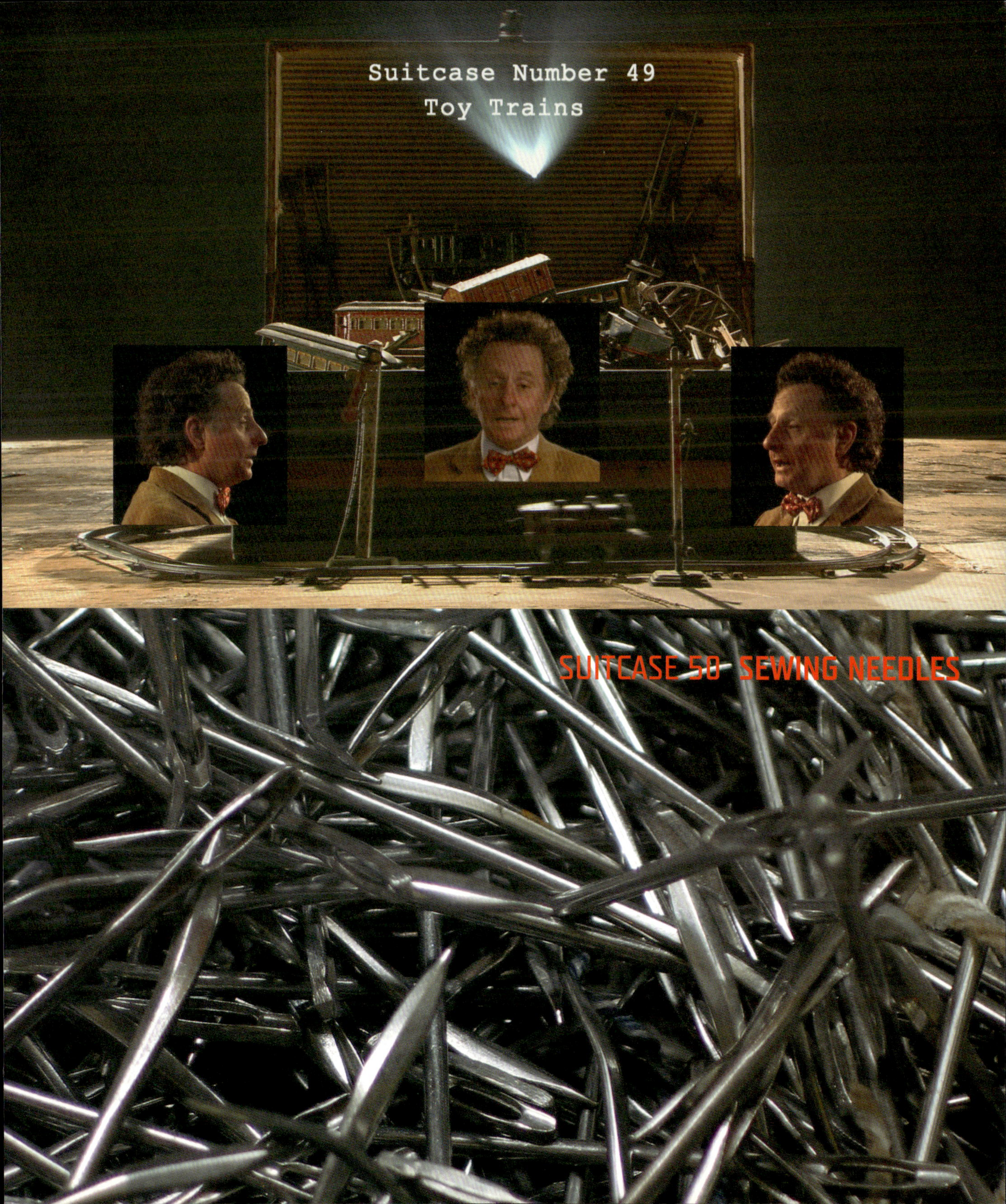
Suitcase Number 49
Toy Trains
SUITCASE 50 SEWING NEEDLES

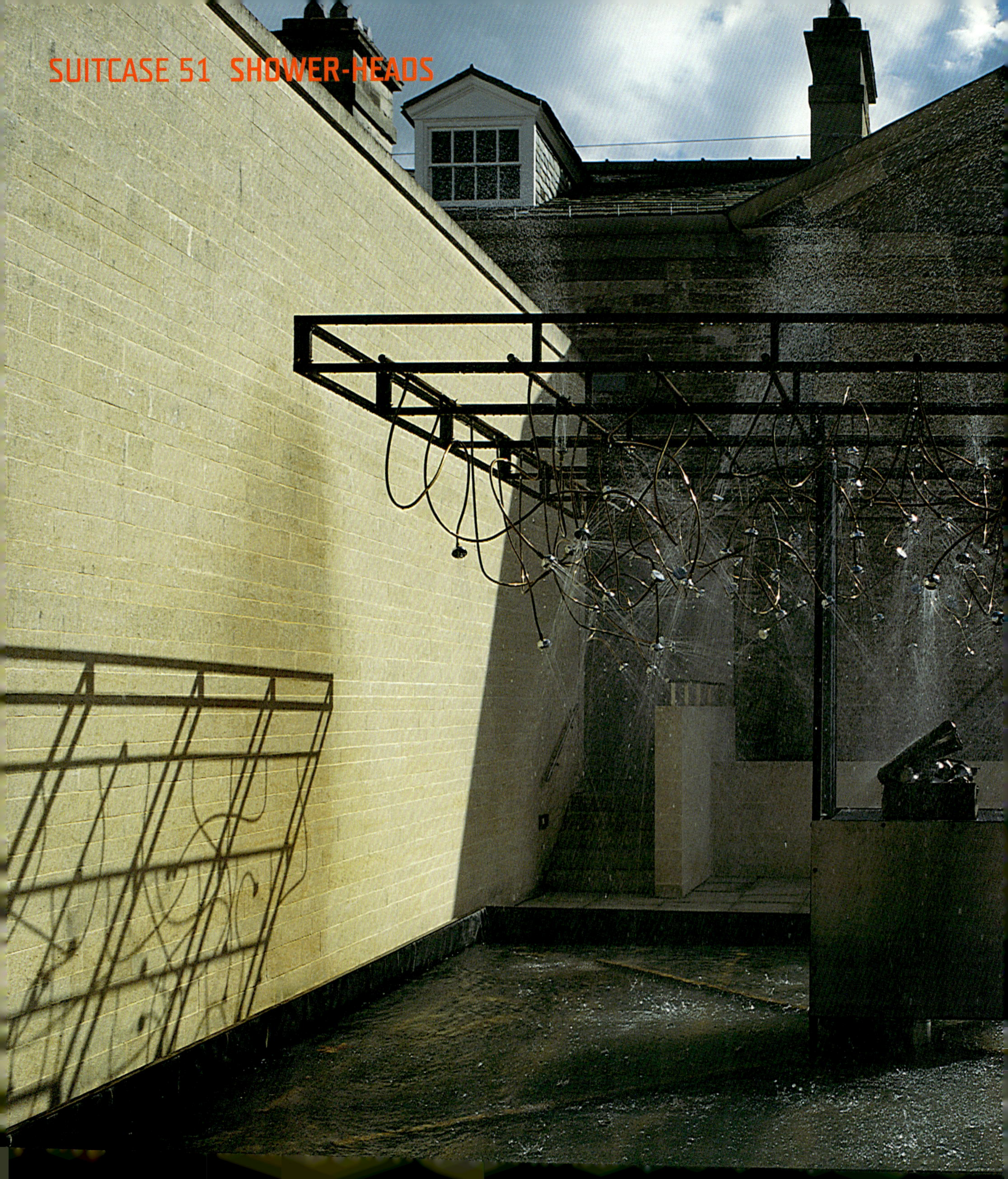

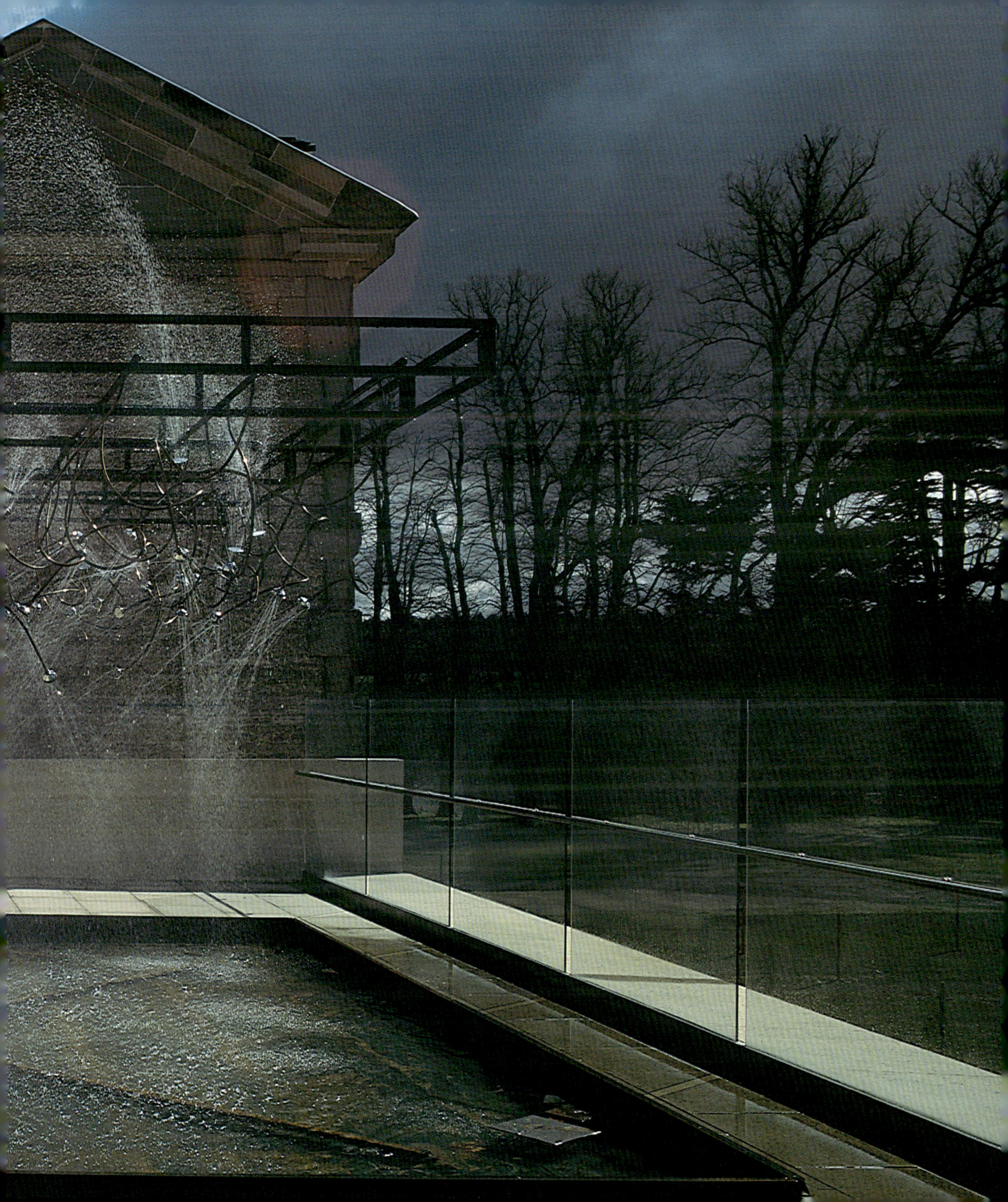

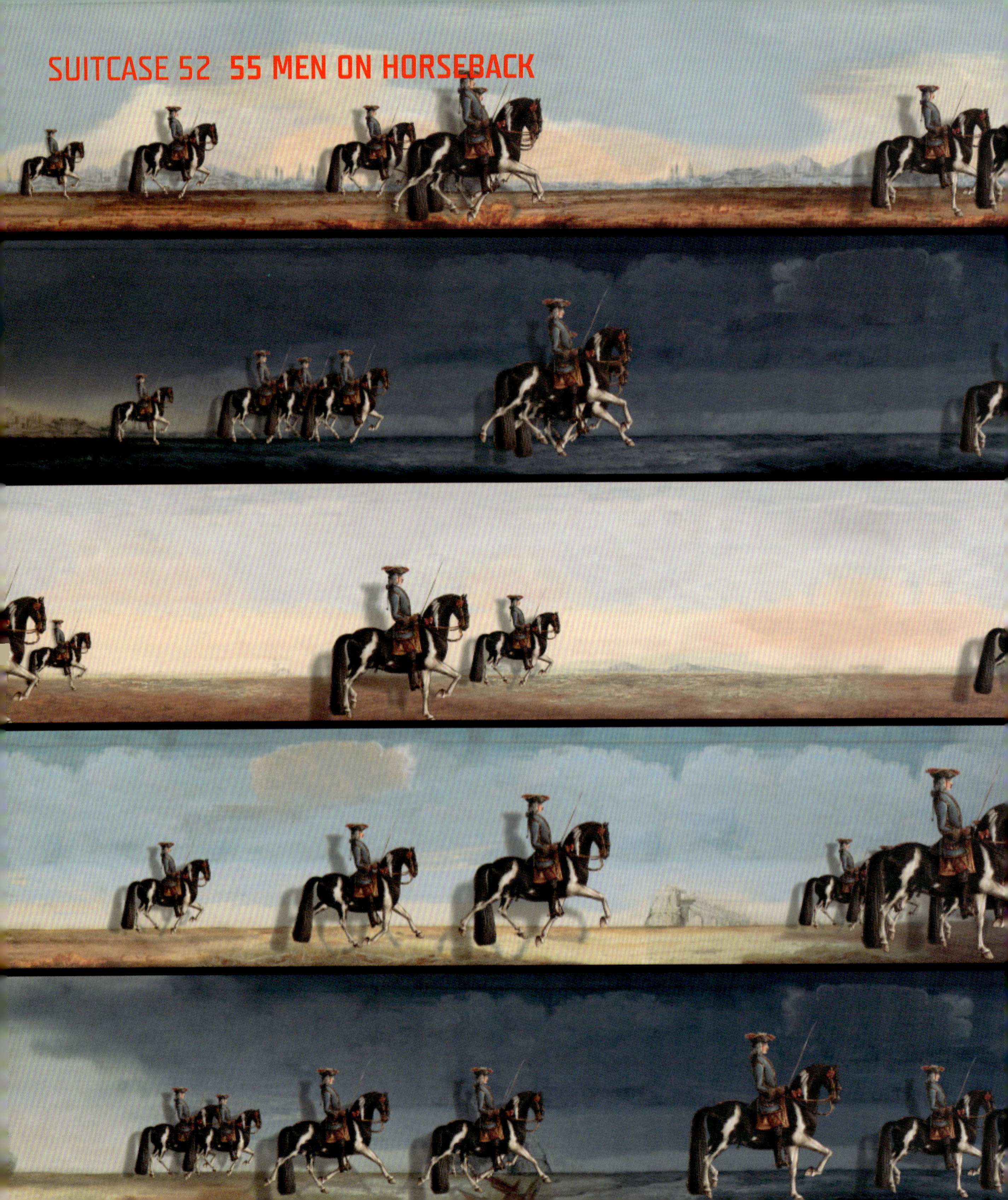
SUITCASE 52 55 MEN ON HORSEBACK

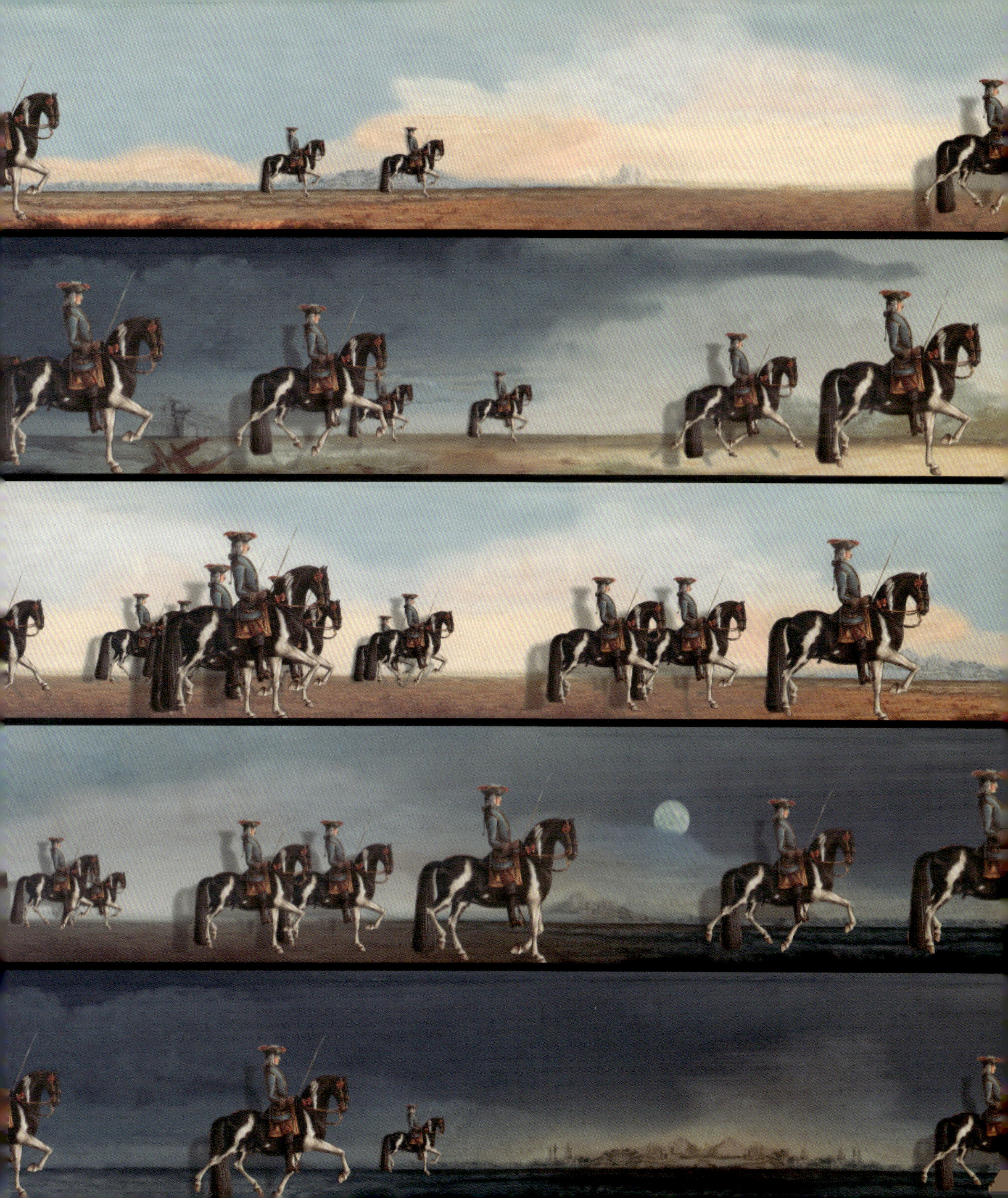

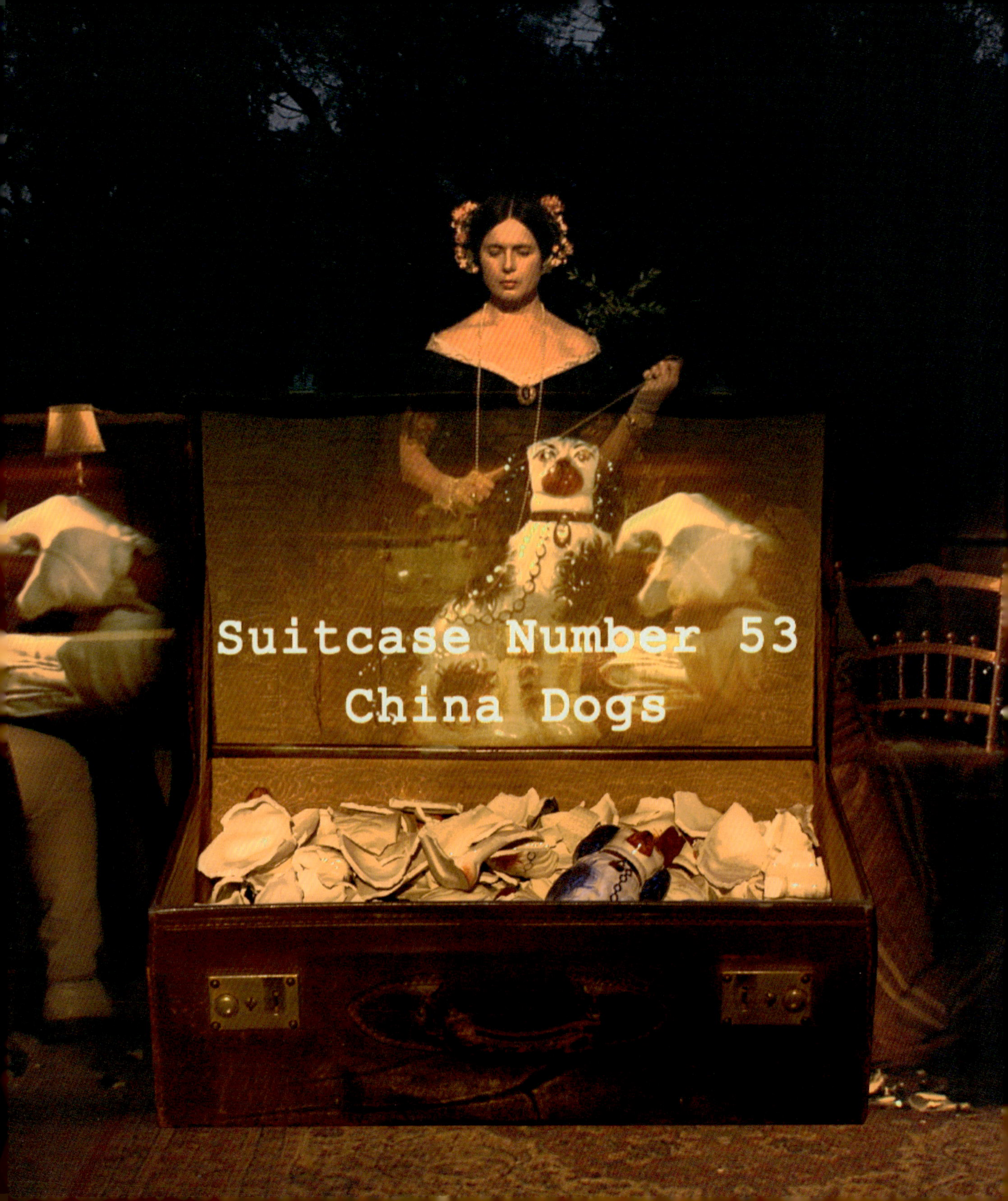

Suitcase Number 53
China Dogs

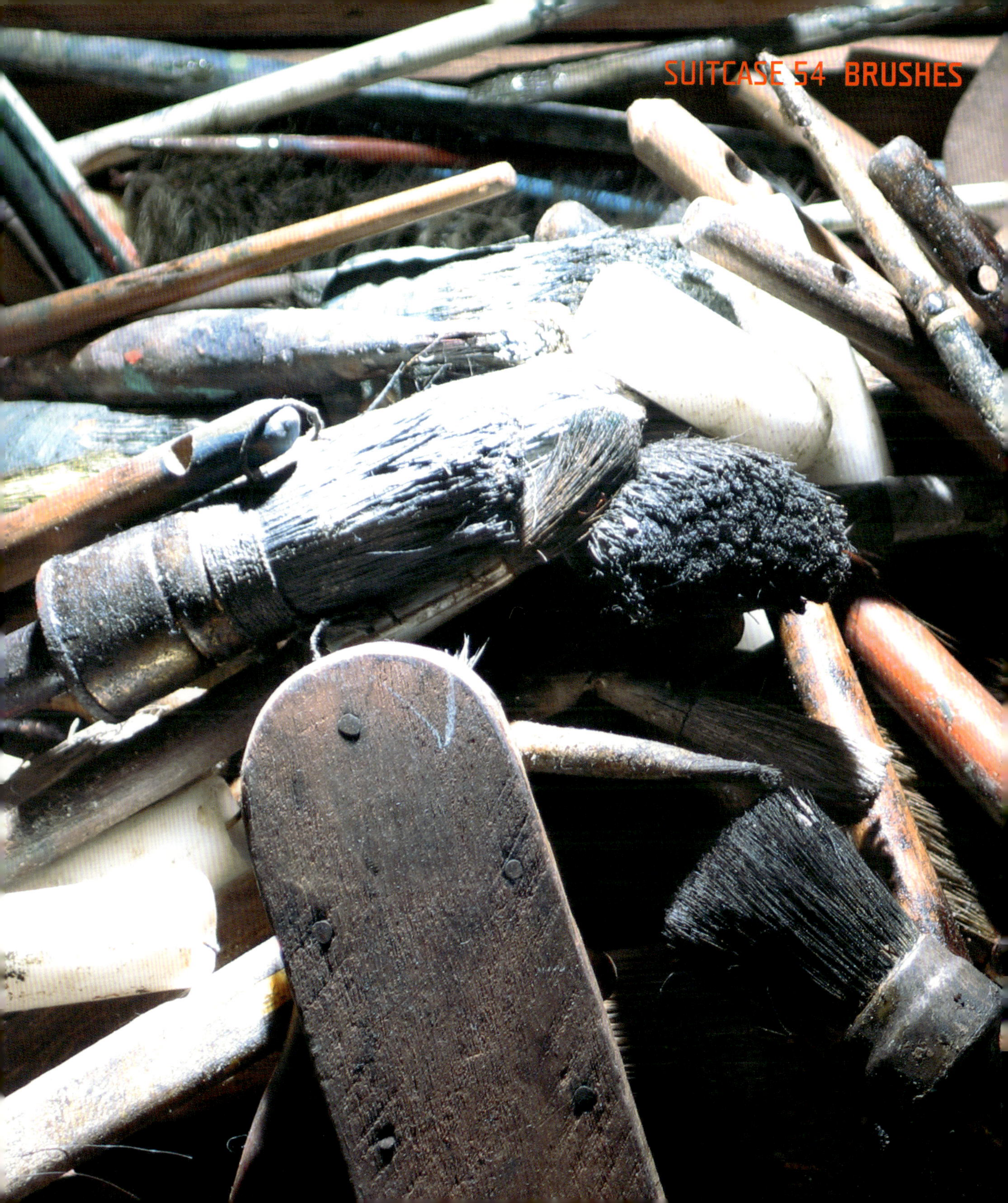

SUITCASE 54 BRUSHES

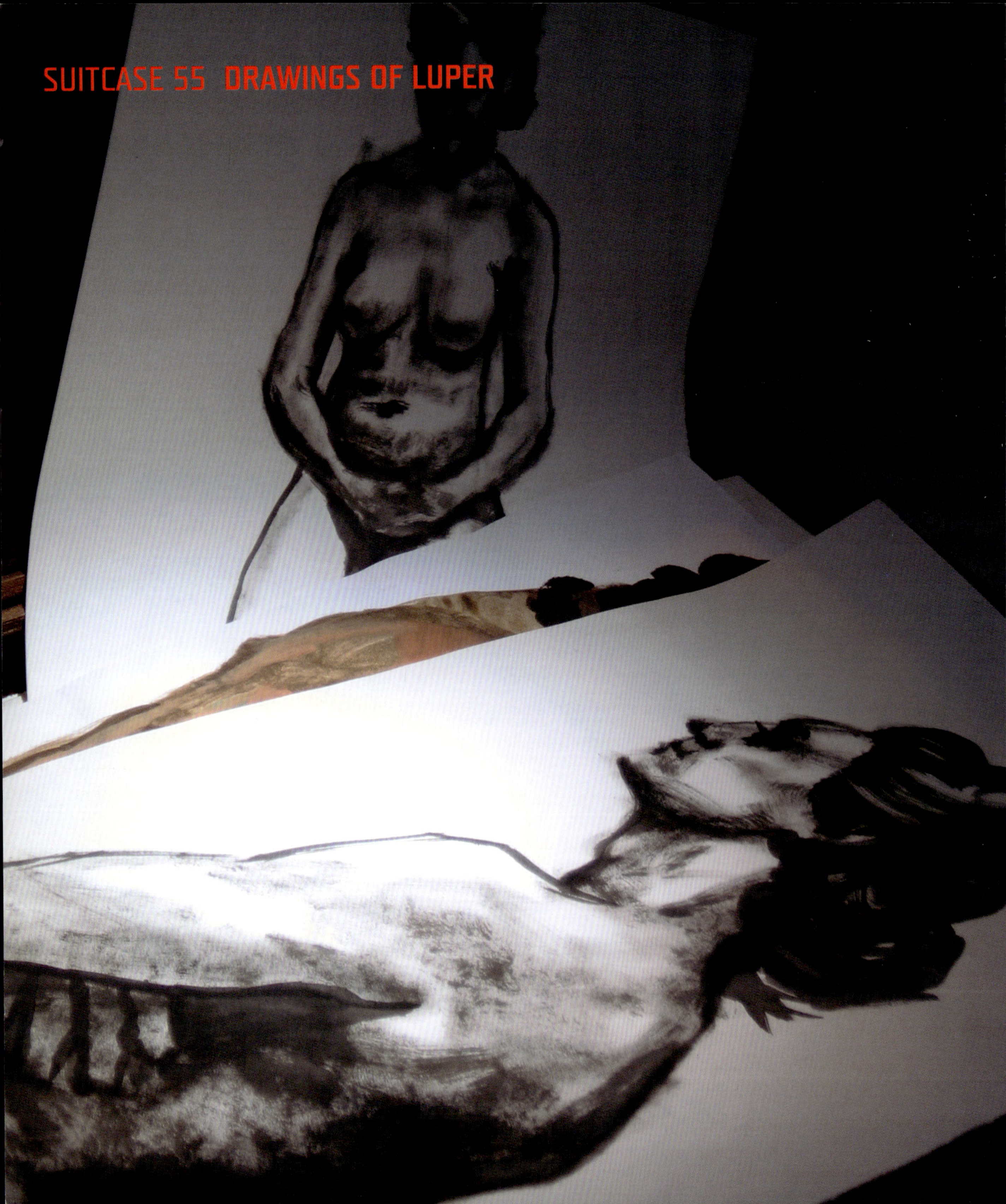
SUITCASE 55 DRAWINGS OF LUPER

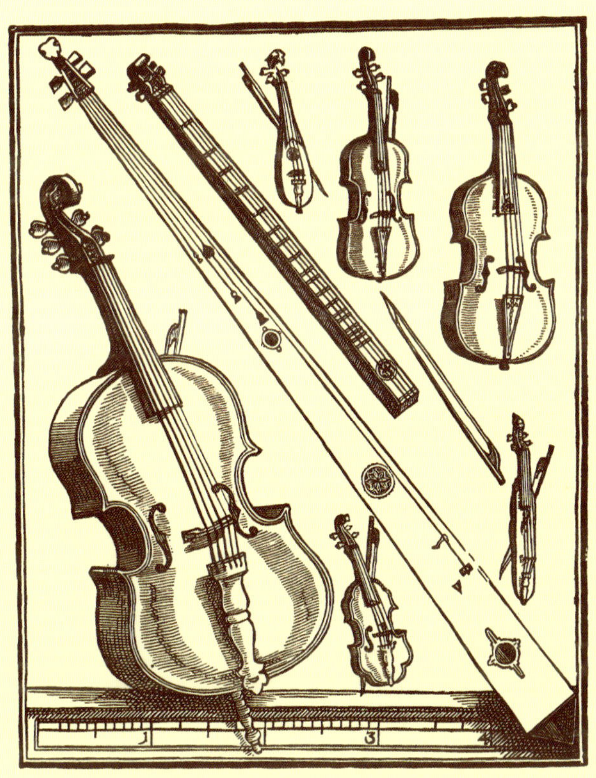
1
3

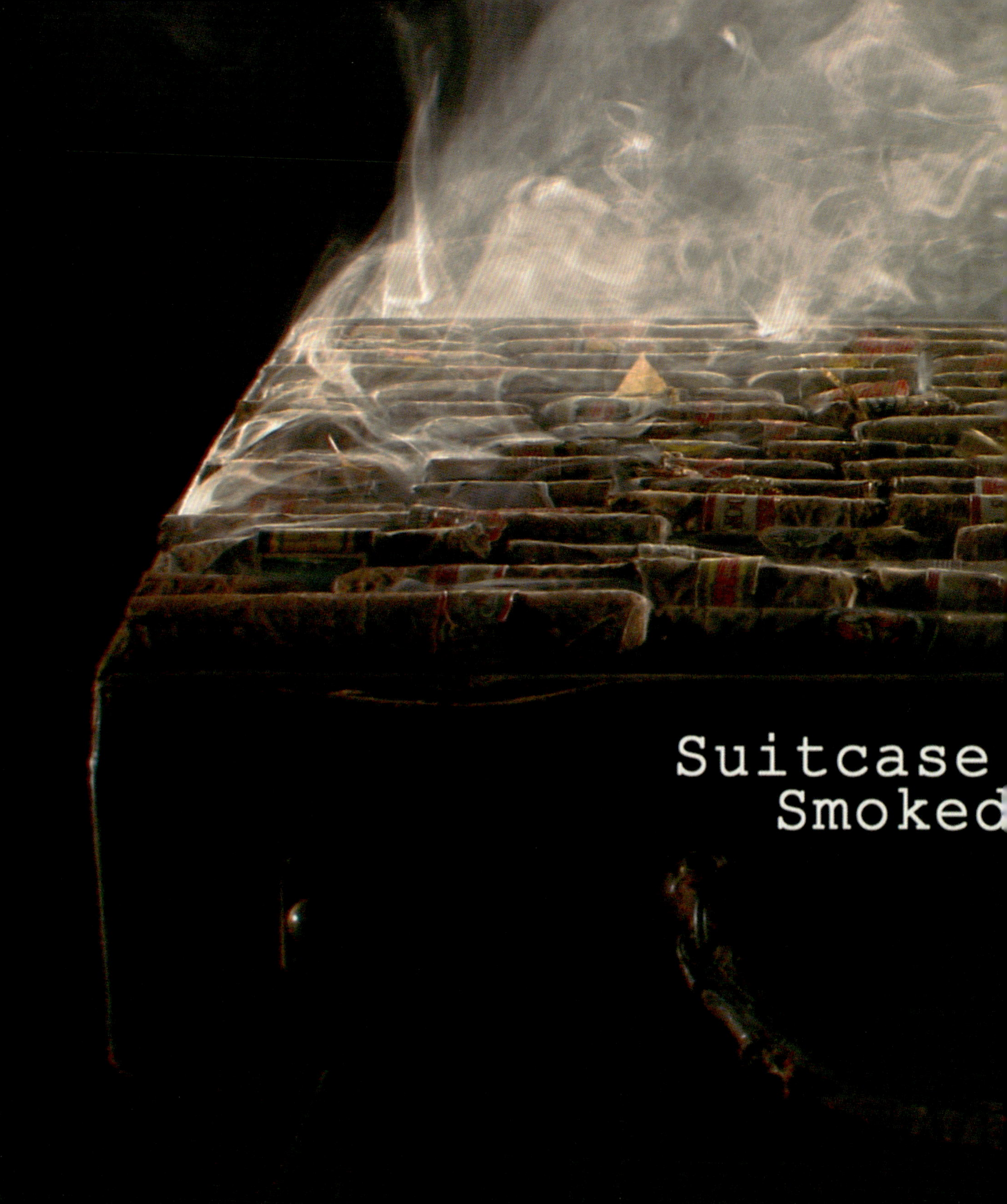
Suitcase
Smoked

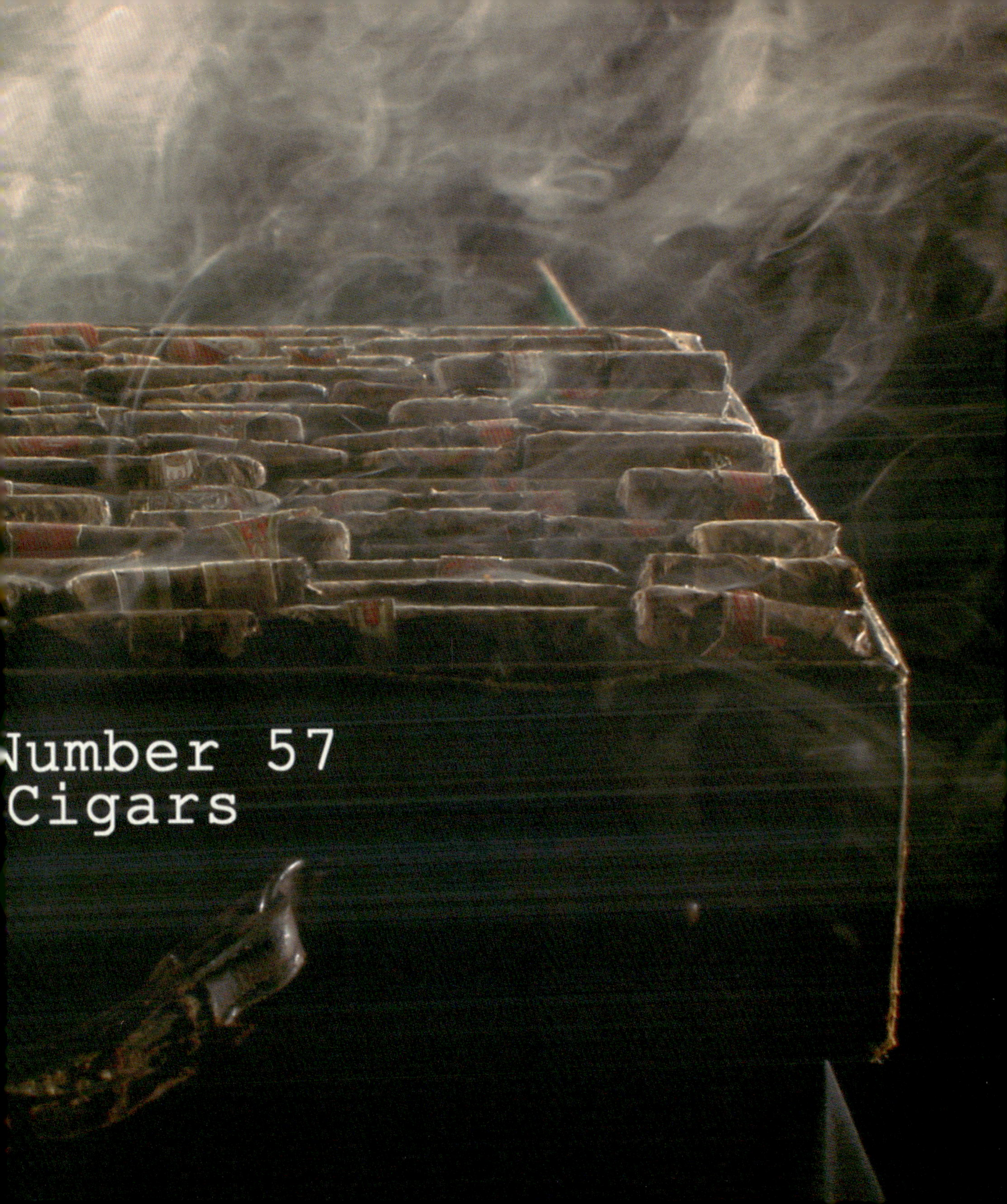
Number 57
Cigars

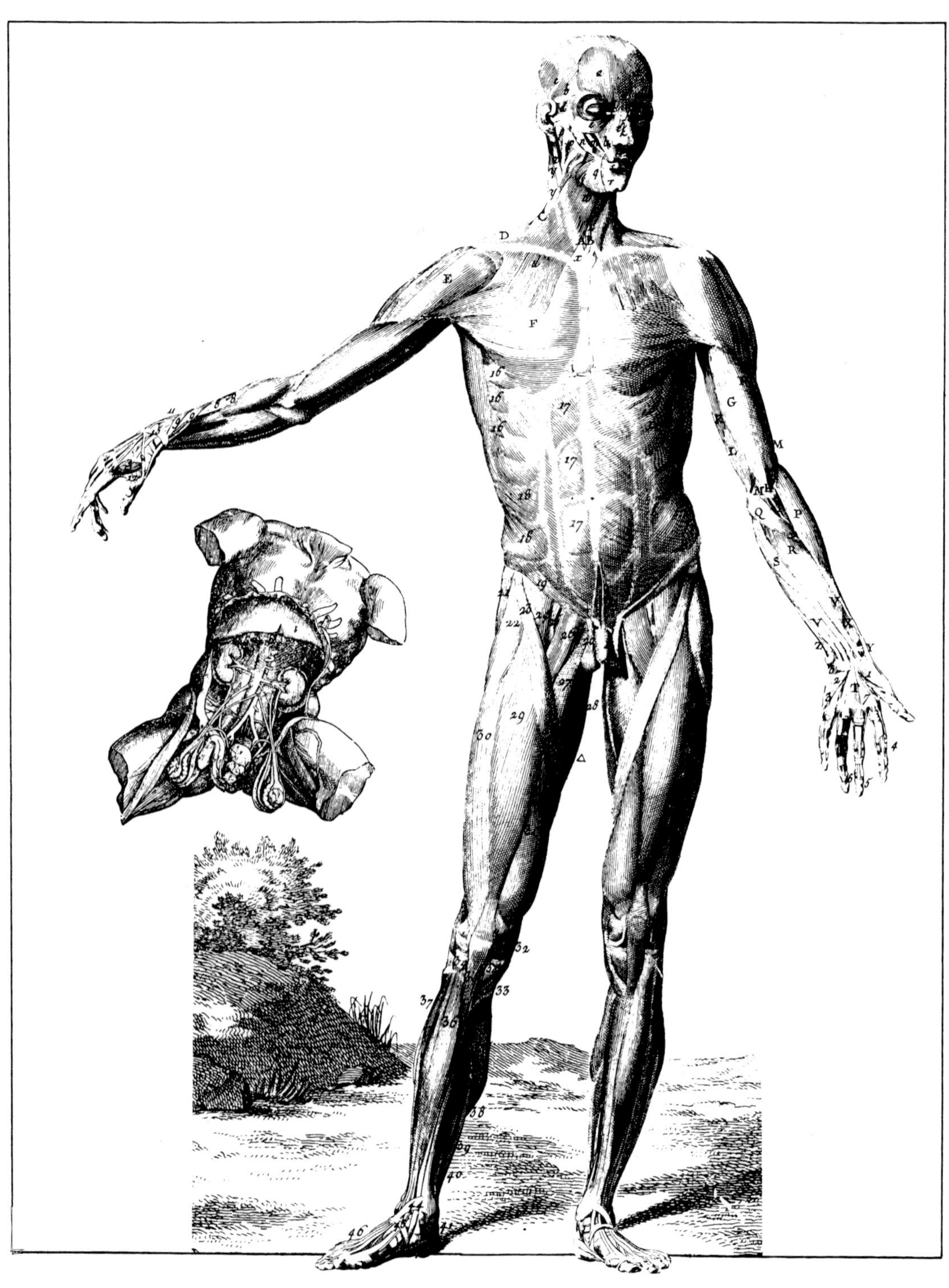

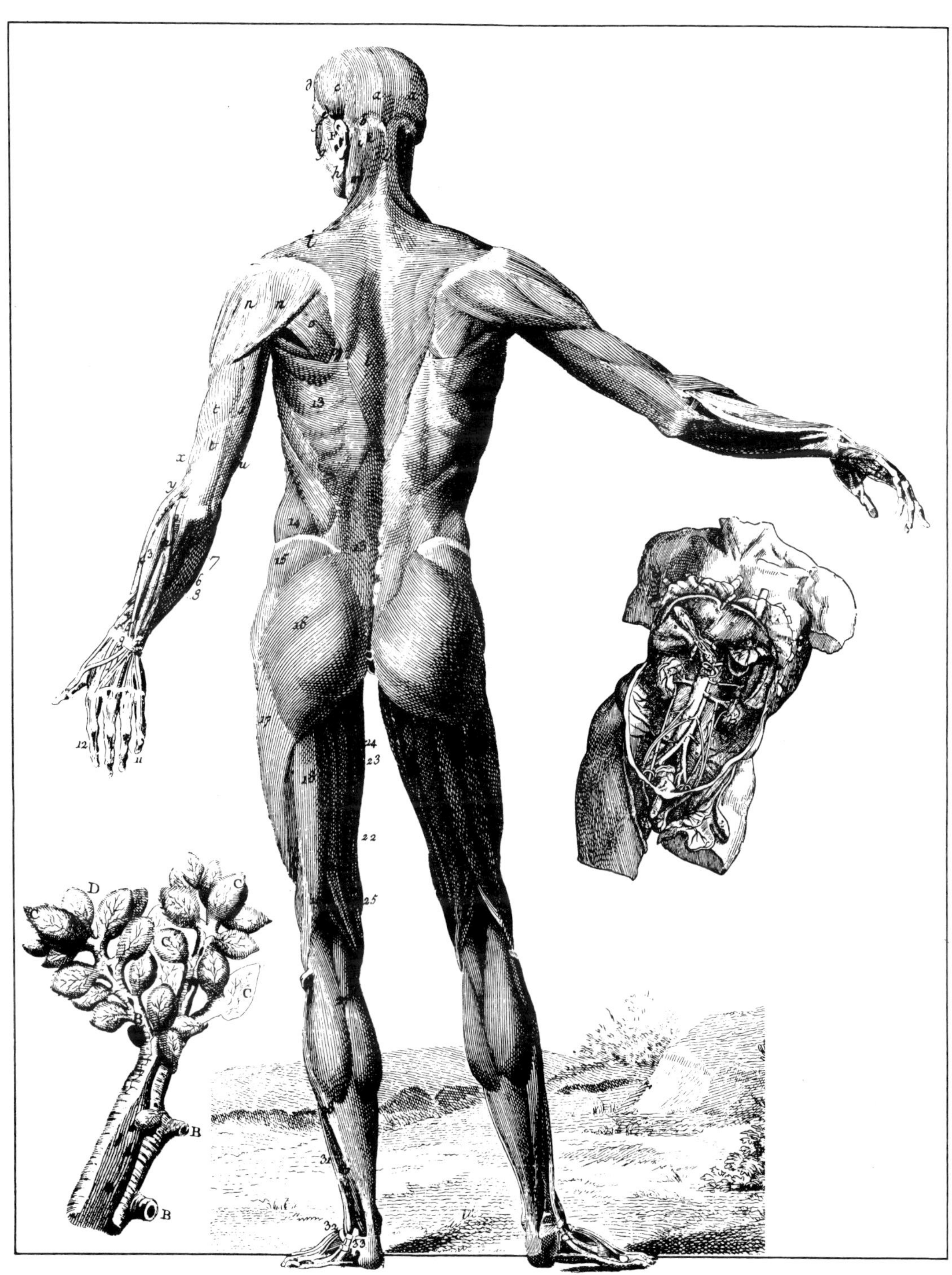

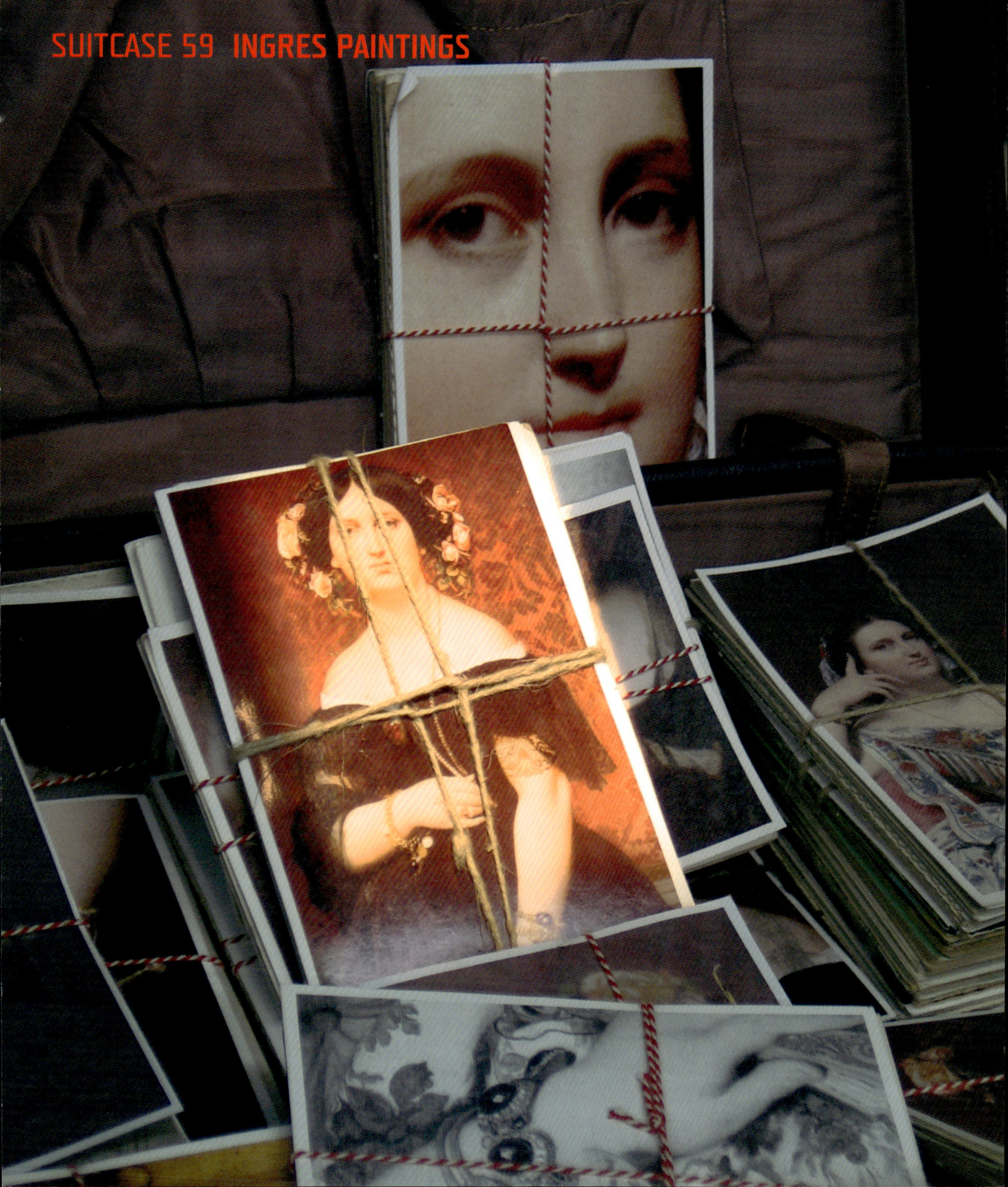
SUITCASE 59 INGRES PAINTINGS

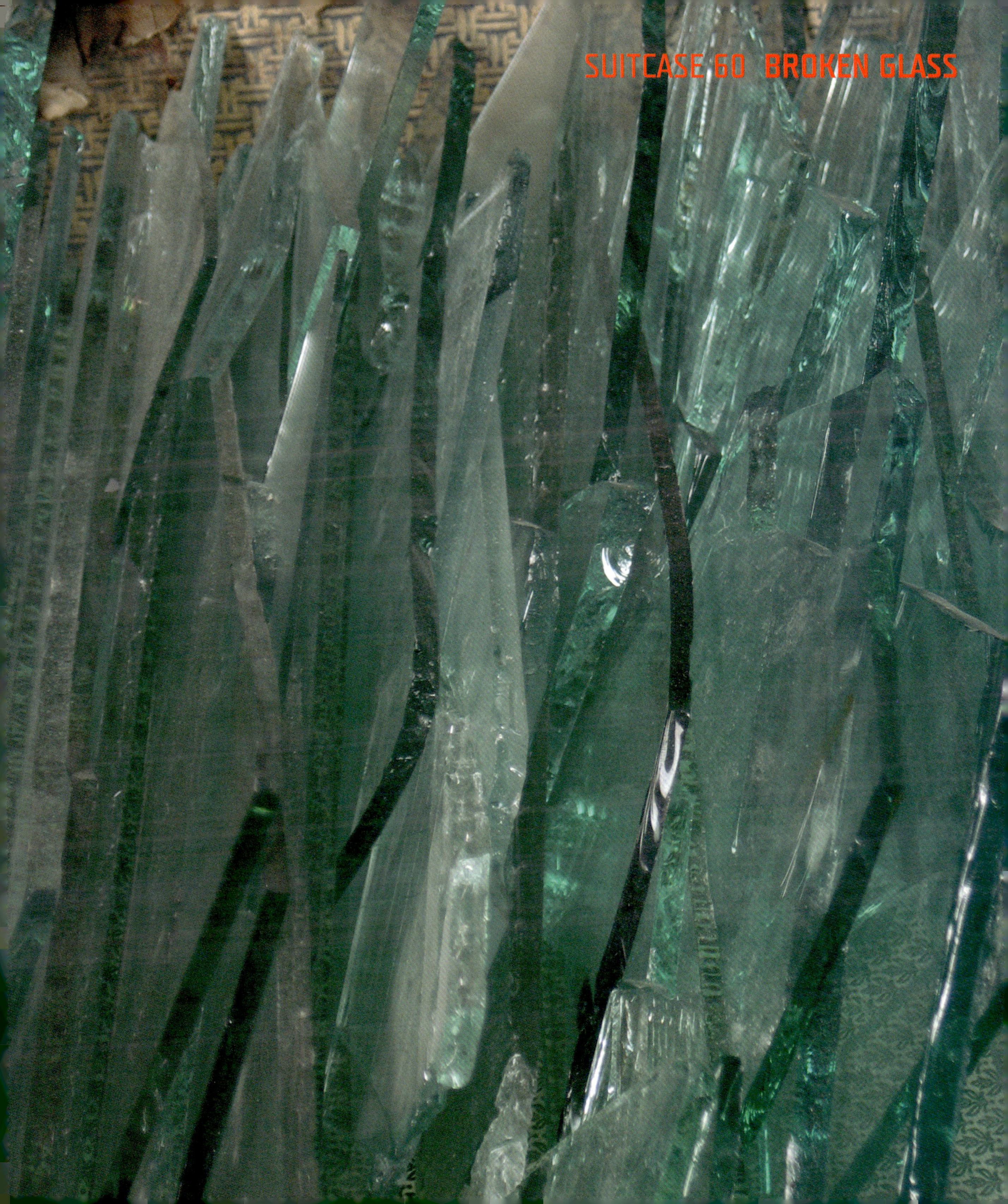
SUITCASE 60 BROKEN GLASS

SUITCASE 61 MOITESSIER GOWNS

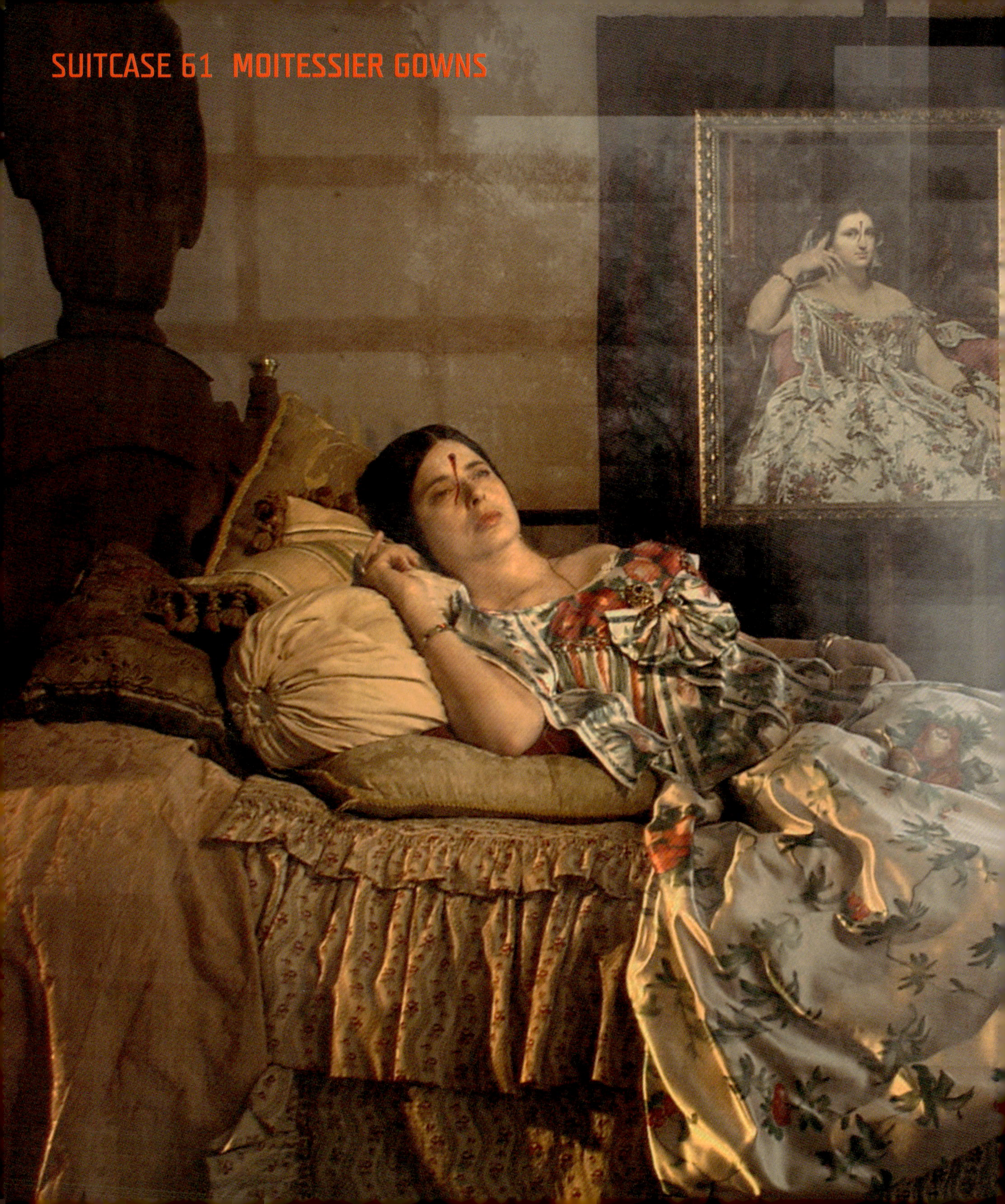

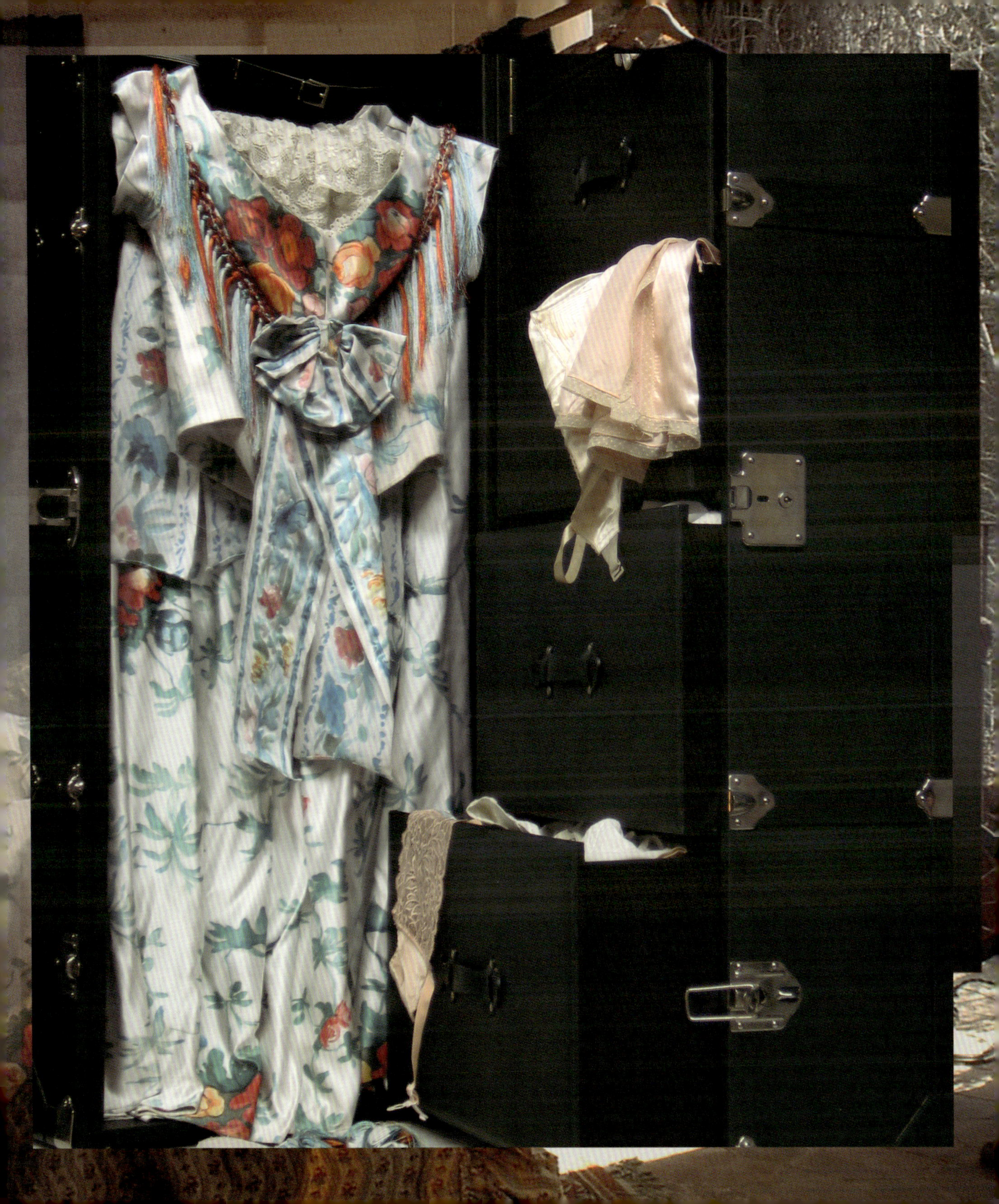

SUITCASE 62 **CRABCLAWS**

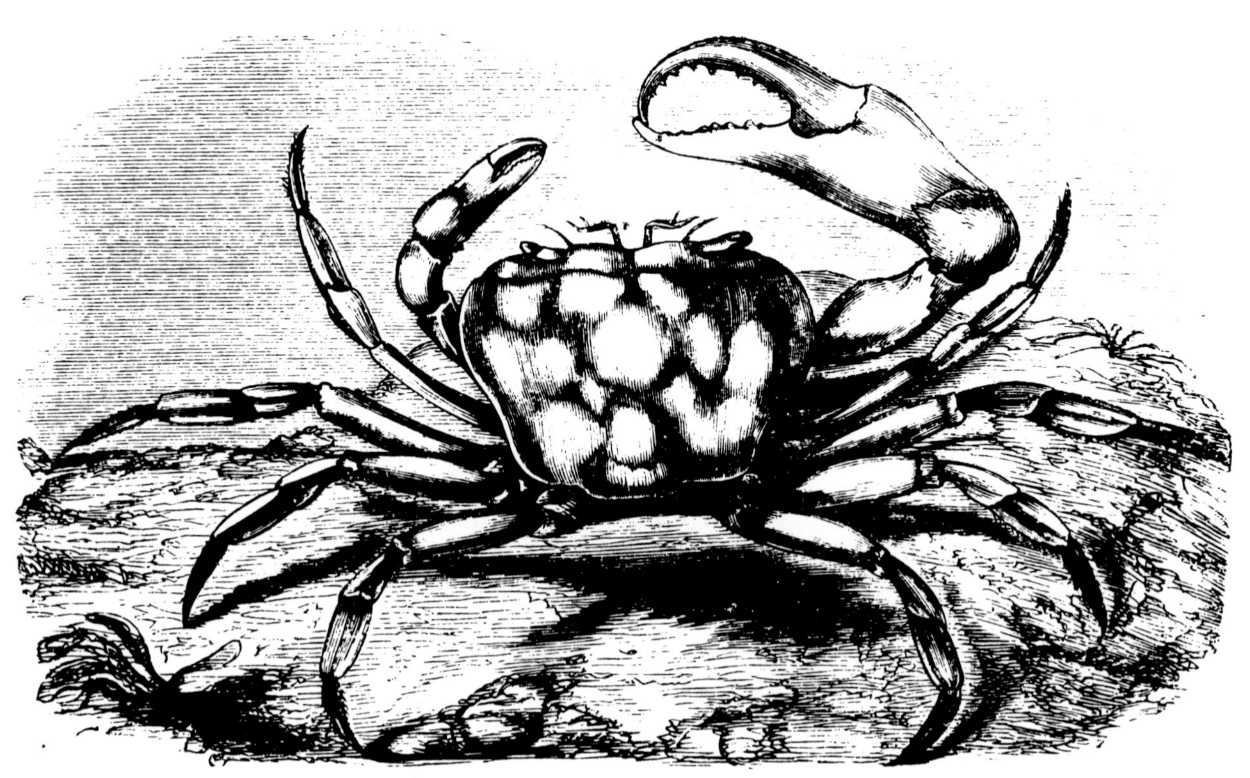

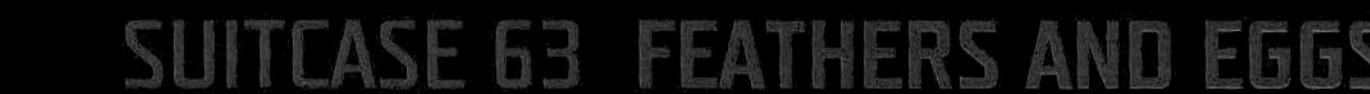
SUITCASE 63 FEATHERS AND EGGS

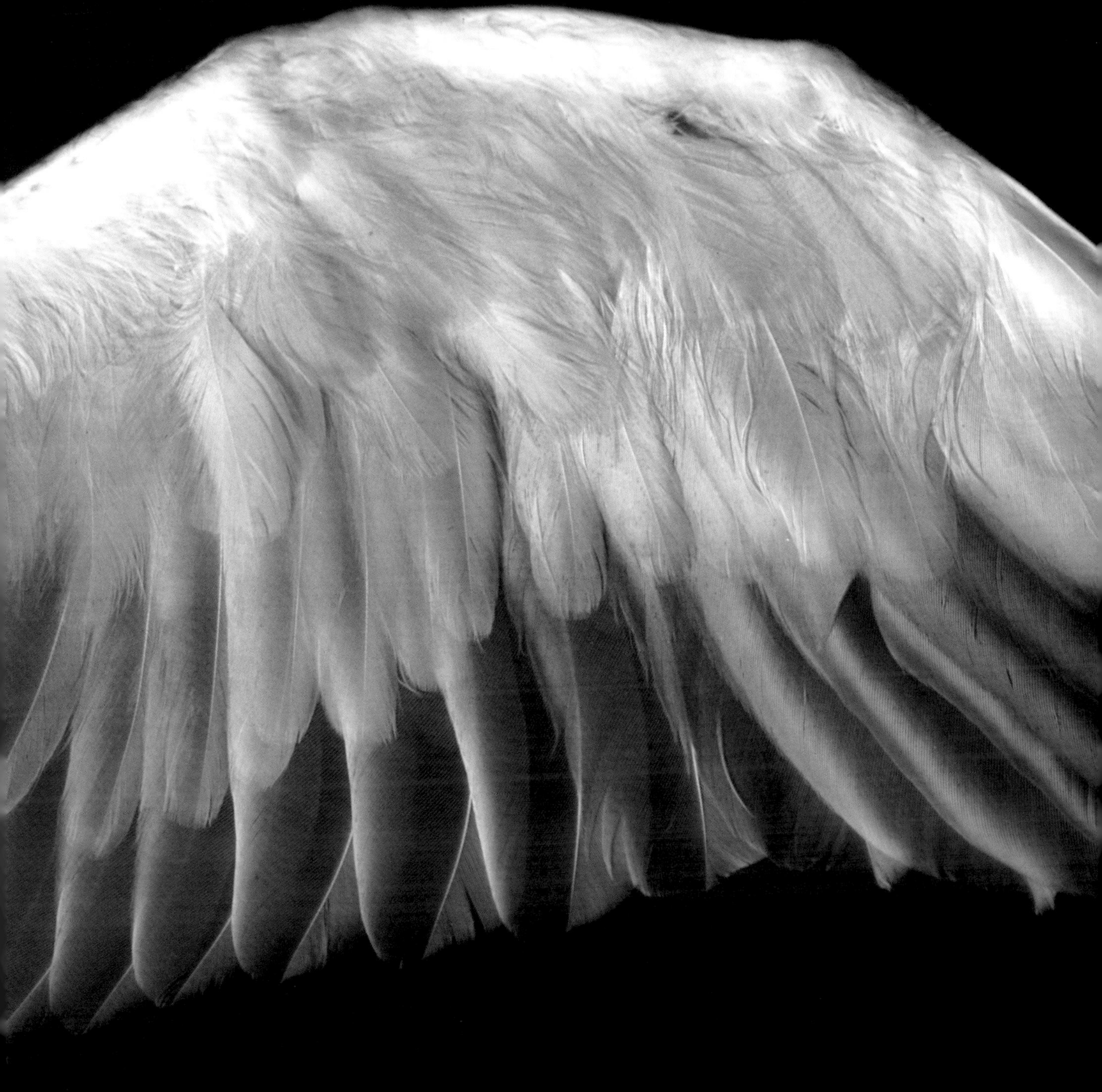

Out of a paint tin.
Calculable,
predictable,
mixable.
From found ingredients

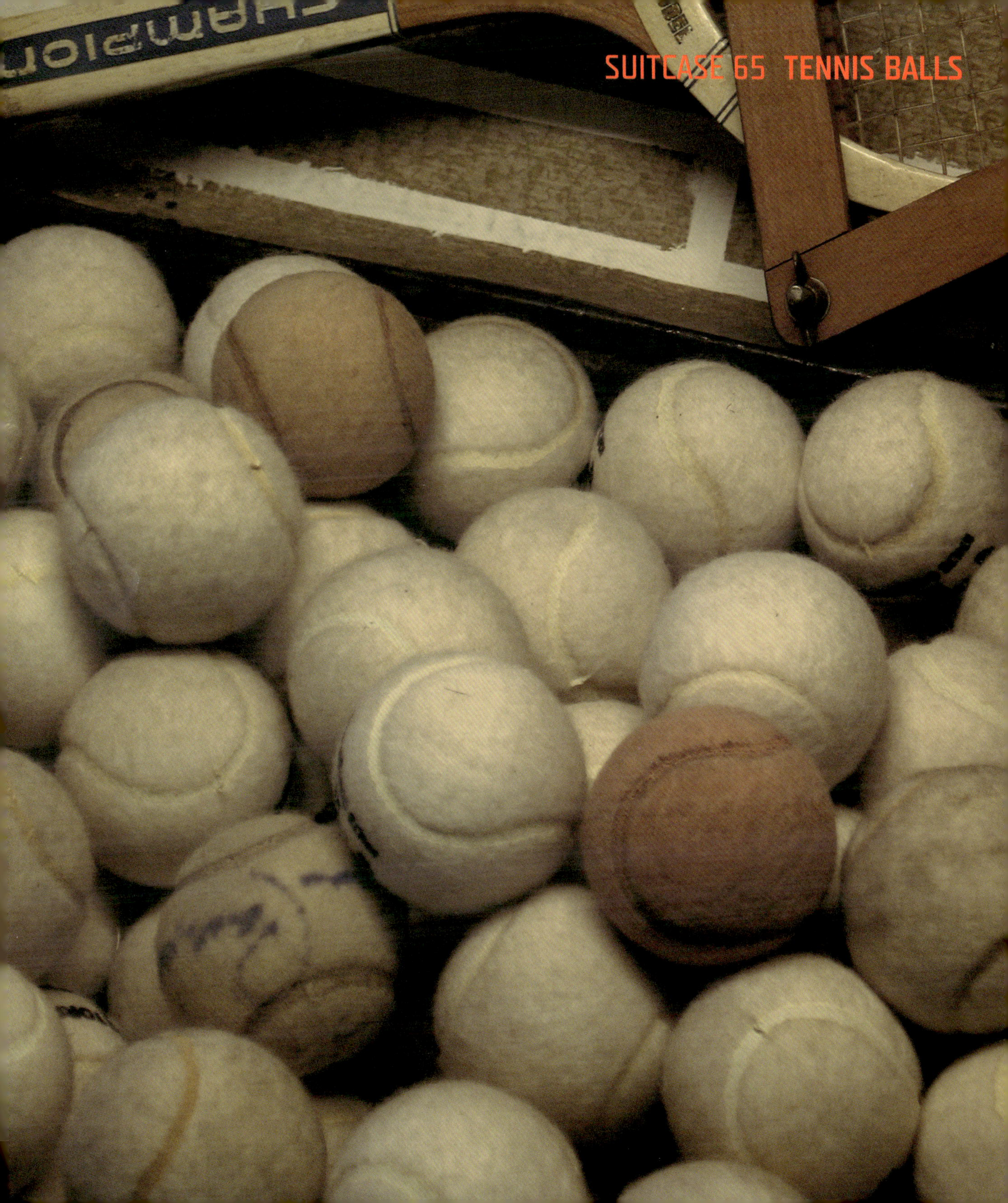

SUITCASE 65 TENNIS BALLS

SUITCASE 66 BOTTLE MESSAGES

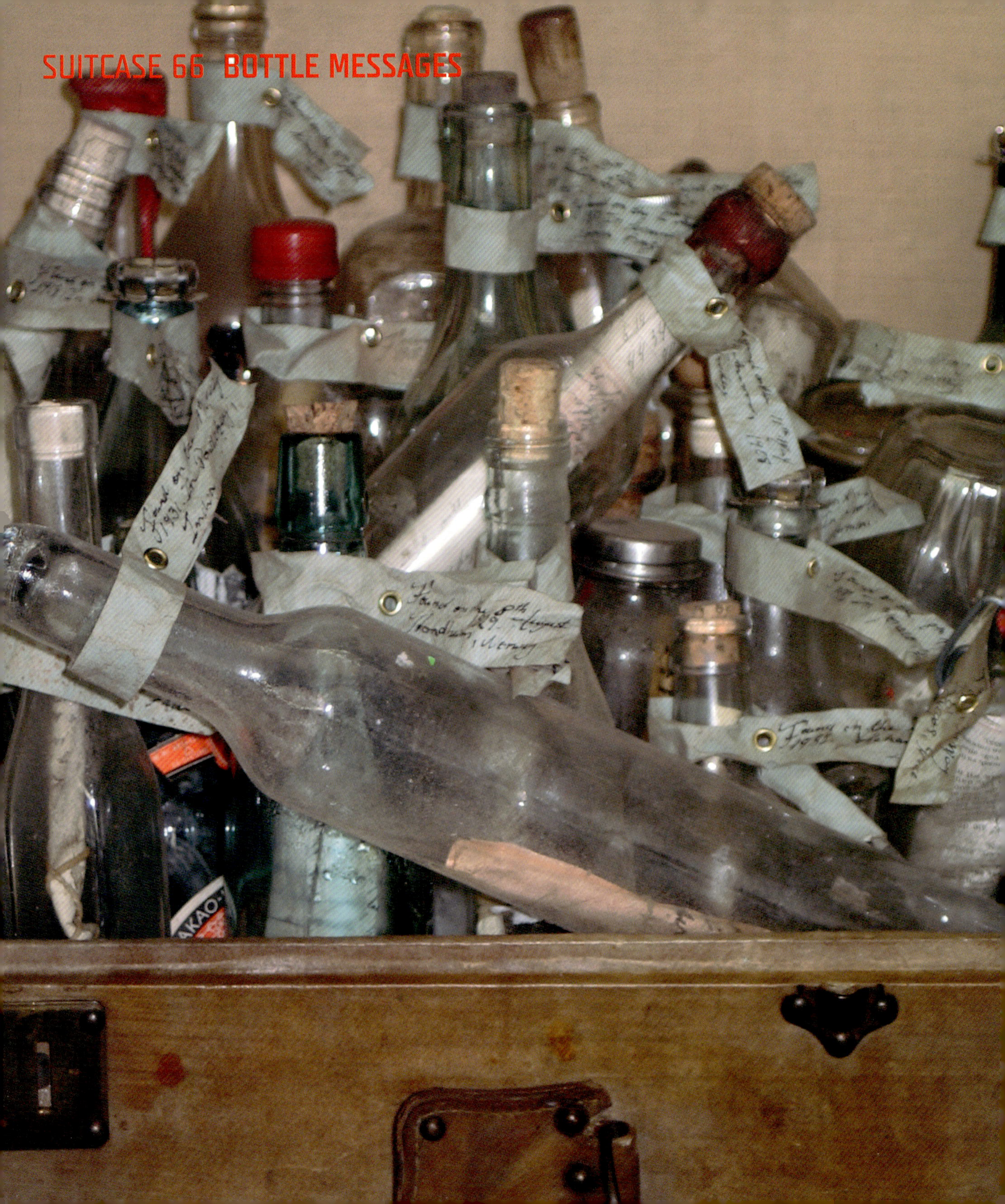

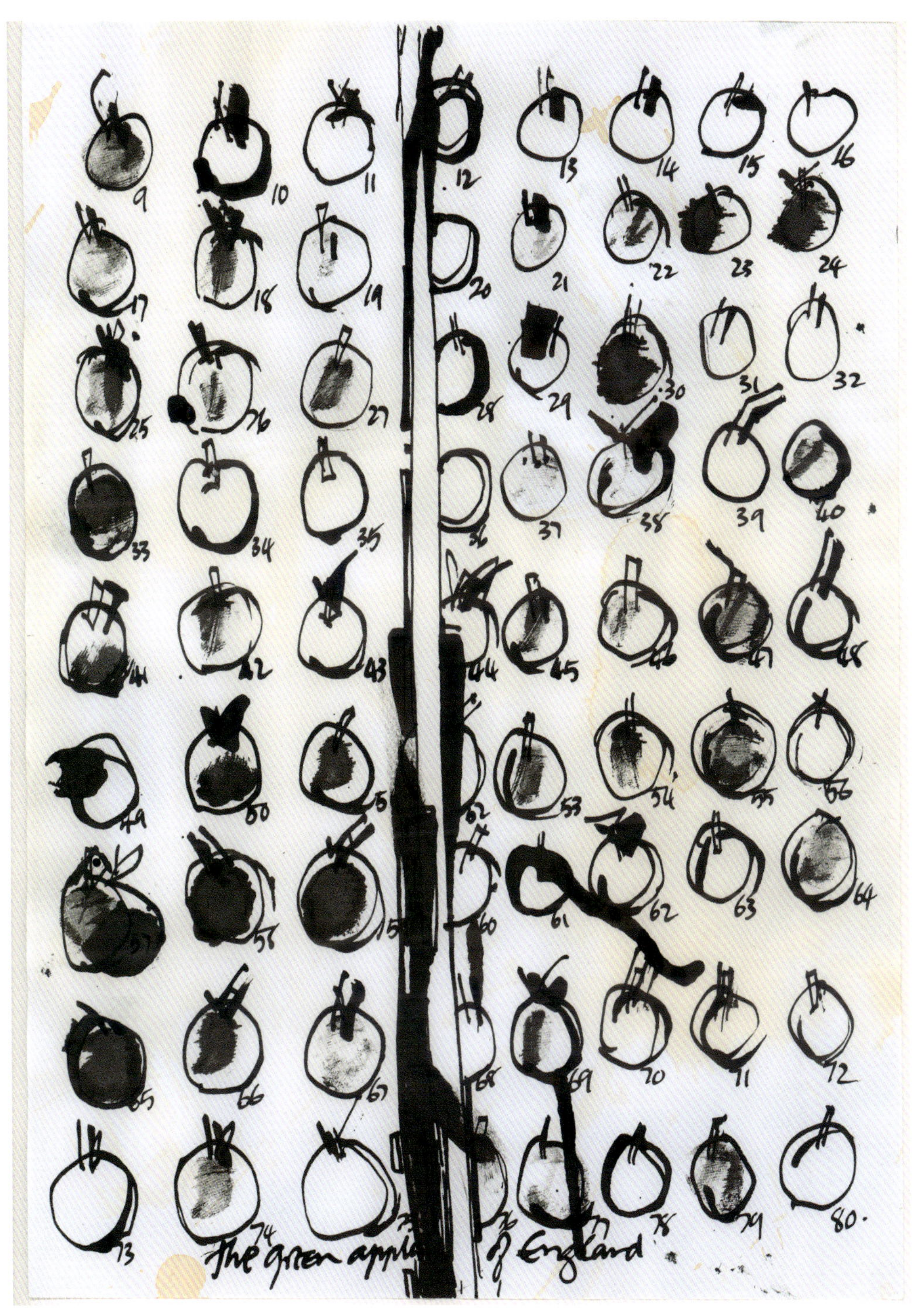
The green appl
of England

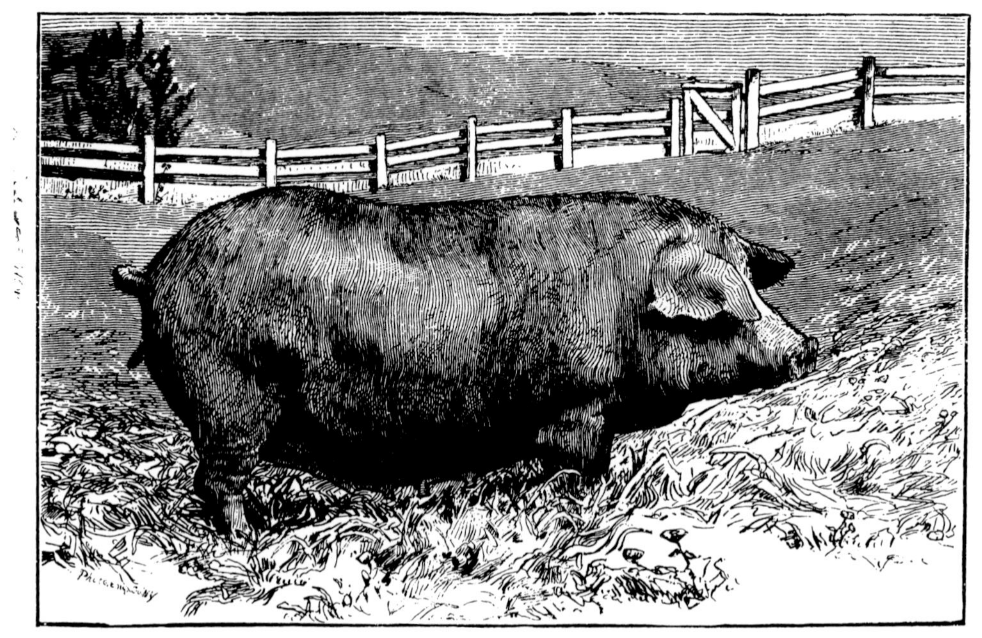

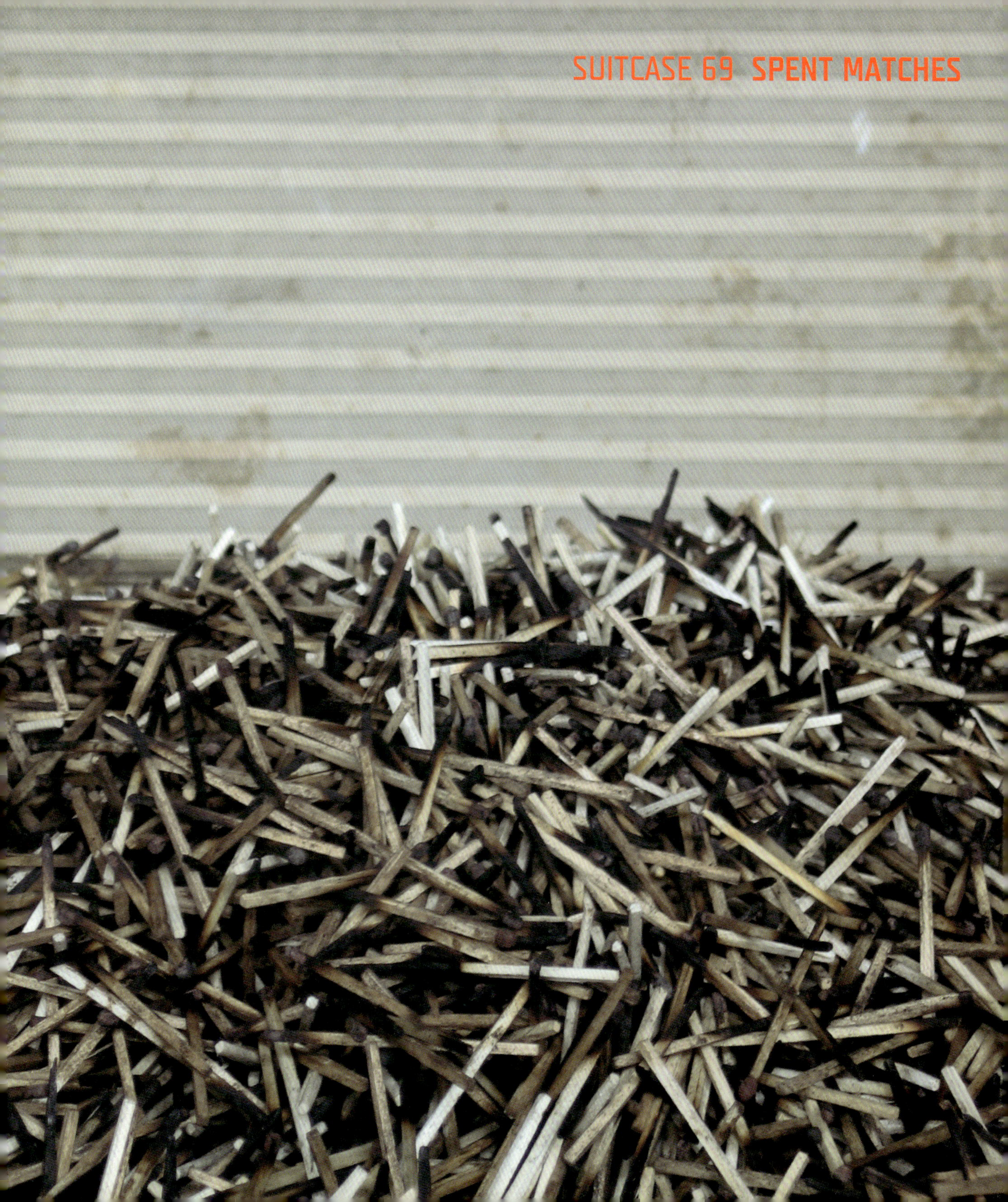
SUITCASE 69 SPENT MATCHES

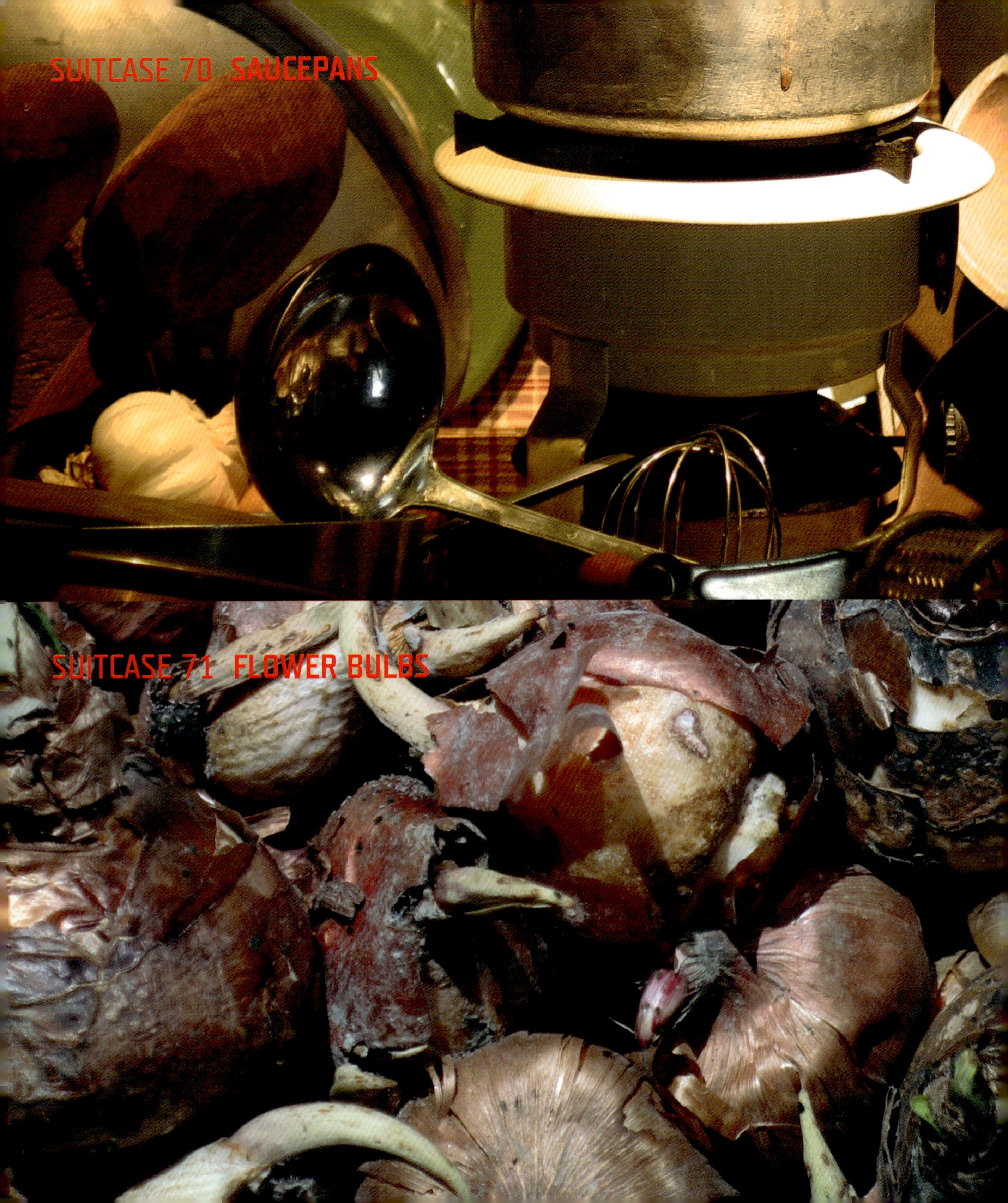
SUITCASE 70 SAUCEPANS
SUITCASE 71 FLOWER BULBS

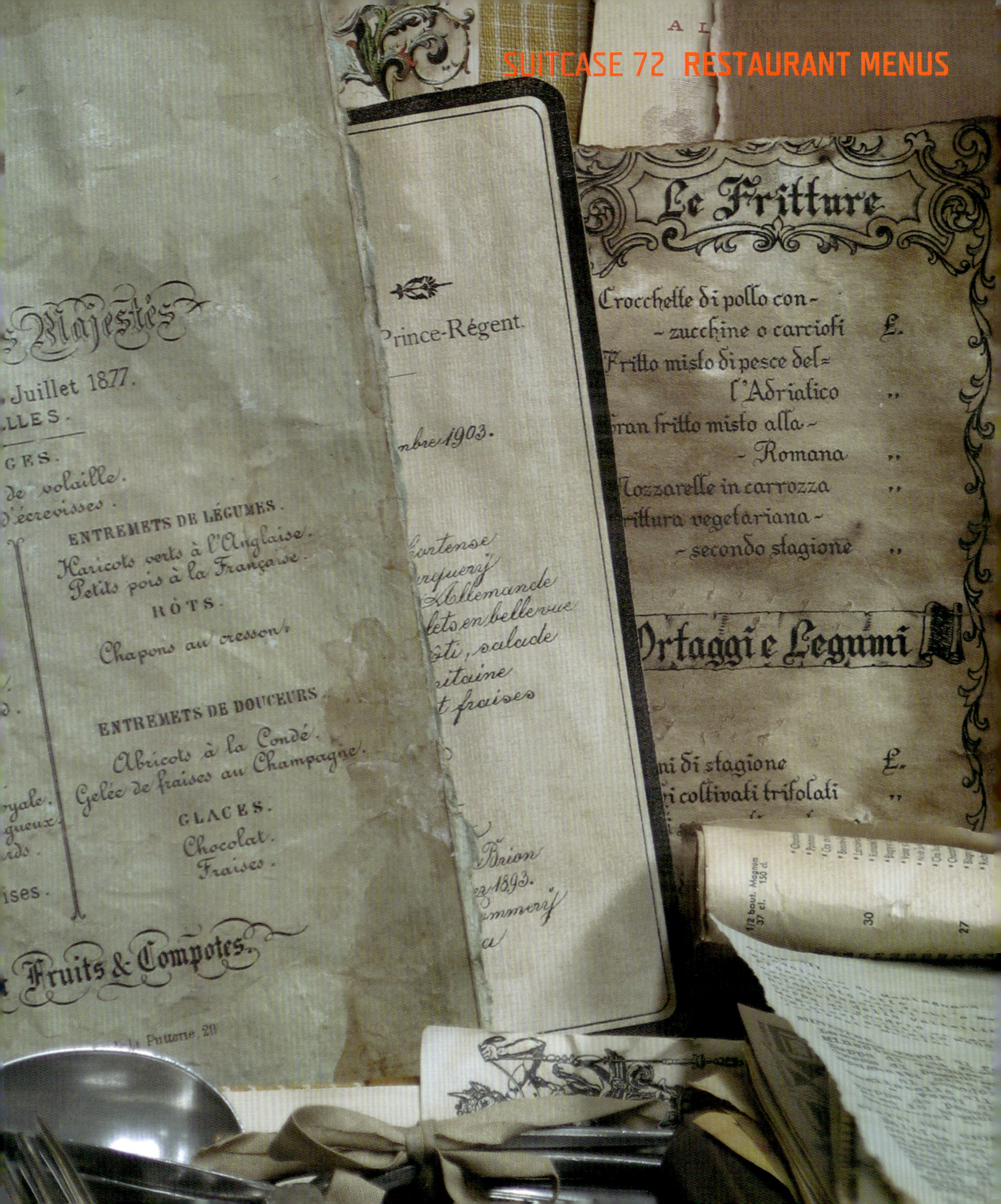
Le Fritture
Crocchette di pollo con-
- zucchine o carciofi £.
Fritto misto di pesce del=
l'Adriatico ,,
Romana ,,
Mozzarelle in carrozza ,,
- secondo stagione ,,
Ortaggi e Legumi
Prince-Régent.
Juillet 1877.
de volaille.
ENTREMETS DE LÉGUMES.
Haricots verts à l'Anglaise.
Petits pois à la Française.
RÔTS.
Chapons au cresson.
ENTREMETS DE DOUCEURS.
Abricots à la Condé.
Gelée de fraises au Champagne.
GLACES.
Chocolat.
Fraises.
Fruits & Compotes.

[illegible]ronegativiteiten, atoomstralen, ionstralen, vanderwaalsstralen

SUITCASE 73 92 ATOMIC ELEMENTS

elektronegativiteit (volgens Little en Jones)	atoomstraal in 10^{-10} m
symbool	
ionstraal (lading van het ion) in 10^{-10} m	vanderwaalsstraal in 10^{-10} m

Symbool	elektronegativiteit	atoomstraal	ionstraal (lading)
Be		1,12	(2+)
Mg		1,60	(2+)
Ca		1,97	(2+)
Sc	1,20	1,60	0,81(3+)
Ti	1,32	1,46	0,90(2+) 0,68(4+)
V	1,45	1,31	0,88(2+)
Cr	1,56	1,25	0,63(3+)
Mn	1,60	1,29	0,80(2+)
Fe	1,64	1,26	0,76(2+) 0,64(3+)
Co	1,70	1,25	0,74(2+) 0,63(3+)
Ni	1,75	1,24	0,72(2+)
Cu	1,75	1,28	0,96(1+) 0,69(2+)
Zn	1,66	1,33	0,74(2+)
Sr		2,15	(2+)
Y	1,11	1,80	0,93(3+)
Zr	1,22	1,57	0,80(4+)
Nb	1,23	1,41	
Mo	1,30	1,36	0,68(4+)
Tc	1,36	1,35	
Ru	1,42	1,33	
Rh	1,45	1,34	
Pd	1,35	1,38	
Ag	1,42	1,44	1,26(1+)
Cd	1,46	1,49	0,97(2+)
Ba		2,17	(2+)
La	1,08	1,88	1,15(3+)
Hf	1,23	1,57	
Ta	1,33	1,43	
W	1,40	1,37	
Re	1,46	1,37	
Os	1,52	1,34	
Ir	1,55	1,35	
Pt	1,44	1,38	
Au	1,42	1,44	1,37(1+)
Hg	1,44	1,52	1,10(2+)
Ra		2,2	
Ac	1,00	2,0	

NH_4^+ : 1,42 · 10^{-10} m

,37 · 10^{-10} m

,71 · 10^{-10} m

symbool	
ionstraal (lading van het ion) in 10^{-10} m	vanderwaalsstraal in 10^{-10} m

H, Li, Be, Na, Mg, K, Ca, Sc, Ti, V, Cr, Mn, Fe, Co, Ni, Rb, Sr, Y, Zr, Nb, Mo, Tc, Ru, Rh, Pd, Cs, Ba, La, Hf, Ta, W, Re, Os, Ir, Pt, Fr, Ra

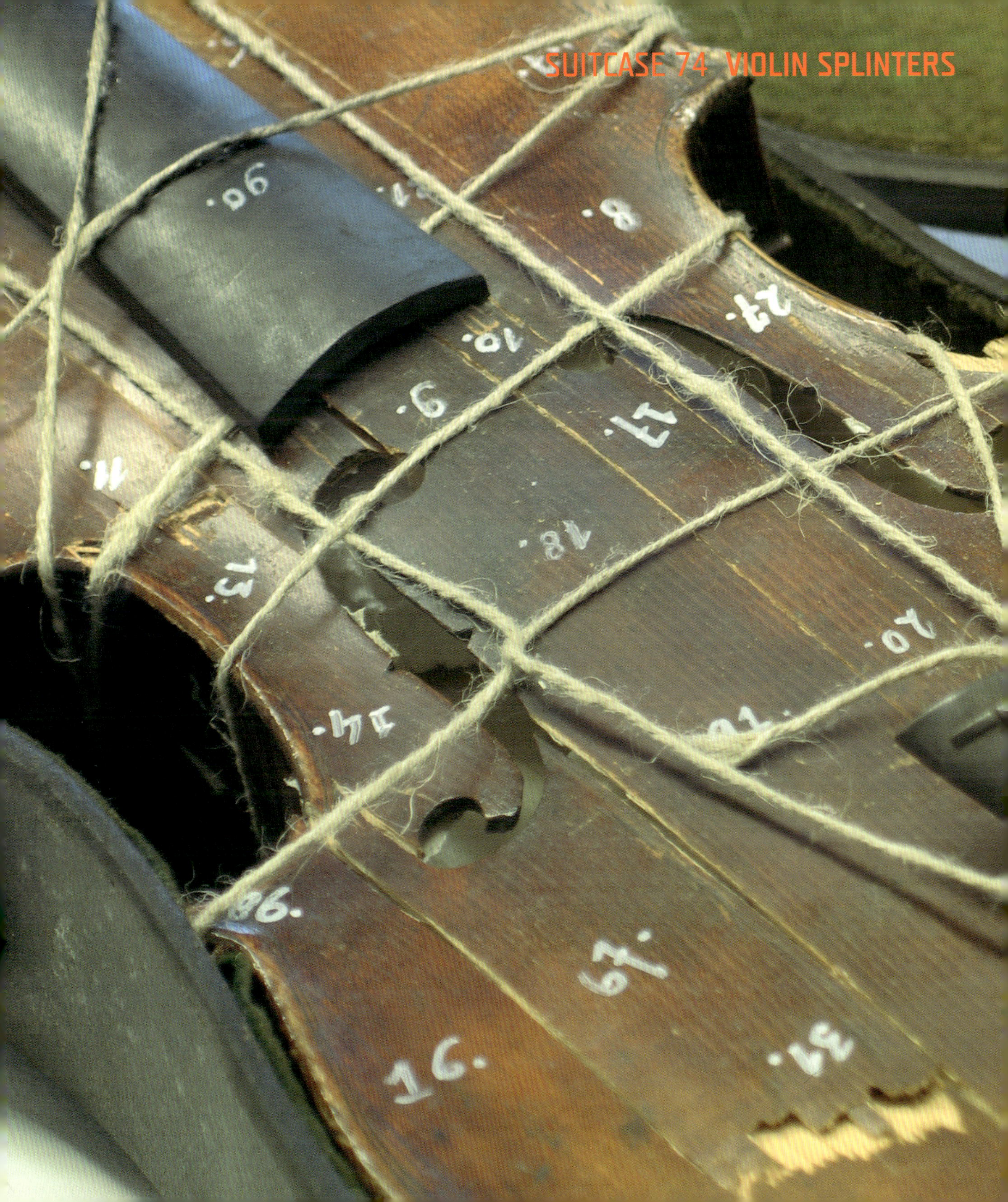

SUITCASE 74 VIOLIN SPLINTERS

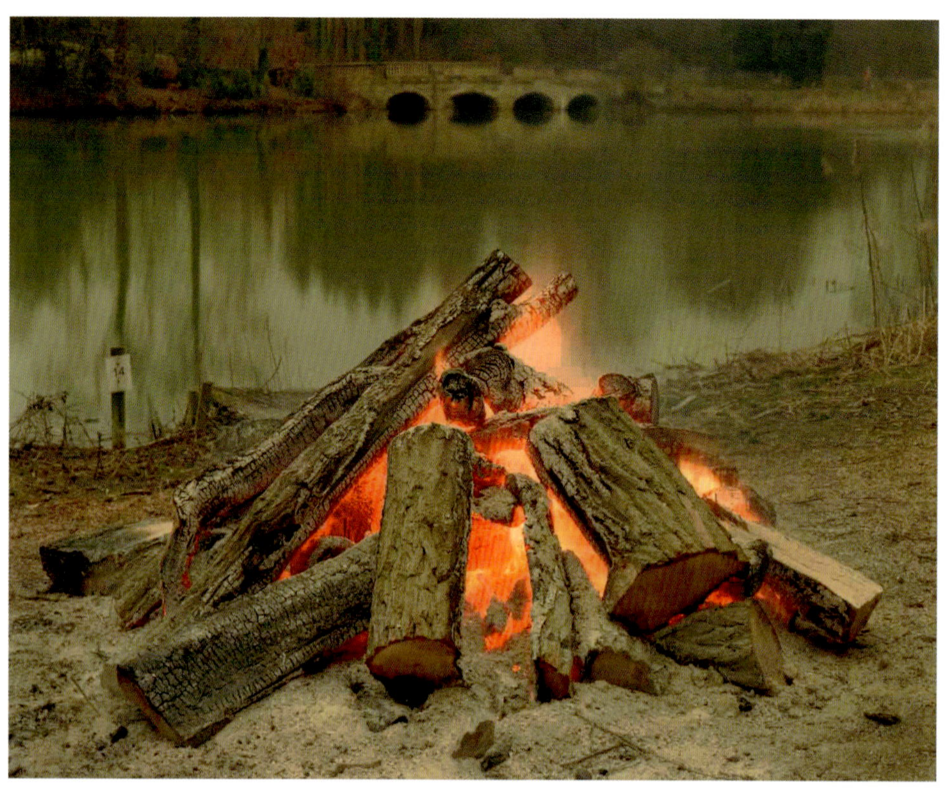

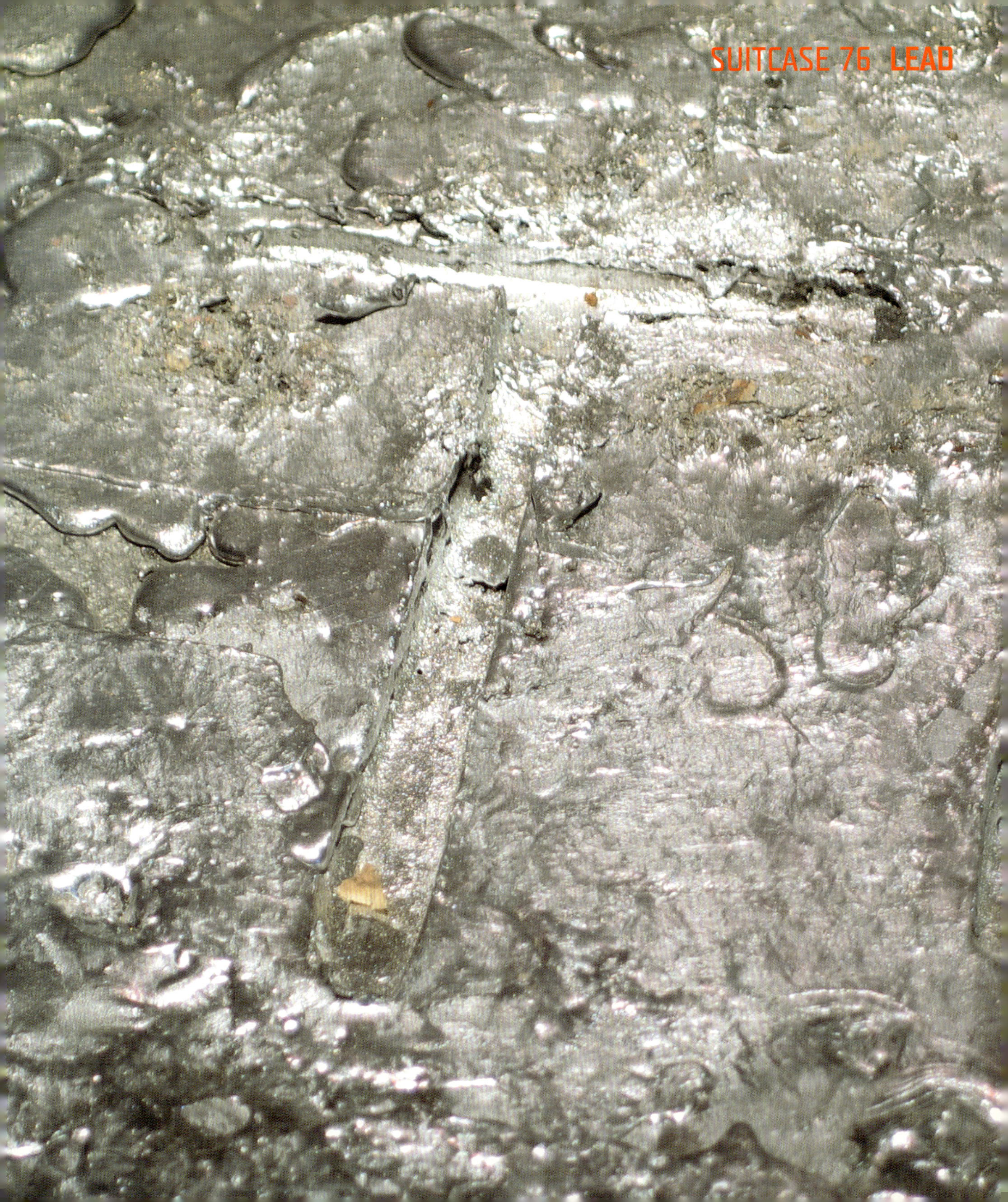
SUITCASE 76 LEAD

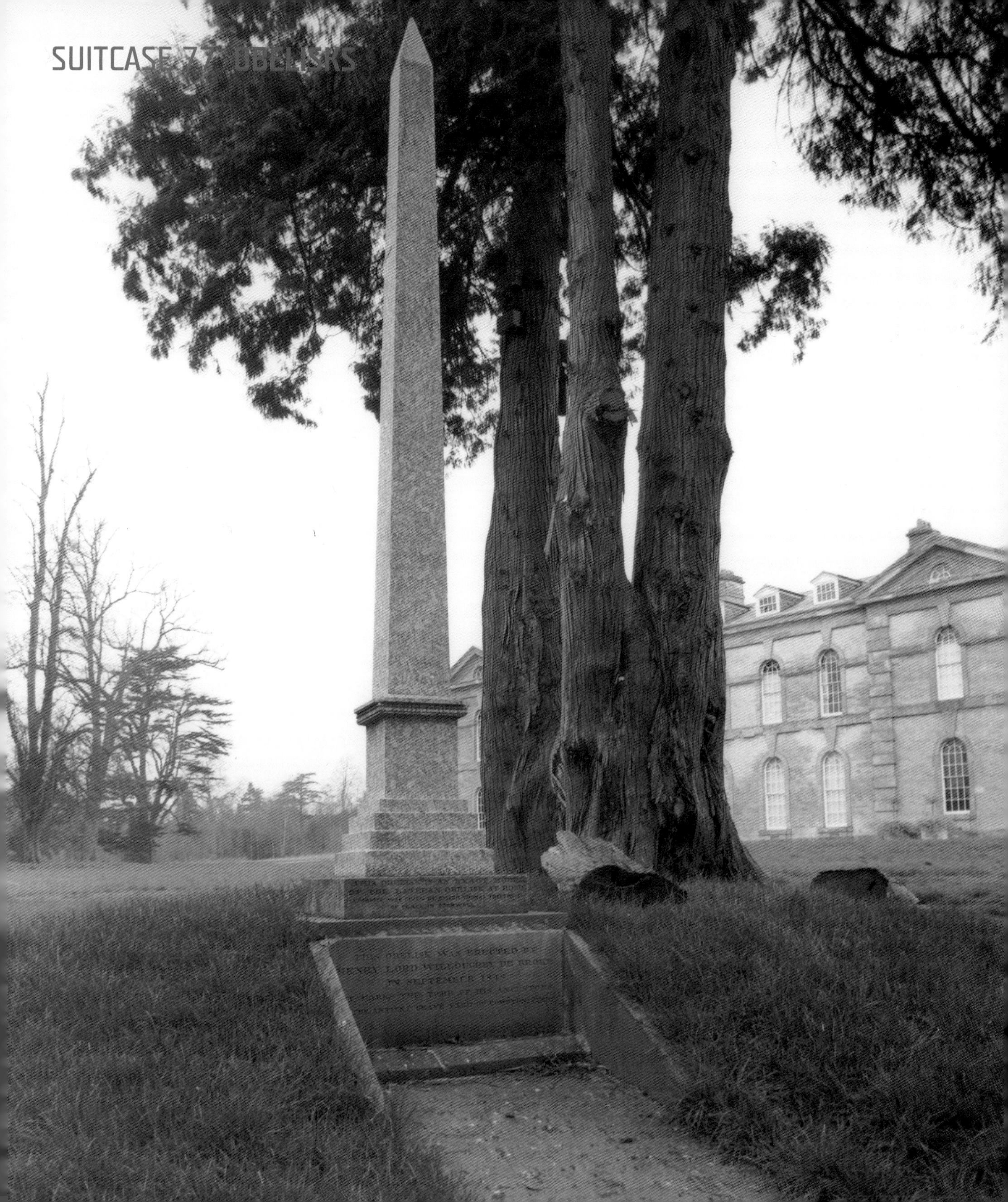

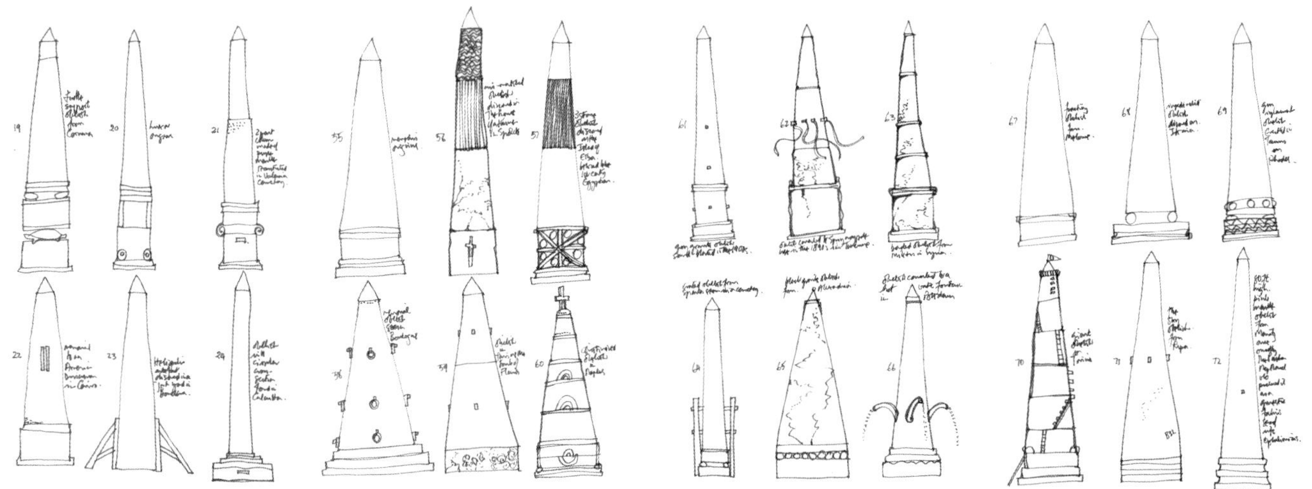

1. Carried by ship from Luxor to Cairo to Naples 2. Floated down the Nile to Alexandria and left in the dock for 600 years before shipped to Verona 3. Shipped to Manchester from Thebes 4. Taken by barge to Cairo and shipped in a French vessel to Paris 5. Shipped to Rome in 120AD and abandoned in Ostia for 700 years before being hauled to Trastevere 6. Reassembled from pieces in Ankara probably transported by ship from Cairo in the 1650s 7. Reconstructed- only the centre stone portion can be authenticated 8. Brought from Thebes by way of Sicily and Italy to St Petersburg in 1841 9. Erected in Turin in the celebrations for the unification of Italy 10. Probably from Thebes erected in Marachese in the 1740s 11. Luxor monument now in Prague 12. Some authorities believe this to be a fake erected in Edinburgh by the Egypt society 13. Shipped from Alexandria to Europe in the 1680s 14. Lost and reconstructed in Phillipi by Antinous in 1720 15. Brought by barge to Boulogne by a wealthy American 16. Erected in a cemetery in Padua in memory of an Egyptian horse 17. Believed to have been touched by Antinous and erected on the Nile banks in his memory 18. A limestone reconstruction in Loughton, Essex, England in memory of a horse that fell in the Battle of Waterloo in 1815 19. Turtle-supported obelisk from Corunna 20. Luxor origins 21. Two-part column made of purple marble reconstructed in Valencia cemetery 22. Memorial to an American businessman in Cairo 23. Heliopolis artefact discovered in a junk yard in Barcelona 24. Obelisk with circular cross-section found in Calcutta 25. Obelisk from Luxor formerly believed to be from Thebes 26. Memorial to Emmanuel III erected in the gardens of Pratolino near Florence 27. Bolted edifice erected in Saragossa 1910 28. Monmouthshire memorial to the dead in the Crimea War, the Crimea being thought to be in Egypt by Welsh artillery 29. Verona marble 30. Fluted obelisk in Riga 31. Granite column from Syracusa 32. Antique Roman obelisk probably from Actium manufactured AD9, supported on a 1719 base with a floral design 33. Decomposed Coptic column discovered in Rubba 34. Brick obelisk in a cemetery in Rheims 35. Possible column of calamine limestone from Mabu 36. Inferior obelisk discovered in the harbour at Jaffa 37. Pink veined marble column lost at sea in 12th century, rediscovered 1927 38. Simple obelisk column of grey granite found in Allissio 39. Double column capped in white porphyr 40. Naval obelisk erected in the Venetian naval docks 41. Obelisk from Memphis adopted as a war memorial in Palermo 42. Celebratory column found in Romania in the 15th century 43. Layered obelisk of tuffa found in Pergamum 44. Cast-iron pinned obelisk found on Minorca shipped there in the 1400s 45. Undressed granite column in the antiqques market Istanbul 46. Yellow sandstone obelisk from Marathon 47. Ship's prows obelisk, Messalina 48. Brown marble column erected in Thessaloniki 49. Obelisk in Malta built into the wall of a Knights of the Cross chapel 50. Milan memorial 51. Decorated obelisk discovered in Sparta, believed to be used as a mile post in the Spartan Marathon 52. Obelisk in St Petersburg erected by Peter the Great 53. From Crete 54. Unidentified obelisk from Cairo 55. Memphis origins 56. Mis-matched obelisk discovered in the house of a tanner in Spoleto 57. Three-stone obelisk discovered on the island of Elba believed to be 1st century BC Egyptian 58. Memorial obelisk seen in Boulogne 59. Obelisk in Paris at the Tomb of Fleuris 60. Christianised obelisk in Naples 61. Gray granite obelisk sand blasted in the 1900s 62. Obelisk converted to Spring Maypole use in the 1890s in Turenne 63. Banded obelisk from Miletis in Syria 64. Crated obelisk from Sparta seen in a cemetery 65. Black granite obelisk from Alexandria 66. Obelisk converted to a hot water fountain in Potsdam 67. 68. 69. 70. 71. 72. 73. 74. 75. 76. 77. 78. 79. Large obelisk discovered in Sinai converted into a local lock-up 80. Sidon obelisk of red sandstone 81. Obelisk for transport manufacture from Heliopolis 82. Discovered in the sea off Messina, believed to be a spoil of war discovered by troops associated with Garibaldi 83. Known as the pillar of Samson and discovered built into the wall of a corn store in Accra 84. White marble obelisk in the museum at Baiae 85. 86. 87. 88. 89. 90. 91. 92

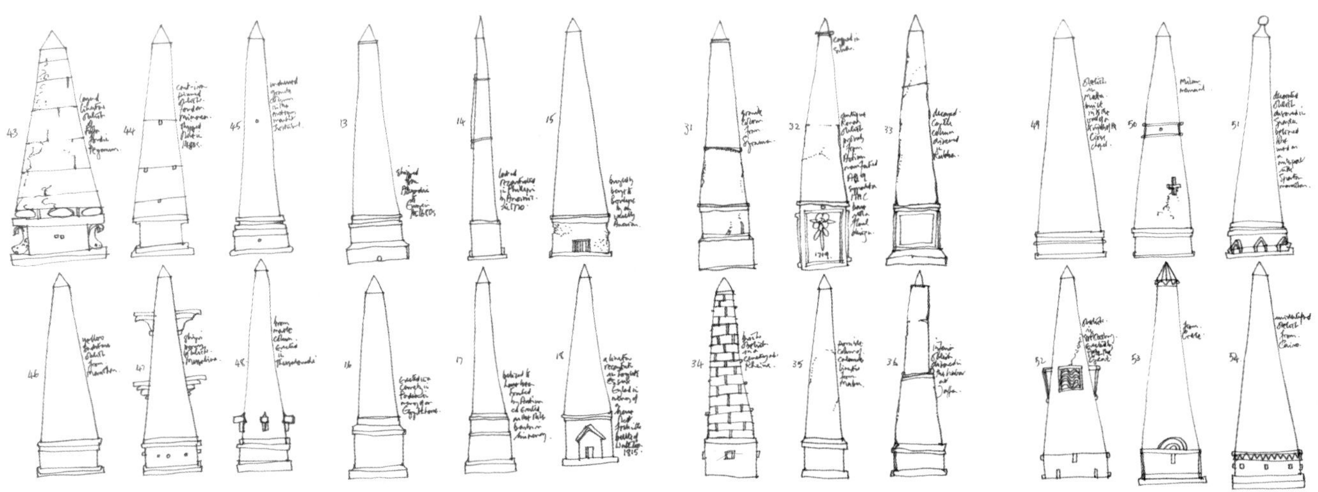

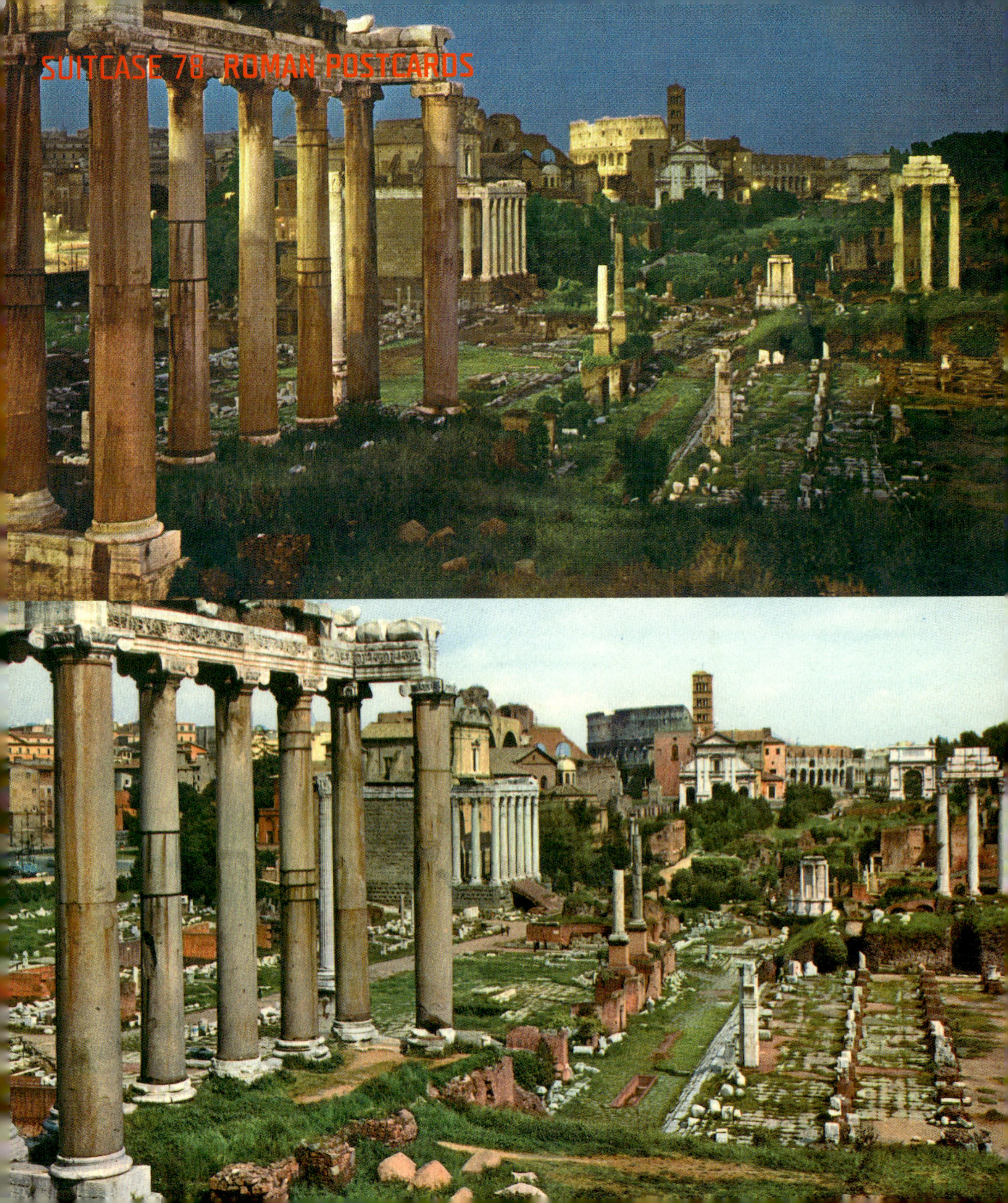

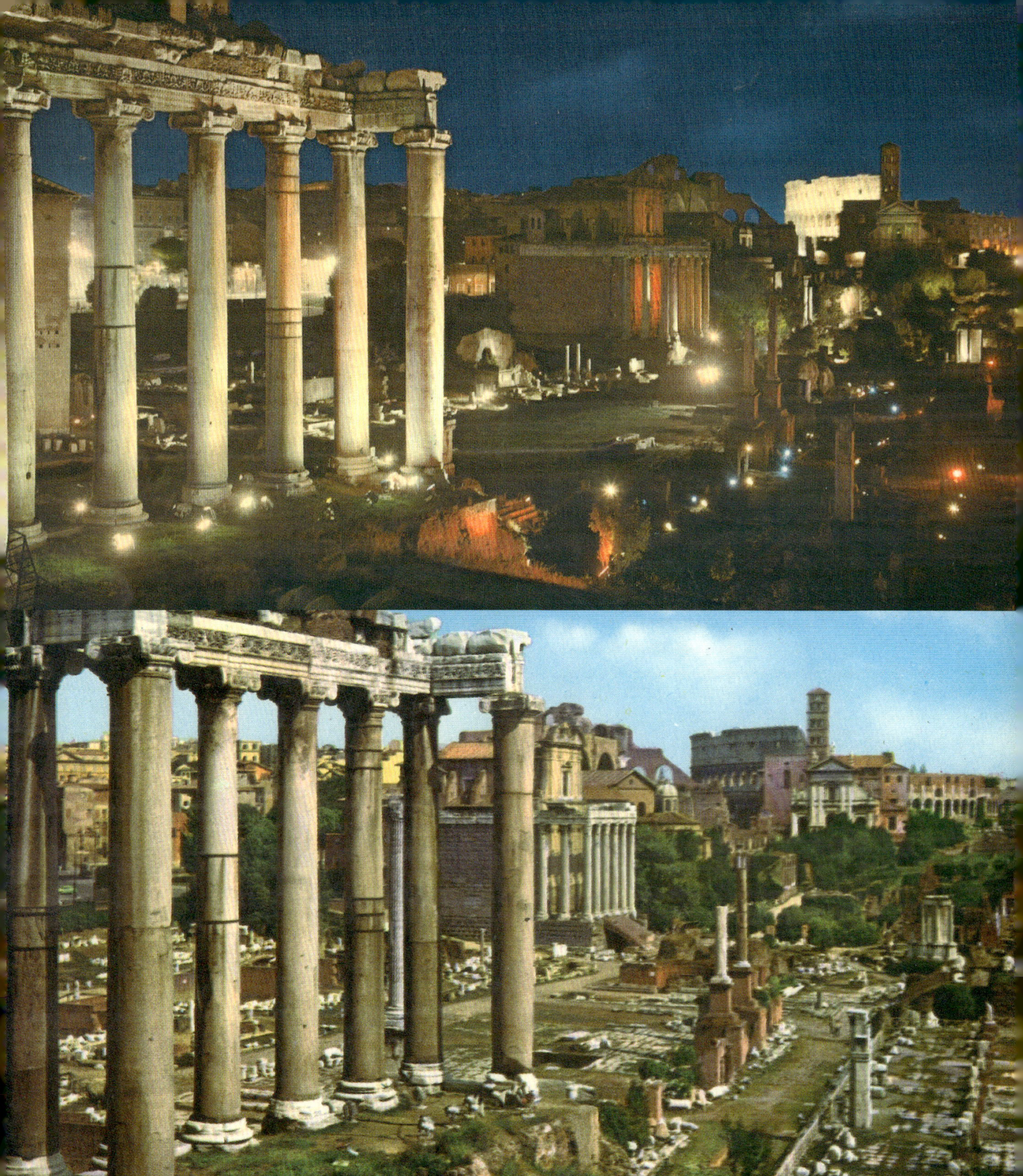

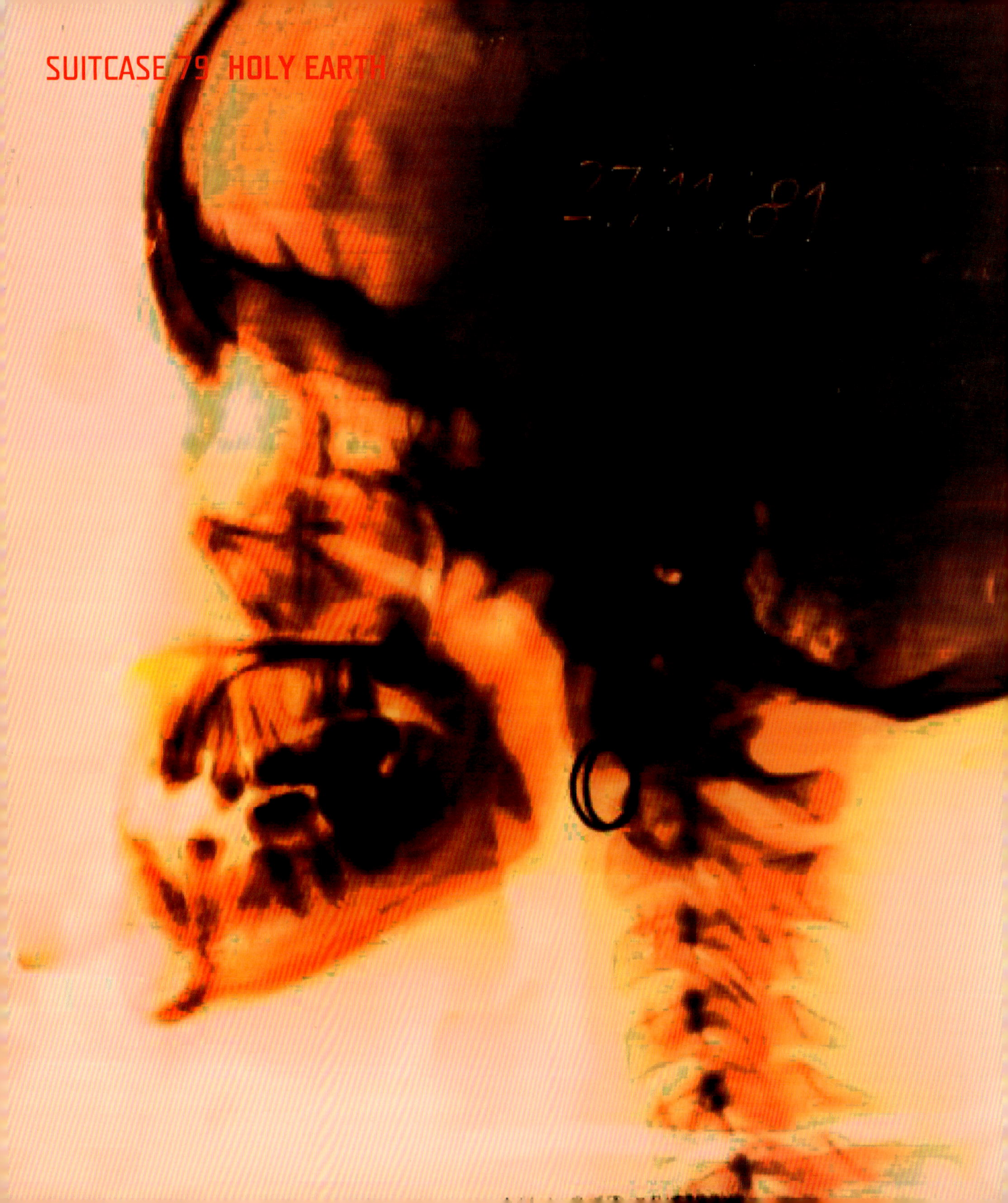
27.11.81

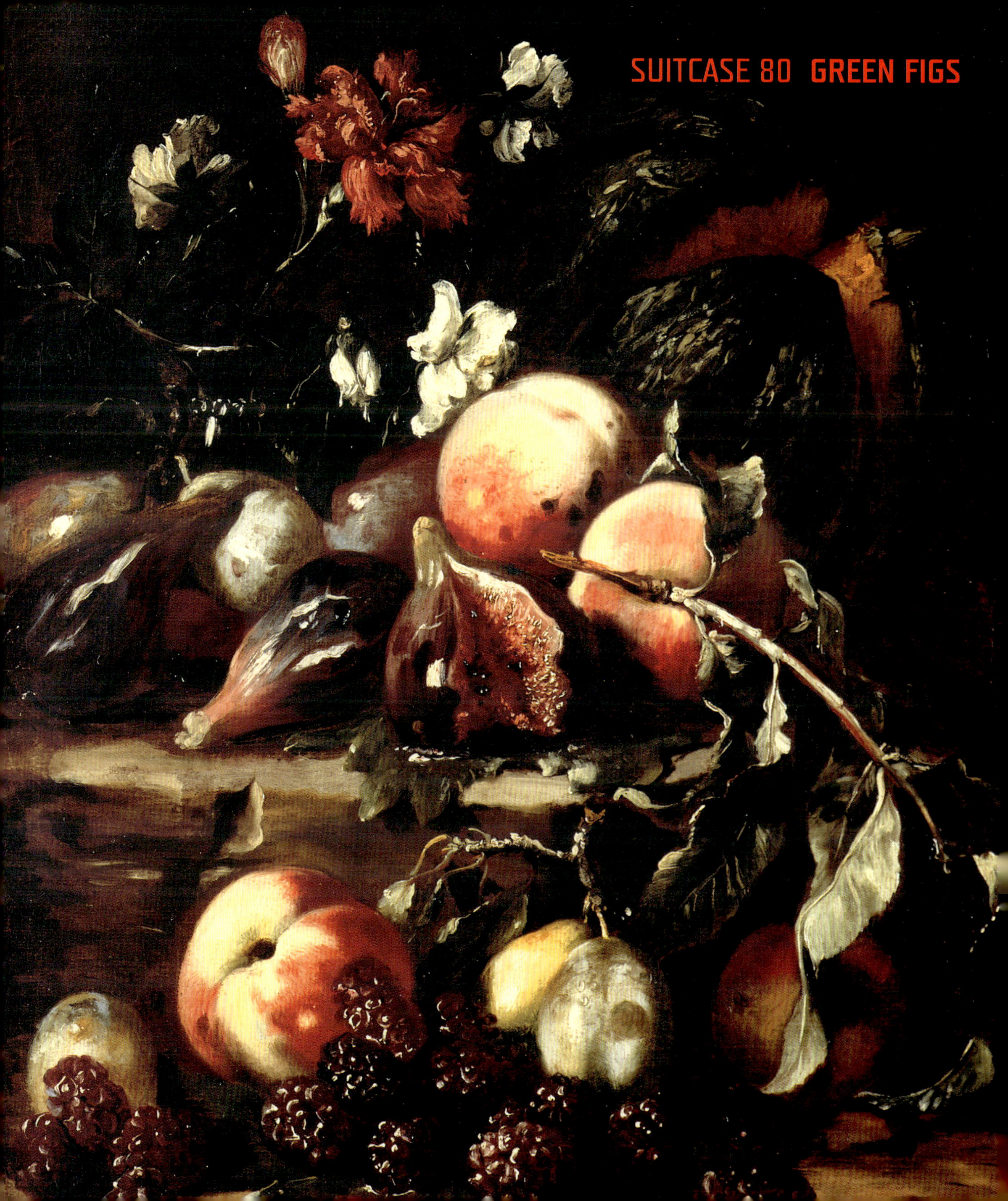
SUITCASE 80 GREEN FIGS

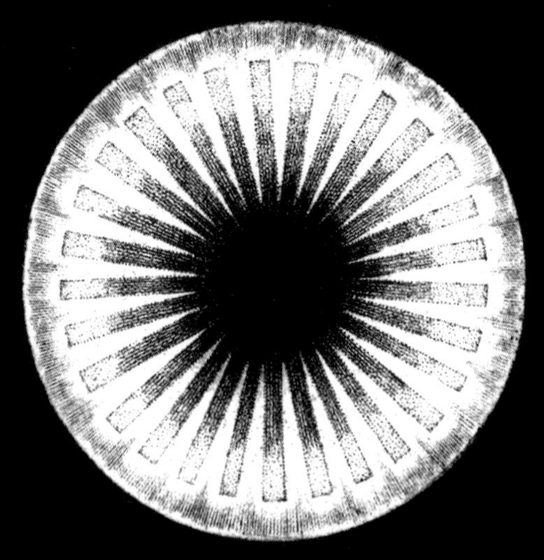

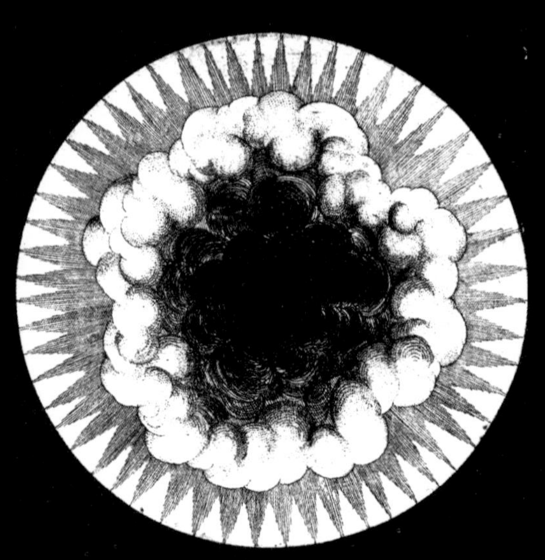

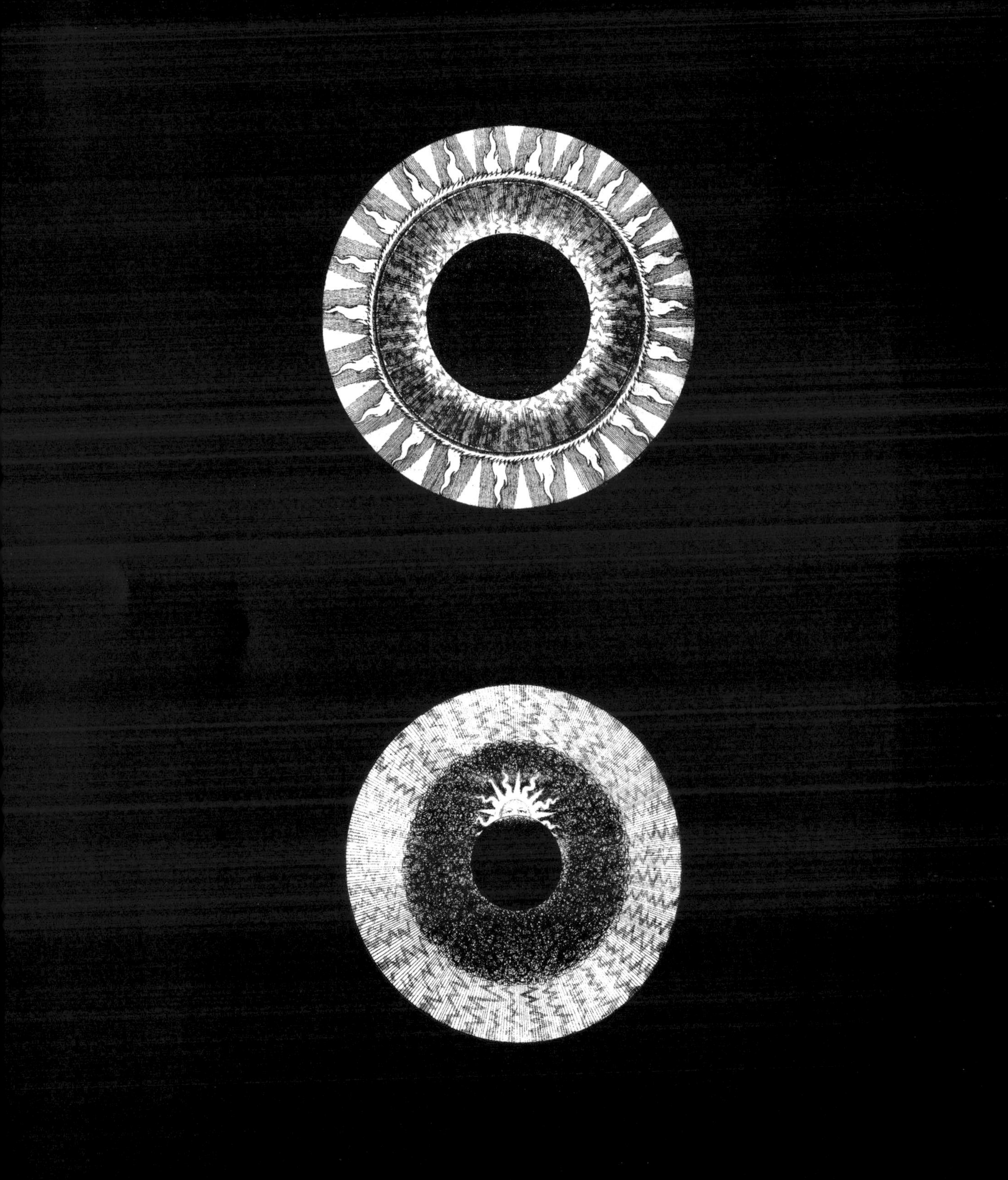

SUITCASE 82 NOTES ON DROWNED CORPSES

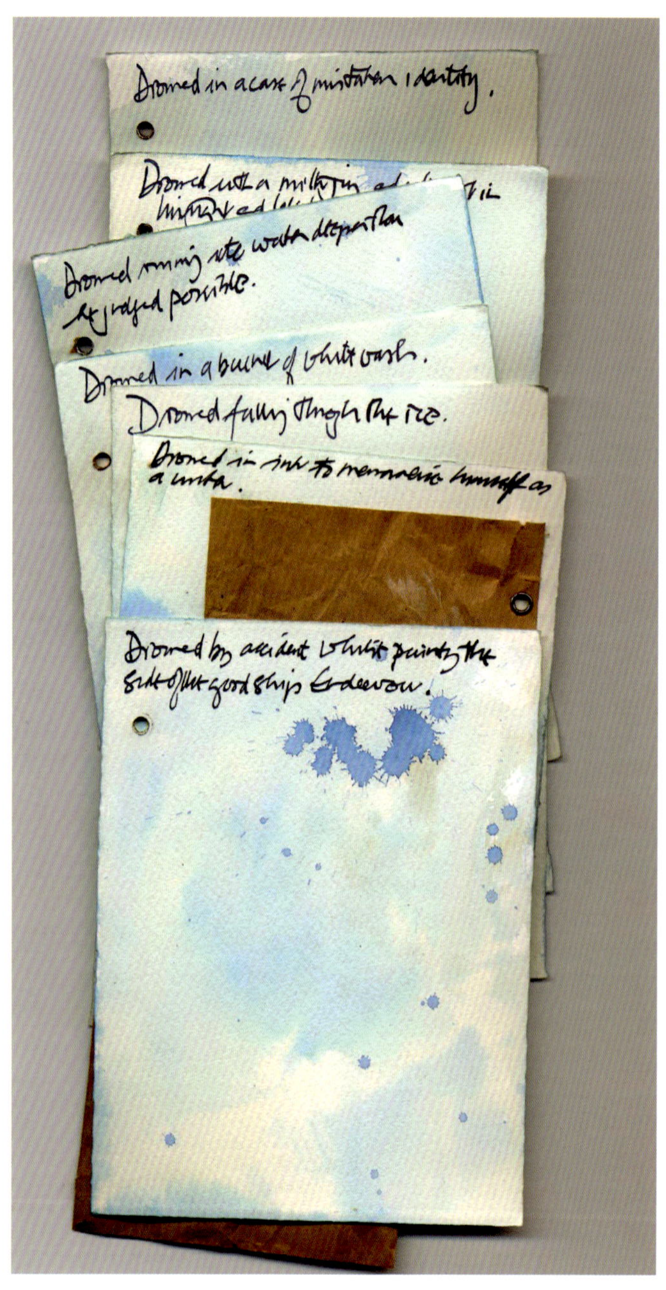

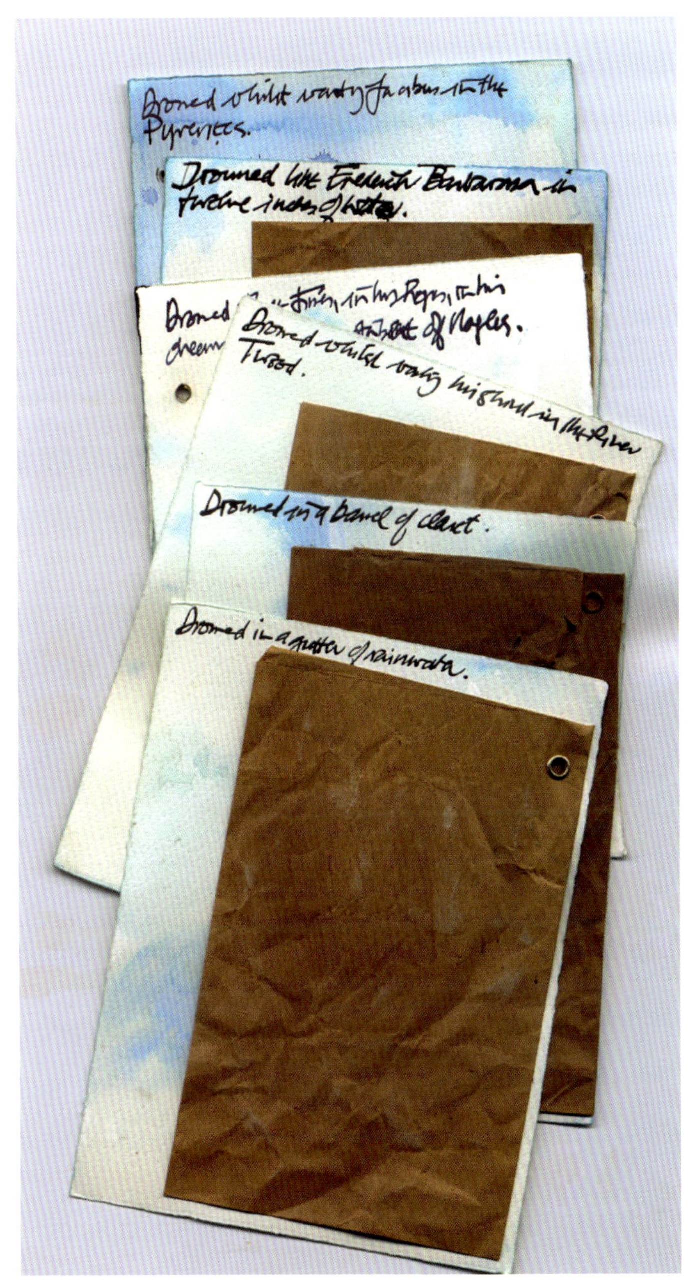
Drowned like Frederick Barbarossa in twelve inches of water.
Drowned in a barrel of claret.
Drowned in a gutter of rainwater.

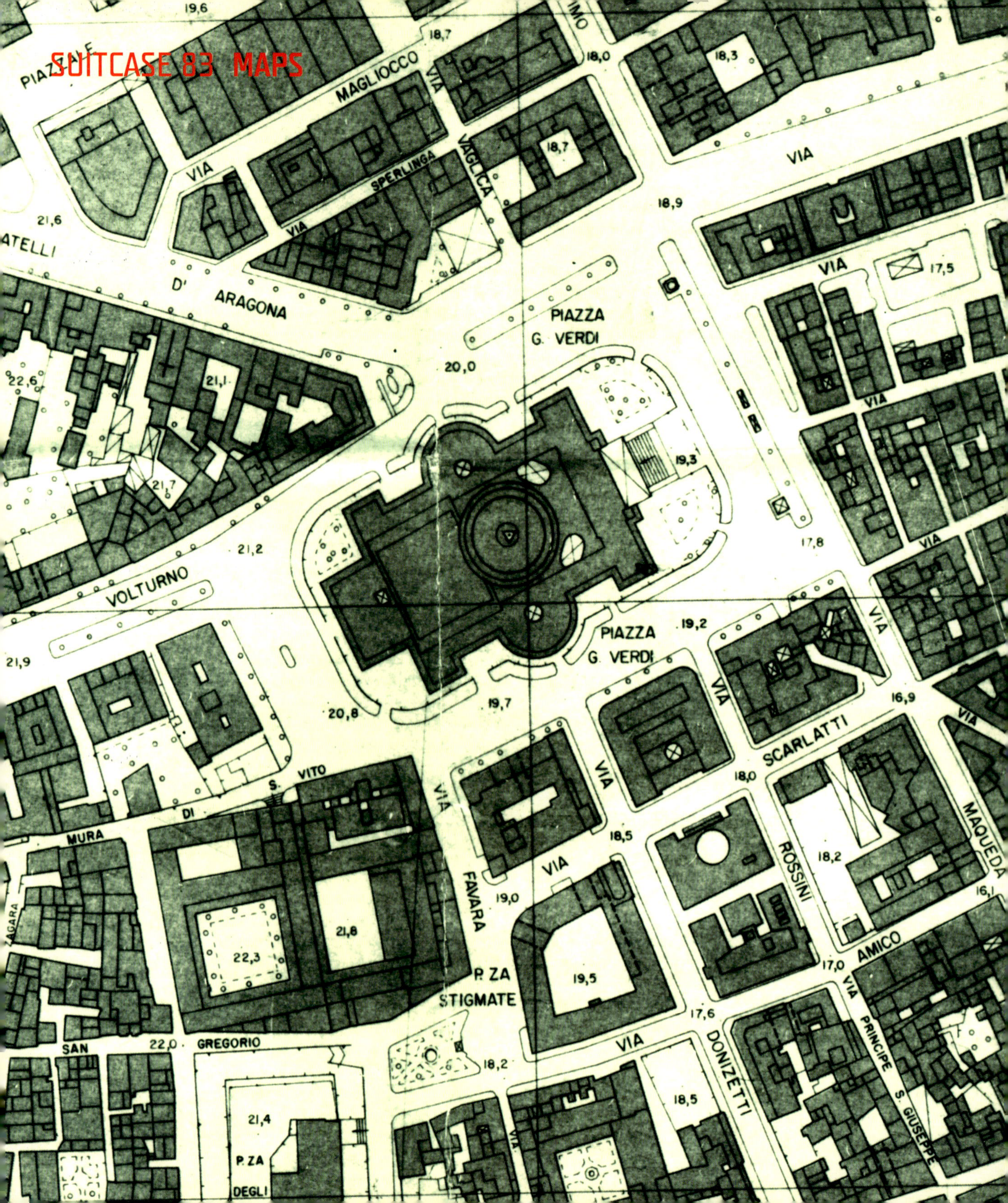

SUITCASE 83 MAPS
PIAZZALE
VIA MAGLIOCCO
VIA VAGLICA
VIA SPERLINGA
VIA D' ARAGONA
ATELLI
PIAZZA G. VERDI
VIA VOLTURNO
PIAZZA G. VERDI
VIA SCARLATTI
VIA MAQUEDA
VIA DI S. VITO
MURA
VIA FAVARA
P. ZA STIGMATE
VIA ROSSINI
VIA AMICO
VIA PRINCIPE S. GIUSEPPE
VIA DONIZETTI
SAN GREGORIO
P. ZA DEGLI
ZAGARA

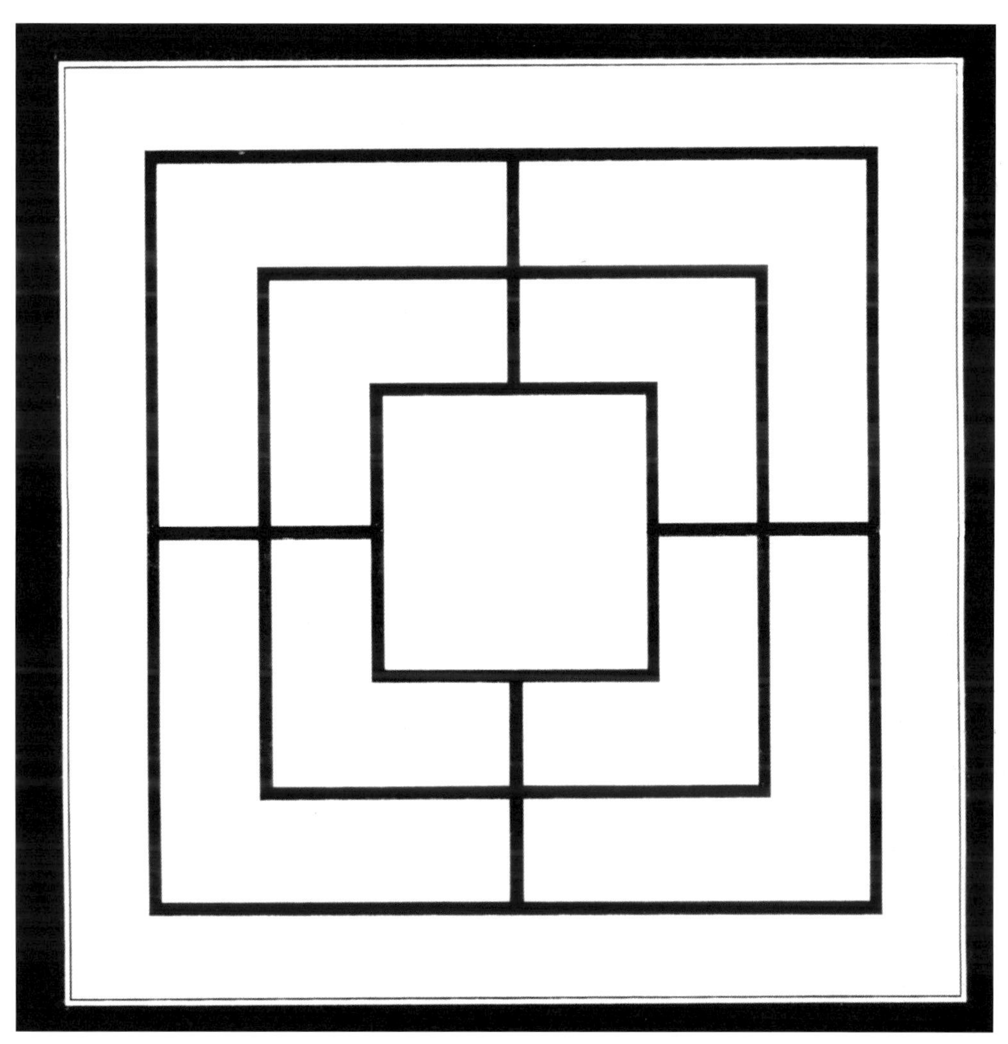

SUITCASE 85 INK & BLOOD

Maybe as much ink has been used in the dispatch of human affairs as blood. You think sometimes that ink and blood could be interchangeable, for it might seem that as much ink has been spilt over blood, as blood over ink. Huge amounts of ink were spilt from the Treaty of Westphalia to the Treaty of Versailles to settle vast amounts of blood-letting. At the Nuremburg Trials there were over fifteen million documents of ink-written evidence to settle the blood-accounts of over fifty-seven million killings to occupy a library of over one million books.

Luper: 100 objects to represent the world.

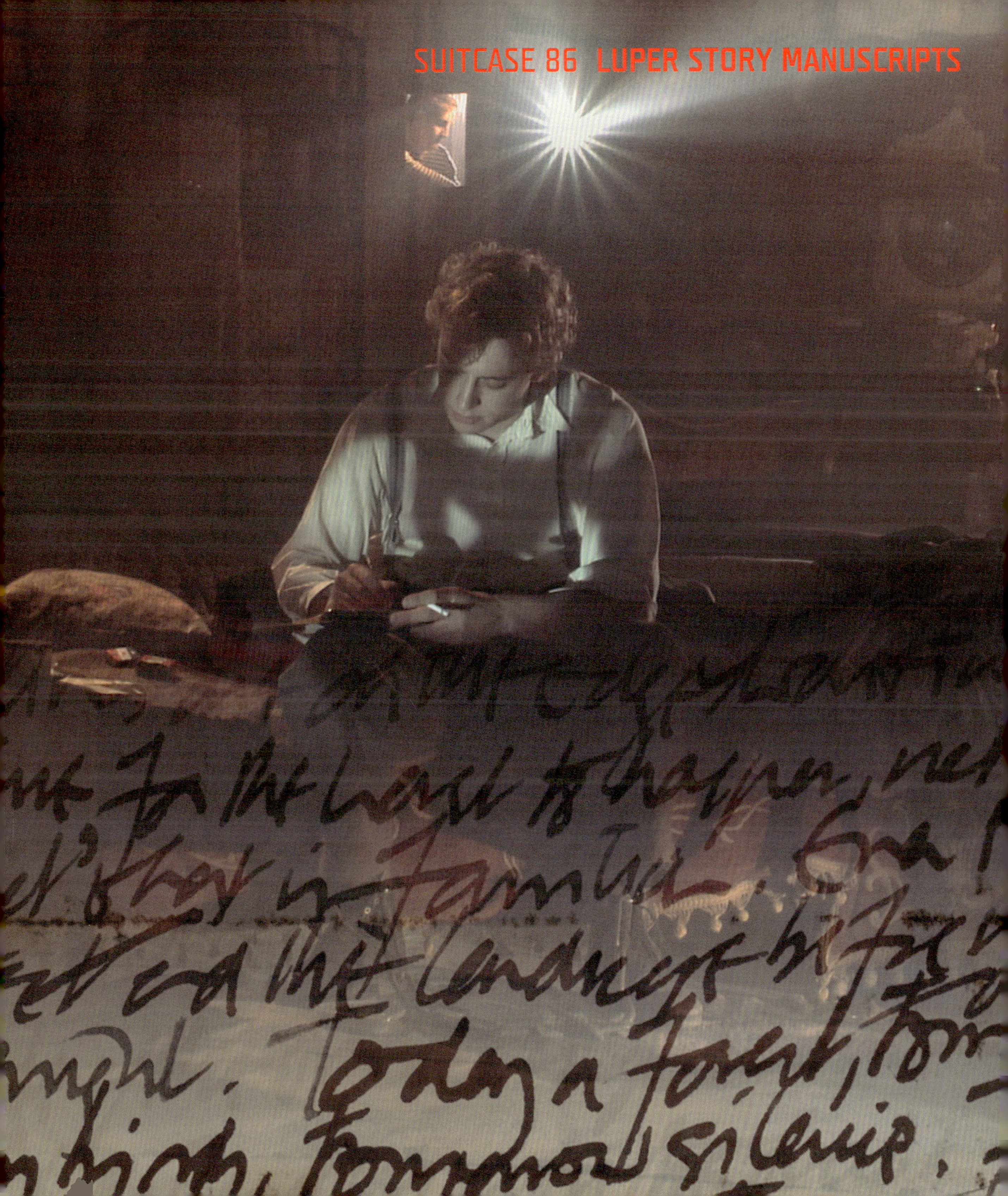
SUITCASE 86 LUPER STORY MANUSCRIPTS

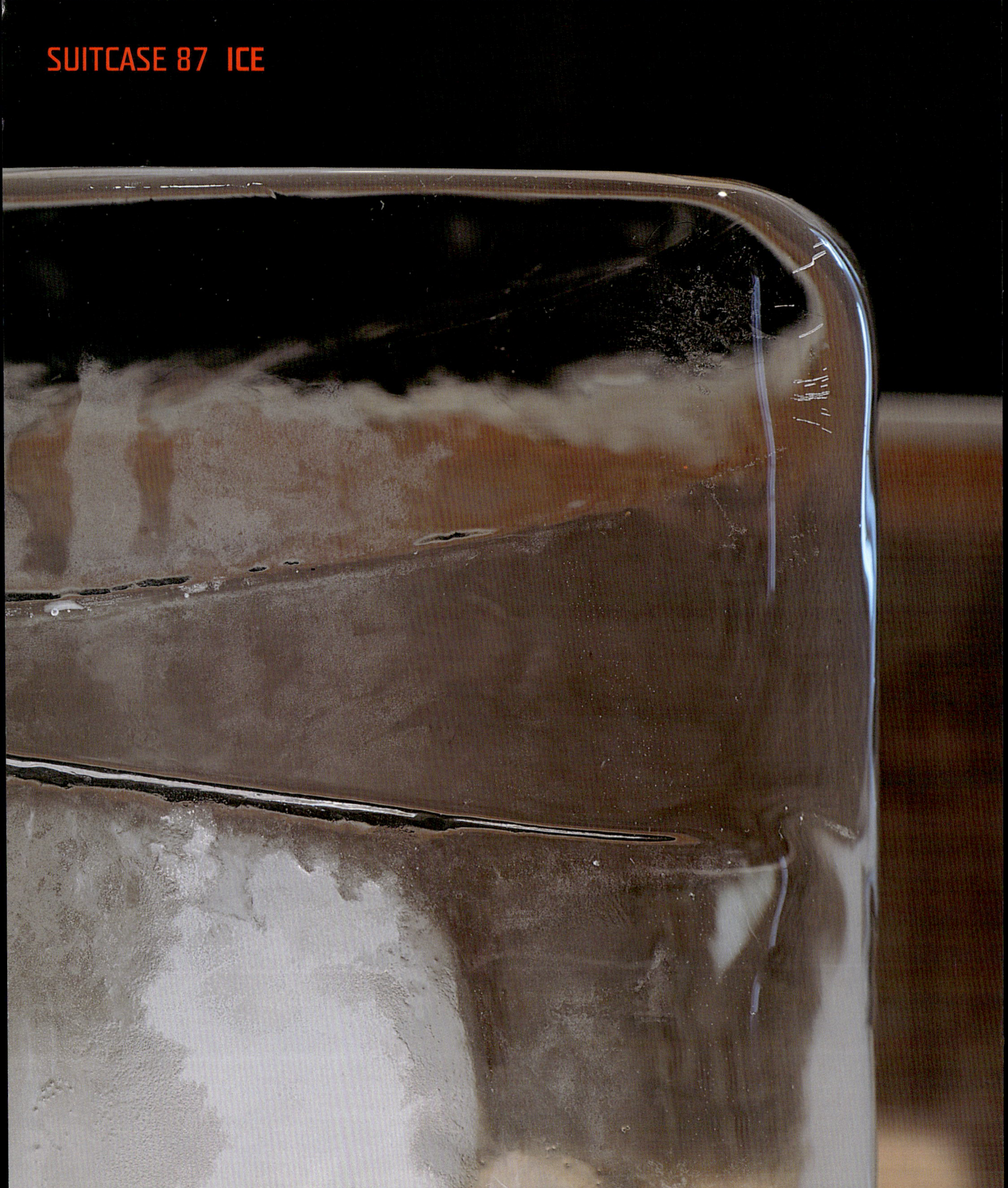
SUITCASE 87 ICE

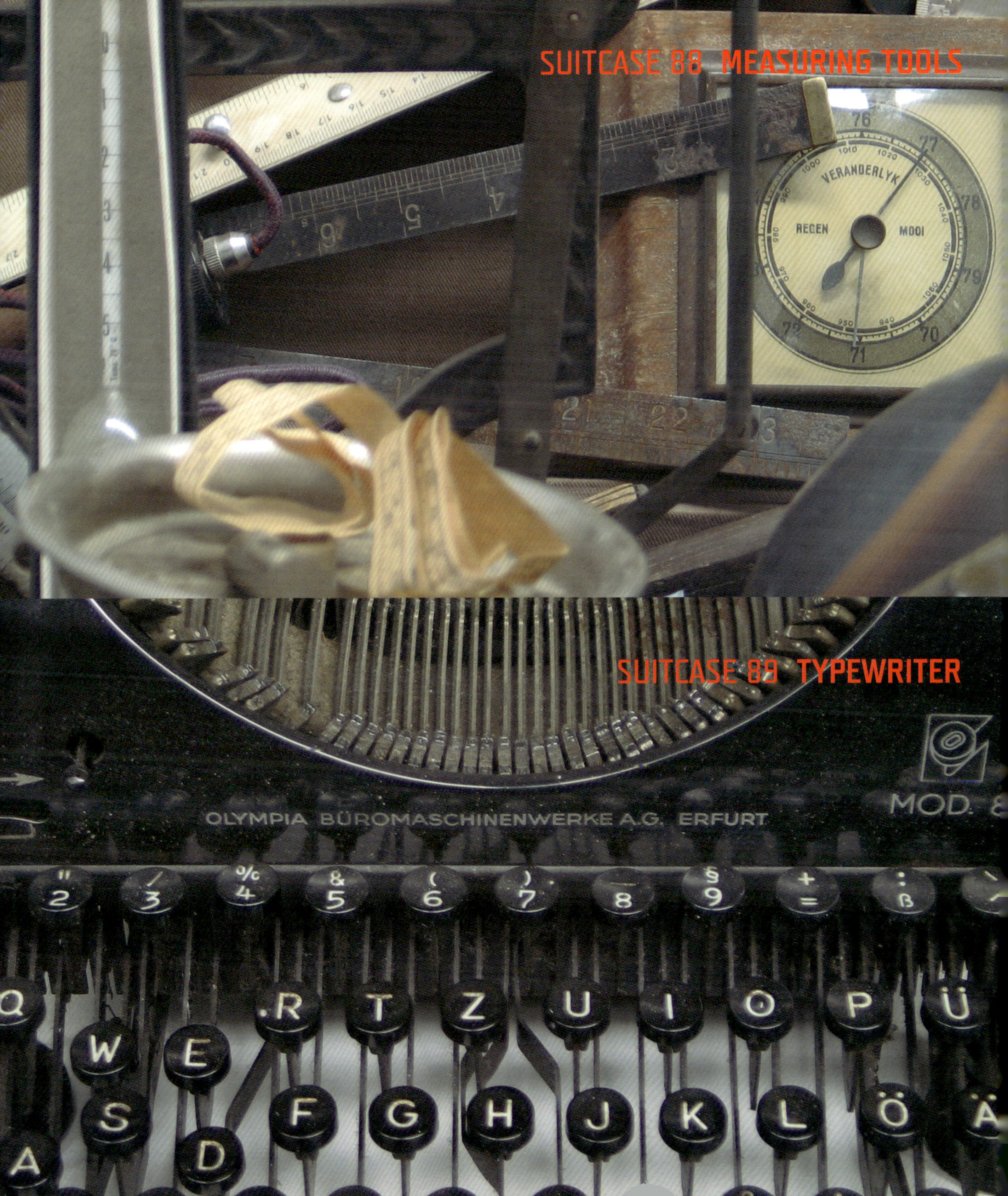

SUITCASE 88 MEASURING TOOLS

SUITCASE 89 TYPEWRITER

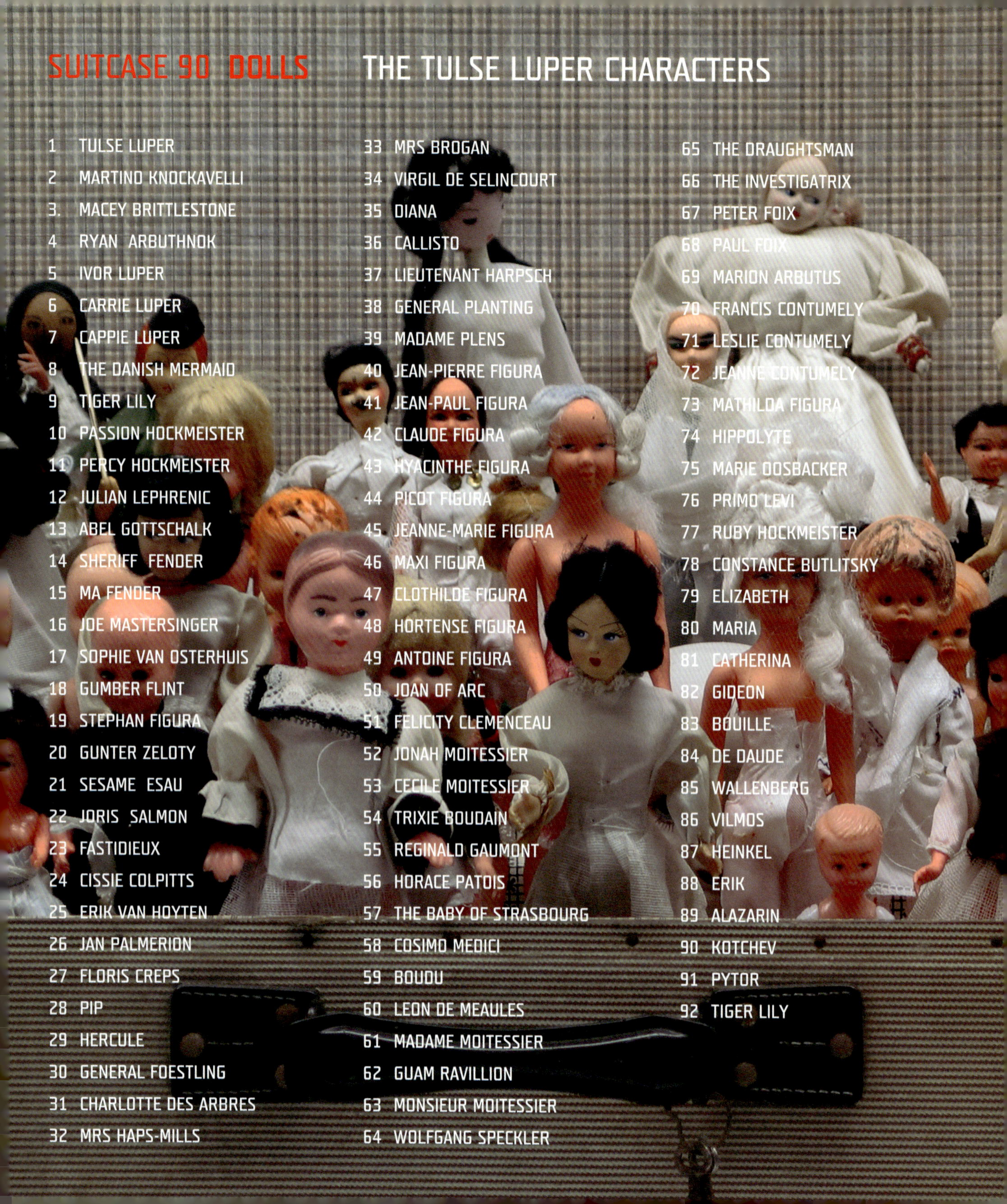

SUITCASE 90 DOLLS

THE TULSE LUPER CHARACTERS

1 TULSE LUPER
2 MARTINO KNOCKAVELLI
3. MACEY BRITTLESTONE
4 RYAN ARBUTHNOK
5 IVOR LUPER
6 CARRIE LUPER
7 CAPPIE LUPER
8 THE DANISH MERMAID
9 TIGER LILY
10 PASSION HOCKMEISTER
11 PERCY HOCKMEISTER
12 JULIAN LEPHRENIC
13 ABEL GOTTSCHALK
14 SHERIFF FENDER
15 MA FENDER
16 JOE MASTERSINGER
17 SOPHIE VAN OSTERHUIS
18 GUMBER FLINT
19 STEPHAN FIGURA
20 GUNTER ZELOTY
21 SESAME ESAU
22 JORIS SALMON
23 FASTIDIEUX
24 CISSIE COLPITTS
25 ERIK VAN HOYTEN
26 JAN PALMERION
27 FLORIS CREPS
28 PIP
29 HERCULE
30 GENERAL FOESTLING
31 CHARLOTTE DES ARBRES
32 MRS HAPS-MILLS
33 MRS BROGAN
34 VIRGIL DE SELINCOURT
35 DIANA
36 CALLISTO
37 LIEUTENANT HARPSCH
38 GENERAL PLANTING
39 MADAME PLENS
40 JEAN-PIERRE FIGURA
41 JEAN-PAUL FIGURA
42 CLAUDE FIGURA
43 HYACINTHE FIGURA
44 PICOT FIGURA
45 JEANNE-MARIE FIGURA
46 MAXI FIGURA
47 CLOTHILDE FIGURA
48 HORTENSE FIGURA
49 ANTOINE FIGURA
50 JOAN OF ARC
51 FELICITY CLEMENCEAU
52 JONAH MOITESSIER
53 CECILE MOITESSIER
54 TRIXIE BOUDAIN
55 REGINALD GAUMONT
56 HORACE PATOIS
57 THE BABY OF STRASBOURG
58 COSIMO MEDICI
59 BOUDU
60 LEON DE MEAULES
61 MADAME MOITESSIER
62 GUAM RAVILLION
63 MONSIEUR MOITESSIER
64 WOLFGANG SPECKLER
65 THE DRAUGHTSMAN
66 THE INVESTIGATRIX
67 PETER FOIX
68 PAUL FOIX
69 MARION ARBUTUS
70 FRANCIS CONTUMELY
71 LESLIE CONTUMELY
72 JEANNE CONTUMELY
73 MATHILDA FIGURA
74 HIPPOLYTE
75 MARIE OOSBACKER
76 PRIMO LEVI
77 RUBY HOCKMEISTER
78 CONSTANCE BUTLITSKY
79 ELIZABETH
80 MARIA
81 CATHERINA
82 GIDEON
83 BOUILLE
84 DE DAUDE
85 WALLENBERG
86 VILMOS
87 HEINKEL
88 ERIK
89 ALAZARIN
90 KOTCHEV
91 PYTOR
92 TIGER LILY

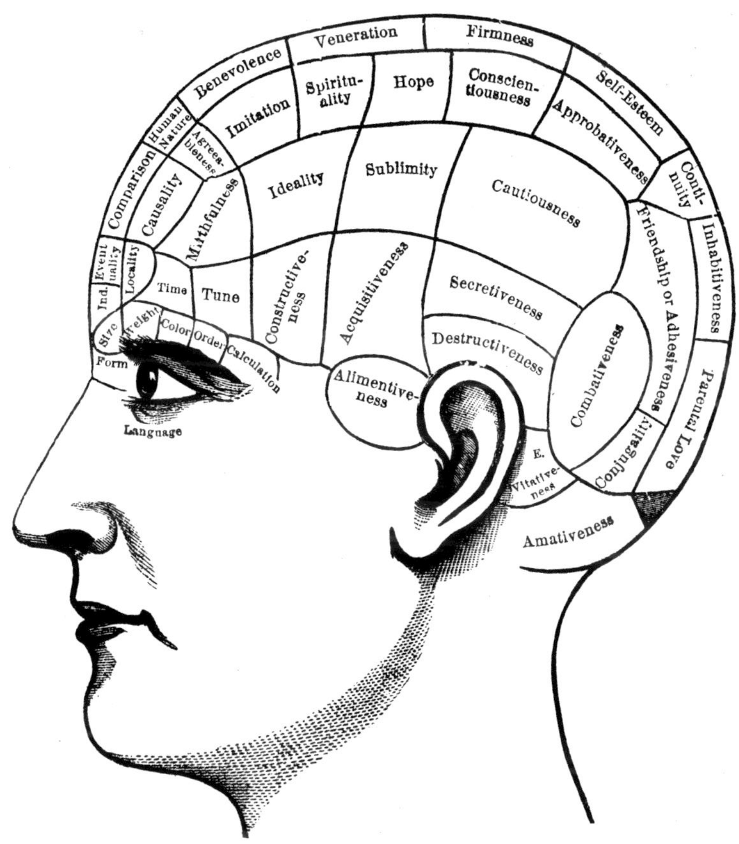

NUMBERING AND DEFINITION OF THE ORGANS.

1. Amativeness, Love between the sexes.
A. Conjugality, Matrimony—love of one. [etc.
2. Parental Love, Regard for offspring, pets,
3. Friendship, Adhesiveness—sociability.
4. Inhabitiveness, Love of home
5. Continuity, One thing at a time.
E. Vitativeness, Love of life.
6. Combativeness, Resistance—defense.
7. Destructiveness, Executiveness—force.
8. Alimentiveness, Appetite—hunger.
9. Acquisitiveness, Accumulation.
10. Secretiveness, Policy—management.
11. Cautiousness, Prudence—provision.
12. Approbativeness, Ambition—display.
13. Self-Esteem, Self-respect—dignity.
14. Firmness, Decision—perseverance.
15. Conscientiousness, Justice. equity.
16. Hope, Expectation—enterprise.
17. Spirituality, Intuition—faith—credulity.
18. Veneration, Devotion—respect.
19. Benevolence. Kindness—goodness.
20. Constructiveness, Mechanical ingenuity
21. Ideality, Refinement—taste—purity.
B. Sublimity, Love of grandeur—infinitude.
22. Imitation, Copying—patterning.
23. Mirthfulness, Jocoseness—wit—fun.
24. Individuality, Observation.
25. Form, Recollection of shape.
26. Size, Measuring by the eye.
27. Weight, Balancing—climbing.
28. Color, Judgment of colors.
29. Order, Method—system—arrangement.
30. Calculation, Mental arithmetic.
31. Locality, Recollection of places.
32. Eventuality, Memory of facts.
33. Time, Cognizance of duration.
34. Tune, Sense of harmony and melody.
35. Language, Expression of ideas.
36. Causality, Applying causes to effect. [tion.
37. Comparison, Inductive reasoning—illustra-
C. Human Nature, Perception of motives.
D. Agreeableness, Pleasantness—suavity.

SUITCASE 92 LUPER'S LIFE

1. a battered bicycle-wheel from Dinard 2. blue feathers from the dancer's dress on board the Portuguese passenger ship 3. photos of Virginia Woolf 4. postcards of the Ingres paintings of Madame Moitessier 5. broken pieces of china dogs 6. Monsieur Moitessier's photographs of his lover 7. female clothing Luper wore at Dinard 8. the revolver used to shoot Madame Moitessier in Dinard 9. cherry-stones 10. the spiked-collar from Strasbourg worn by the dog Titan 11. film-stills of Joan of Arc 12. pink and blue cinema tickets from the Arc en Ciel 13. packets of black and white 35mm film-clips (held up to the light) 14. manuscripts of The Baby of Strasbourg 15. the water-logged watch once belonging to the twin Paul 16. a dried and withered bunch of roses from the cinema in Strasbourg 17. bleached and gnawed dog bones 18. postcards of Strasbourg Cathedral 19. Radio parts from Vaux with station-identity dials showing exotic locations 20. the Kodak camera belonging to Mrs Haps-Mills and many of the photos she took of German soldiers in the park at Vaux 21. a metal fly swat 22. Manchester Guardian from 1940 23. an erotic print by Goltzius 24. Luper's manuscript of The Pairing 25. the quilted nightdress of Charlotte des Arbres worn by Cissie at Vaux 26. the eleven photos of Figura's children 27. a Belgian Fascist Cadet Force uniform 28. a silver whistle threaded on a cord 29. desert sand from Moab packed in a brown envelope 30. Moab Mormon maps 31. three dead locusts 32. newspaper cartoons of Rupert Bear and Tiger Lily 33. bundles of the love letters sent from Luper's father to his mother 34. the lump of chalk used by the 10-year old Luper to write on the Newport wall wrapped together with string with the lump of coal used by Martino to do the same 35. a medical model of the human brain 36. Monsieur Moitessier's cigarettes 37. Luper's red dress from Dinard 38. a set of a child's distressed red building blocks 39. a cork-stoppered bottle of water 40. a perfume bottle from Paris 41. a distressed and browned human skull 42. a bundle of used pencil stubs wrapped around with string 43. a ceramic egg-cup in the shape of a chicken 44. a snowstorm toy of Milan cathedral 45. a pack of used playing cards 46. a triangular kaleidoscope – the kind with mirrors 47. a child's model of a stork carrying a baby in a sling from its beak 48. a glass eye in a blue glass eyeglass 49. a toy bath 50. a dried eidelweis flower 51. a black and white portrait photograph of Raoul Wallenberg 52. a small squat bottle of black ink 53. an Anna Karenina novel in any language other than Russian 54. a bar of brown carbolic soap 55. a blown ostrich egg dated 5th April 1942 in black indian ink 56. a bunch of dried lavender tied with a pink ribbon 57. a bold red ribbon 58. a 1940s black telephone 59. a large false moustache 60. a dental tool with vicious intent 61. a pair of World War II motorcycle goggles 62. a transparent envelope of white dust 63. a rusty spring 64. a toy or miniature easel 65. a red dyed handkerchief 66. a much-used leather football boot 67. pieces of coloured glass from a stained glass window 68. a pair of metal handcuffs 69. a green-painted wooden apple 70. a school hand-bell with a wooden handle 71. a man's leather trouser-belt with a metal buckle coiled like a snake 72. a framed and glazed photograph of the bearded Charles Darwin 73. an abacus distressed from over-use 74. a circular hand mirror in a wooden frame 75. a man's blue folded shirt with chest pockets 76. a wooden police truncheon 77. a vinyl gramophone record of dance music still in a cardboard sleeve 78. a heavy metal model sphinx that can be used as a paper-weight 79. a pair of sugar tongs 80. a small microscope suitable for a child or a beginner studying biology at home 81. a bunch of keys 82. a bunch of glass grapes 83. a sheet of pink blotting paper blotted with blue fountain-pen ink 84. a metal mask for the eyes 85. a crucifix 86. a blue ceramic teapot 87. a wooden chair leg turned on a lathe 88. an English dictionary published before 1950 89. an empty bottle of Dom Perignon champagne 90. a large sheet which could be a shroud or then again a make-piece screen for the projection of films 91. an imitation Roman helmet 92. a film-can. It is a little rusty. Inside is a 16mm film wound on to a metal spool.

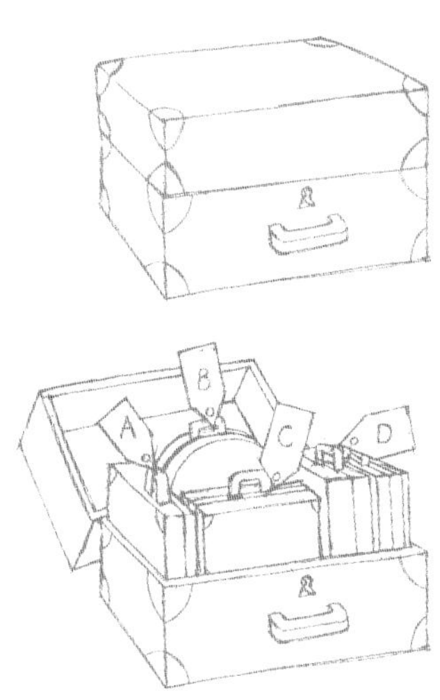
A
B
C
D

92 SUITCASES

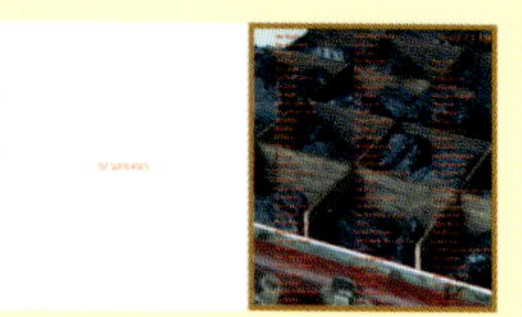

SUITCASE 1 COAL

A Suitcase of 92 coal lumps packed by the 10-year old Tulse Luper whilst he was imprisoned by his father in the coal house of his home in Newport, South Wales in 1921. The 92 coal lumps were to prophetically represent the major landscapes, real and metaphorical, of Luper's life – a suitcase to represent the geography of Tulse Luper's life.

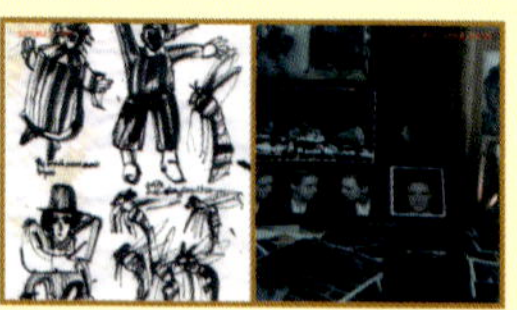

SUITCASE 2 TOYS

A suitcase of toys packed by Luper's mother in 1924 after her 12 year old son had left home. The toys were a collection assembled out of the assortment of objects assembled by Luper, relative to his many future interests, most of them associated with the disciplines of measuring and collecting, classifying and ordering. It is a suitcase to represent the interests of Luper's life.

SUITCASE 3 LUPER PHOTOS

A suitcase of photographs of Tulse Luper discovered in 1987 at the London offices of the Knockavelli Ice-Cream Company. It is a suitcase containing the visual record of Luper's appearance during 92 years.

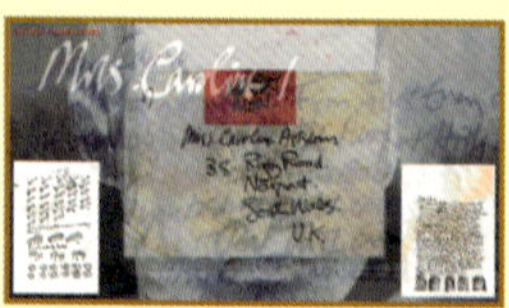

SUITCASE 4 LOVE LETTERS

A suitcase of 92 letters written by Luper's father, Ivor, to Luper's mother, Carrie Ashdown, in 1916 and 1917, and sent from the Flanders trenches to Newport in South Wales. The letters, acquired, read, studied and treasured by the 18 year old Luper, gave him an insight into questions of loyalty and endurance, and emotional and erotic love. It is a suitcase to represent Luper's emotional life.

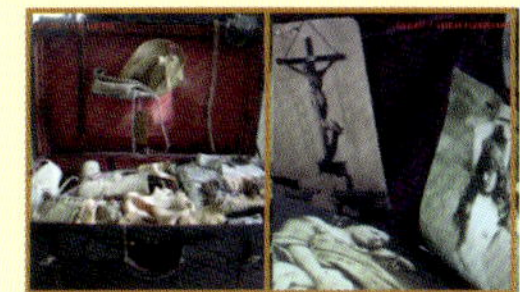

SUITCASE 5 & 6 CLOTHES

Two suitcases of clothes confiscated from Jewish lovers on the border-crossing railway-station at Ventimiglia in 1939, a Luper discovery when he was imprisoned in the Mole Antonelliana in Turin. The suitcases were a stimulus for historians of Luper's life to make a collection of all of Luper's clothes from the cradle to the grave, from birth-sheet to shroud.

SUITCASE 7 VATICAN PORNOGRAPHY

A suitcase of erotic photographic stills and film associated with the archives of the Vatican. They were discovered in 1985 in the Victor Emmanuel Building in Rome at the time of the making of a film called The Belly of an Architect. This is a suitcase to represent the iconoclasm, anticlericalism and eroticism of Luper's life.

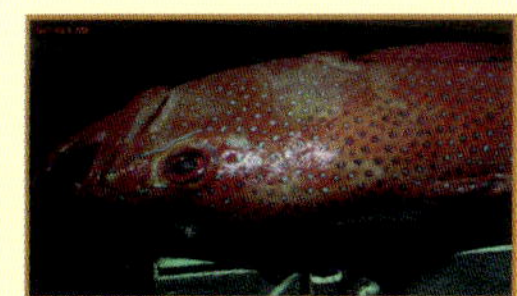

SUITCASE 8 FISH

A suitcase of fish discovered in a refrigerator in a fish-restaurant at Rimini in 1962, a wry reference to Luper's belief in positive red herrings and a poetic reminder of all the fishy events of his life.

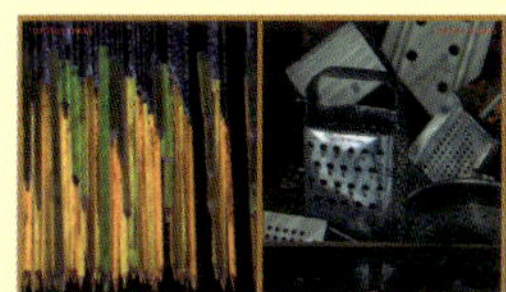

SUITCASE 9 PENCILS

A suitcase of pencils discovered in Moab, Utah in 1934, used by the 11-year old Ruby Hockmeister, cousin of Passion Hockmeister, to make a series of prophetic drawings, seeing through a child's innocent eye, the events and anxieties of Luper's life.

SUITCASE 10 HOLES

A suitcase of holes, 92 objects of negative space, a laconic joke packed by Luper after his political experiences in Europe in the 1960s.

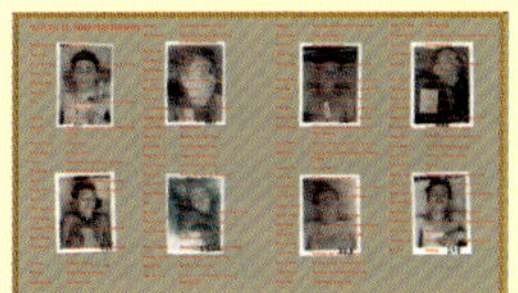

SUITCASE 11 MOAB PHOTOGRAPHS

A suitcase of photographs taken by the Italian-born Moab Photographer, Mastersinger, of the community of Moab law-breakers, malcontents and petty criminals, collected by Luper as an essay on mediocrity and small-time criminality.

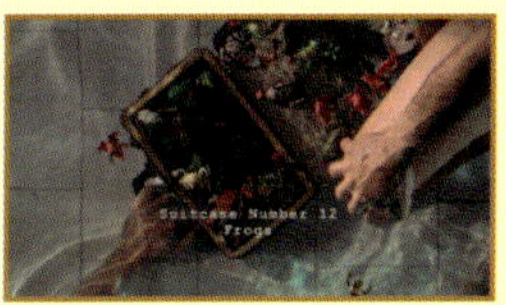

SUITCASE 12 FROGS

A suitcase of 92 collected emblematic frogs, manufactured in many materials, found in the bath of an electrocuted rapist in Zagreb in 1957. A wry universal comment on the proposition of the necessity to kiss the frog to obtain happiness.

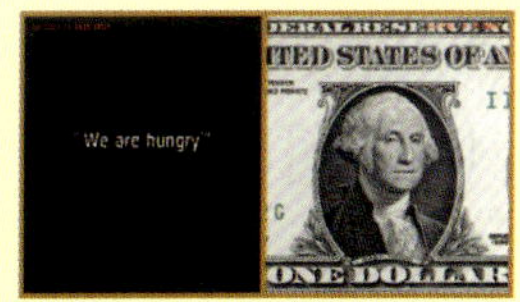

SUITCASE 13 FOOD DROP

A suitcase of food items dropped from a US Army bomber into Potsdammer Platz in September 1961 on the occasion of the East German isolation of West Berlin. Hoarded by Luper as a symbol of the idea of sequestering rations for life's survival.

SUITCASE 14 DOLLARS

A metal suitcase of small denomination US dollars given to Luper by William Gottschalk as an inducement for his assistance in keeping an eye on the activities of his Mormon relatives in Europe, though Luper was fully aware that it was laundered money offered to him as a bribe. Luper took the money and it financed the first years of his European career.

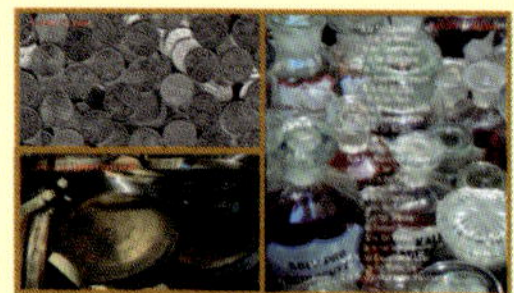

SUITCASE 15 COINS

A suitcase of small currency coins kept by the front door of Luper's apartment in Antwerp from 1936 till 1940, a bulwark against needless poverty. In theory anyone was allowed to take what he or she needed for cigarettes, pastries, newspapers, Belgian chocolates, French condoms, a glass of wine, a tram ticket, or flowers for visiting the sick.

SUITCASE 16 LUPER'S LOST FILMS.

This suitcase contained 23 16mm films, many of them incomplete, the evidence of Luper's filmic interests before he left for Europe in 1938.

SUITCASE 17 ALCOHOL

A suitcase of bottles of alcohol arranged according to the alphabet – 92 ways to drink a way to Heaven or Hell.

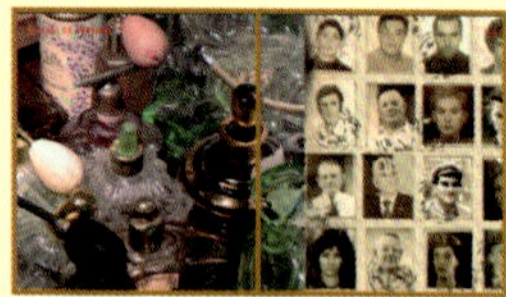

SUITCASE 18 PERFUME

A suitcase of bottles of perfume emblematic of 92 good smells of the world.

SUITCASE 19 PASSPORTS

A suitcase of materials for the making of false identities to permit the possessor access to illusive freedom.

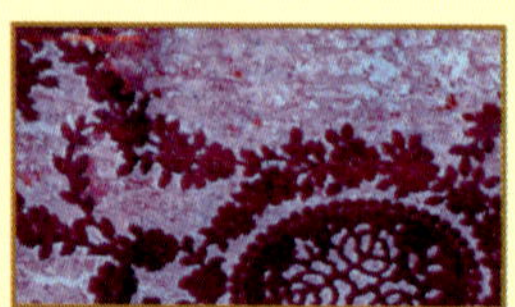

SUITCASE 20 BLOODIED WALLPAPER

A suitcase of wallpaper fragments soaked in blood, long considered to be Luper's blood, but probably the blood of cattle from the cattle trucks arriving from Germany and Poland at Antwerp Railway Station.

A reminder of the violence of Luper's imprisonment.

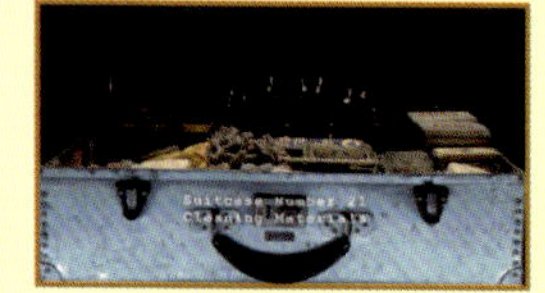

SUITCASE 21 CLEANING FLUIDS

A suitcase of cleaning fluids supposedly collected by Knockavelli on the occasion of an attempted escape by Luper from his bathroom arrest prison in Antwerp Railway Station in 1939, emblematic of Luper's optimistically naive campaigns to clean up evil.

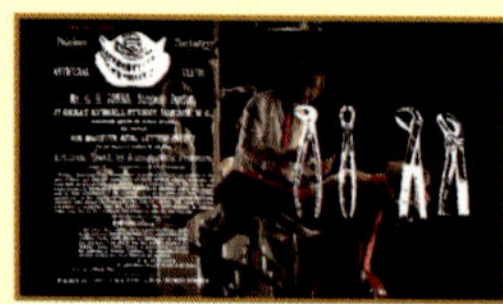

SUITCASE 22 DENTAL TOOLS

A suitcase of dental instruments once owned by Palmerion.

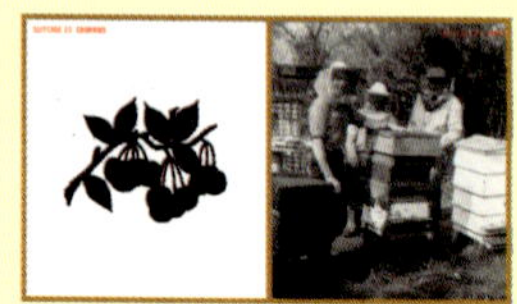

SUITCASE 23 CHERRIES

A suitcase of black cherries given as a gift to Luper in his bathroom arrest imprisonment in Antwerp Railway Station. Luper saw it as a memento of lost happiness and irrecoverable innocence.

SUITCASE 24 HONEY

A suitcase filled with honey, given as a prophetic gift to Luper whilst he was imprisoned in the bathroom of a hotel suite of the Antwerp Grand Station Hotel in 1940. It was evidence both of lost happiness and sexual humiliation.

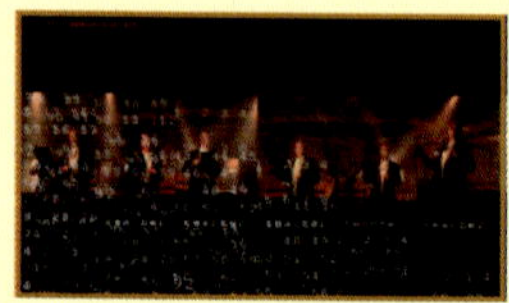

SUITCASE 25 NUMBERS & LETTERS

A suitcase of three-dimensional numbers and letters. To Luper, an apocryphal writer, the three dimensional characteristics turned letters, and therefore possibly words, into tangible, holdable, portable objects.

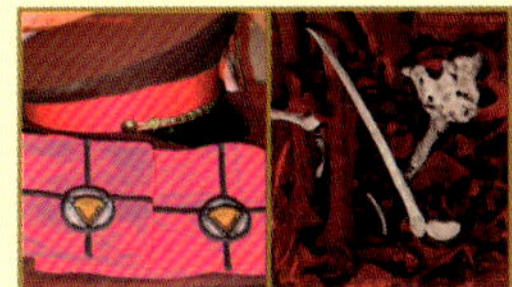

SUITCASE 26 LUPER UNIFORMS

A suitcase containing Luper's clothing from his imprisonment in the Antwerp Railway Station Hotel, it certainly once contained his Fascist uniform and the paper suit he made from Belgian Railway train time-tables.

SUITCASE 27 DOG BONES

Luper was amused that God spelt backwards was dog, and what of His bones?

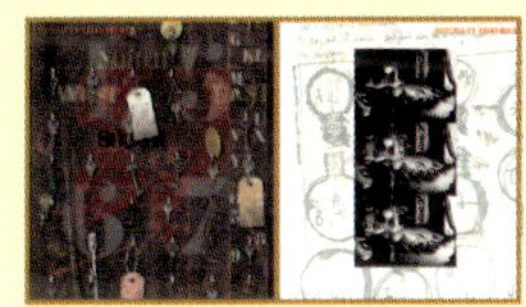

SUITCASE 28 LOCKS AND KEYS

A suitcase full of locks and keys, symbolic of Luper as a perpetual professional prisoner.

SUITCASE 29 LIGHT-BULBS

A suitcase of light-bulbs, witnesses of ambiguous events in conditions of poor light and total darkness.

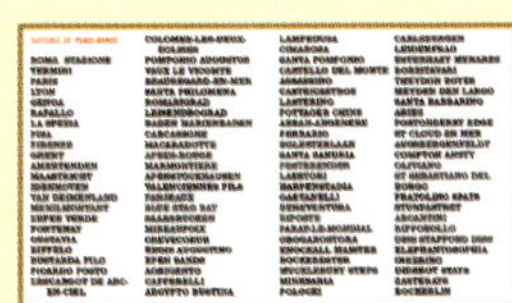

SUITCASE 30 PLACE-NAMES

A suitcase of place-names invented by Cissie Colpitts for the amusement of Luper at Antwerp, a compendium of the places of Paradise on Earth reachable by the international railway network of Europe before Fascism takes over travel and turns out all the lights.

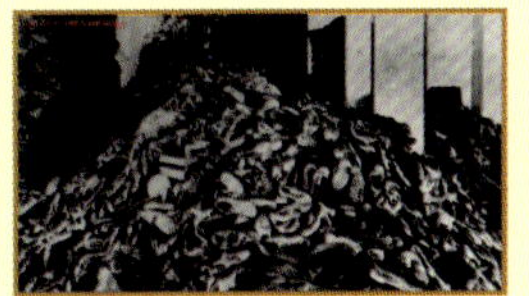

SUITCASE 31 BOOTS AND SHOES

A suitcase of Luper's boots and shoes symbolic of Luper as a restless traveller.

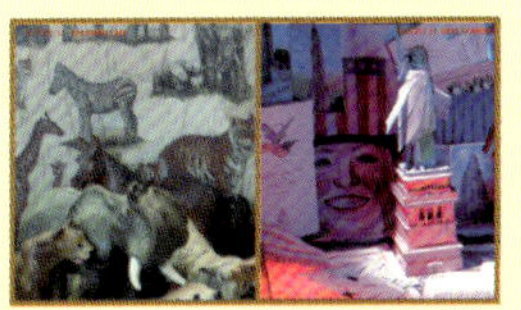

SUITCASE 32 ZOO ANIMALS ARK

A suitcase of miniature animals. Luper was fascinated by shere diversity from a single idea.

SUITCASE 33 IDEAS OF AMERICA

Luper, even in 1940, had an unsettled equivocal idea of America. He packed a suitcase to contain his equivocations. Such equivocations had been presented to his jailers in Antwerp to either convince them to go to there at once, or stay completely away and try to forget that such a place had ever existed.

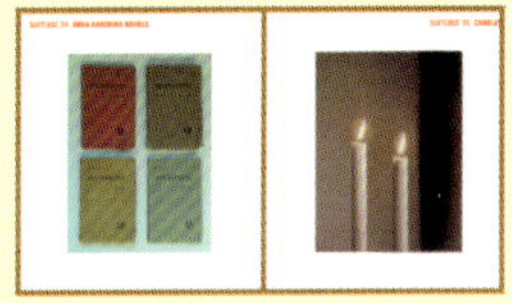

SUITCASE 34 ANNA KARENINA NOVELS

A suitcase of Tolstoy's Anna Karenina novels translated into many languages. Luper had chosen this novel of tragic love to write his own fictions between the lines of each printed page.

SUITCASE 35 CANDLES

A suitcase of candles for symbolically lighting every kind of darkness.

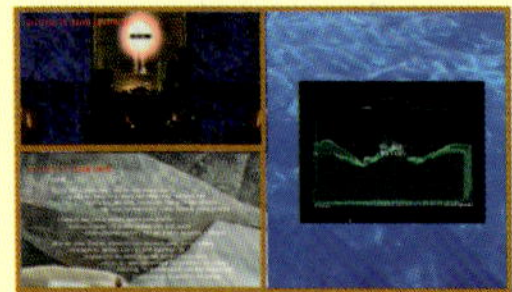

SUITCASE 36 RADIO EQUIPMENT

A suitcase of radio equipment from Vaux packed by Figura on Luper's behalf in the knowledge that Luper and Cissie could continue their love affair across the air-waves wherever they were.

SUITCASE 37 CLEAN LINEN

A suitcase of freshly laundered clean white linen, a symbol of ecstasy to Luper who never ceased dreaming of the allure of clean sheeted beds and fresh underwear. The suitcase was packed at Vaux near Paris on Luper's behalf in 1941 by Mrs Haps-Mills, who dreamt of a life of servile domestic devotion to a man of her dreams.

SUITCASE 38 WATER

A suitcase reinforced to hold water, redolent of Luper's fascination with water and his fear of drowning.

SUITCASE 39 CODE

A suitcase of code-books

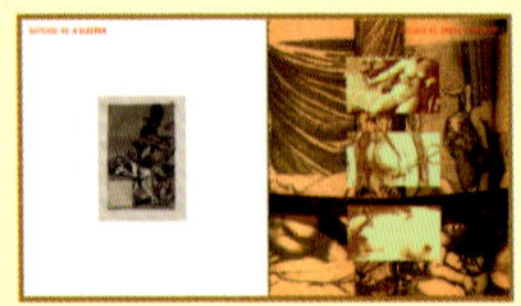

SUITCASE 40 A SLEEPER

A suitcase large enough to pack Charlotte des Arbres, a woman so desperate in love, she slept in a suitcase ready to be immediately mailed to her lost lover.

SUITCASE 41 EROTIC ENGRAVINGS

A suitcase of late 16th century erotic prints stolen from the walls of the Vaux Chateau by Luper and his jailers in 1940. The engravings are by Hendrik Goltzius who sought commissions in Europe to keep his workshop from bankruptcy. Luper, imprisoned in a Moscow jail, wrote a scenario of the commissioning of these engravings as an excuse for contemplating Old Testament tales and Ovid's Metamorphosis as erotic dramas.

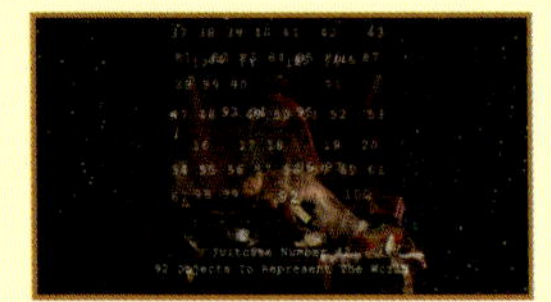

SUITCASE 42 92 OBJECTS TO REPRESENT THE WORLD

A collection of lost property items Luper found beneath the seats of the Arc en Ciel cinema in 1941. Luper eventually increased this collection to make a suitcase of 92 objects that represented the world and all that was in it.

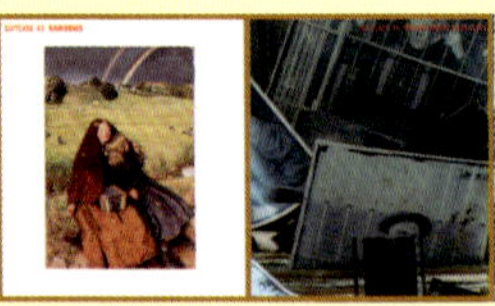

SUITCASE 43 RAINBOWS

A suitcase of rainbows, most unusable, unbuyable, unpriceable commodity, and a promise that the world would never perish through drowning.

The rainbow is an unnecessary phenomenon of which no live thing has taken advantage. No animal is parasitic on a rainbow, no-one colonises a rainbow. No-one uses a rainbow like they use a cloud or hot air or the mountains of the wind or geysers or hot water springs or snow. Rainbows are supremely unused. No-one can exploit them to measure anything by, test anything by. The only exploiters, and that for the idea and not the reality are writers, painters and fabulist theologians.

Luper: 100 objects to represent the world.

SUITCASE 44 PRISON MOVIE FILM-CLIPS

A suitcase of film-clips of feature films of prisons and prisoners and prison escapes. The film-clips were appropriated by Luper whilst imprisoned at the Arc en Ciel cinema in Strasbourg in 1942.

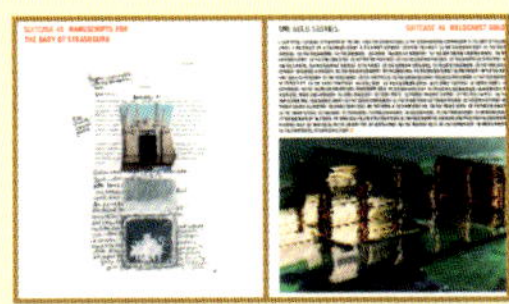

SUITCASE 45 MANUSCRIPTS FOR THE BABY OF STRASBOURG

A suitcase containing the drawings and manuscripts of a project Luper called The Baby of Strasbourg, much later made into a film under the name of a different city. It was a story of the making of a child saint suffocated in order to dismember his body to make Holy Relics. Luper had been much disturbed by the death of his jailer Figura who had left eleven children behind at the mercy of the world.

SUITCASE 46 HOLOCAUST GOLD

A suitcase of 92 bars of gold reconstituted from the stolen property of victims of The Third Reich between 1930 and 1945. Each gold bar has a story.

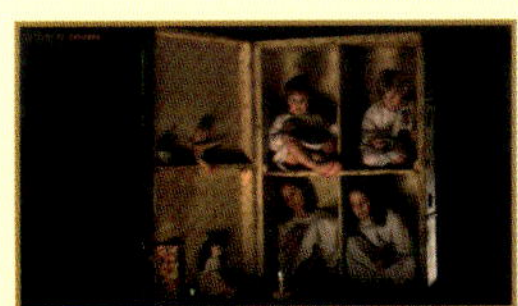

SUITCASE 47 CHILDREN

A large suitcase that imprisoned the abandoned children of Figura in Strasbourg. Madame Plens later filled it with their toys.

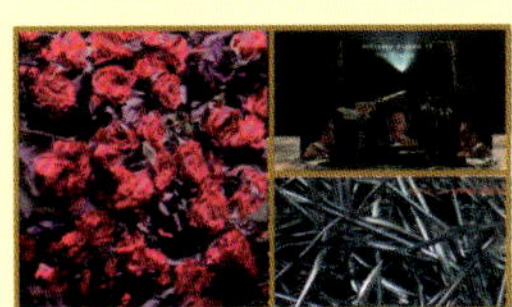

SUITCASE 48 DEAD ROSES

A suitcase of dead red roses, the collected sentimental items of love exchange left in the Strasbourg cinema by the unrequited lover, Horace Whirlpool, who later was inveigled into a false suicide pact from which he did not survive. Luper was known to have preserved the dead flowers as a symbol of hopeless love.

SUITCASE 49 TRAINS

A suitcase of toy trains.

SUITCASE 50 SEWING NEEDLES

A suitcase of sewing needles stained with blood.

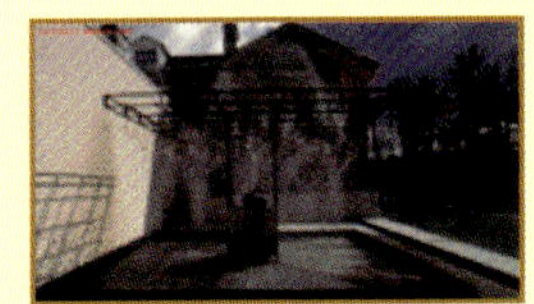

SUITCASE 51 SHOWER-HEADS

A suitcase of shower-heads stolen from washrooms, shower-rooms and bathrooms in memory of the deception of the Holocaust.

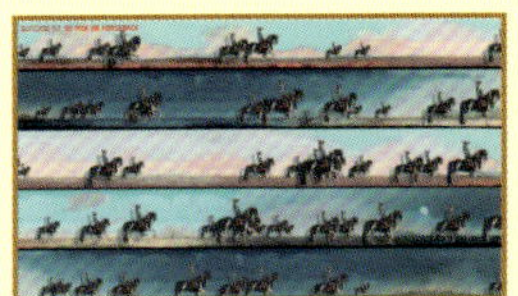

SUITCASE 52 55 MEN ON HORSEBACK

A suitcase of 55 equestrian paintings which inspired Luper to write a scenario for a project he called 55 Men on Horseback.

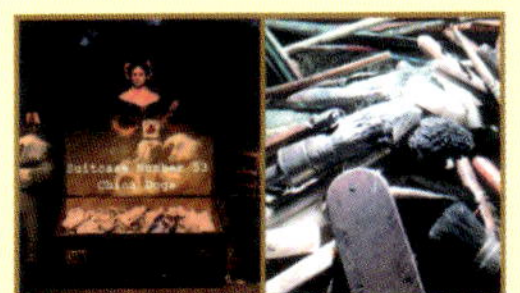

SUITCASE 53 CHINA DOGS

A suitcase of broken china dogs kept by Madame Moitessier at her house in Dinard.

SUITCASE 54 BRUSHES

A suitcase of paint-brushes. Luper had always wanted to be a painter. Someone later added the candles to suggest that a painter's prime concern was to paint light.

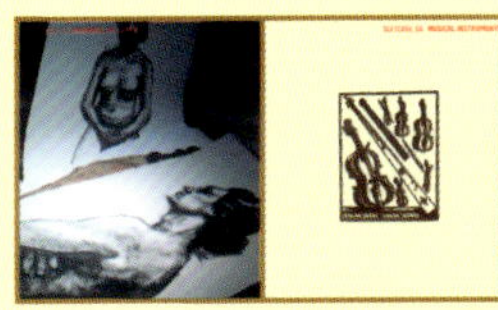

SUITCASE 55 DRAWINGS OF LUPER

A suitcase of drawings of Luper posing naked in a garden at Dinard. The drawings demonstrated a quandary of whether a draughtsman should draw what he sees or what he knows, a proposition that Luper later wrote as a play called The Draughtsman's Conflict.

SUITCASE 56 MUSICAL INSTRUMENTS

A suitcase of assorted musical instruments that seemed to Luper to indicate ideal camaraderie.

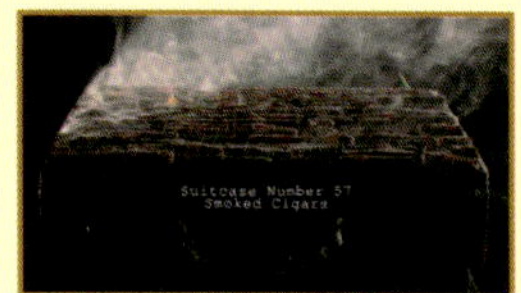

SUITCASE 57 SMOKED CIGARS

A suitcase of smoked cigars, the clue to the death of two composers, Wolfgang Decker and Anton Webern. Luper was in Bolzano when he heard of the death of Webern; he served Webern's apparent assassin, US Army Sergeant W. Bell, with a glass of creme de menthe, and later wrote a fiction about the deaths of composers, which later surfaced as an opera performed in Amsterdam in 1998 called Rosa.

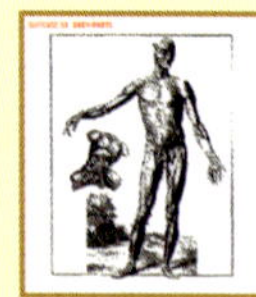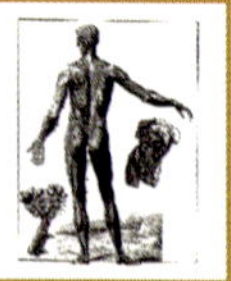

SUITCASE 58 BODY-PARTS

A suitcase of body-parts, an illustration to a story called Body Parts that Luper wrote to exorcise a horror of dismemberment.

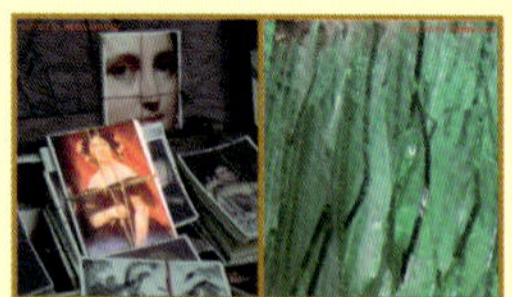

SUITCASE 59 INGRES PAINTINGS

A suitcase of postcard reproductions of portrait paintings by Ingres.

SUITCASE 60 BROKEN GLASS

A suitcase of broken glass and broken mirrors, Luper's representation of chance escapes and bad luck.

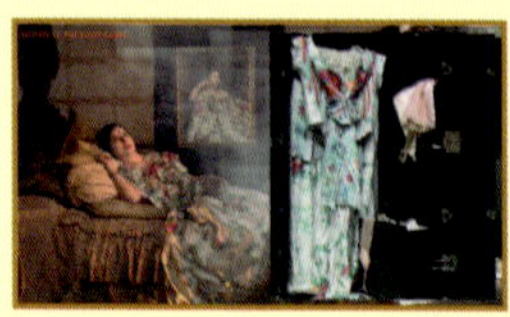

SUITCASE 61 MOITESSIER GOWNS

A suitcases of clothes worn by the portrait sitters of the French painter Ingres, collected by Madame Moitessier in association with her Ingres namesake.

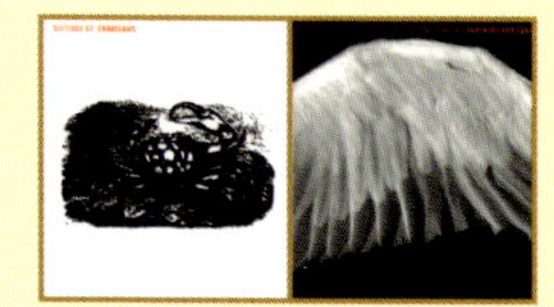

SUITCASE 62 CRABCLAWS

A suitcase of crab-claws, evocative symbol of highly specialised evolutionary Natural Selection at work.

SUITCASE 63 FEATHERS AND EGGS

A suitcase of feathers and eggs to memorialise Icarus, first successful pilot and victim of the first flying accident, a symbol of Luper's passion for personalised flight.

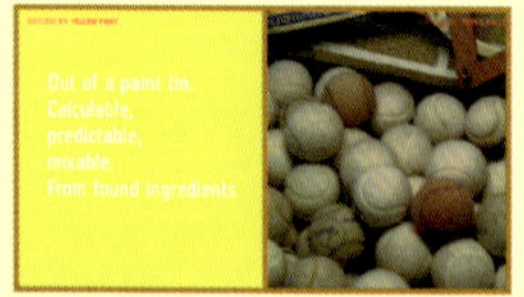

SUITCASE 64 YELLOW PAINT

A suitcase of yellow paint.

SUITCASE 65 TENNIS BALLS

A suitcase of 92 tennis balls taken from the sea. They reminded him of Henry VIII endlessly playing tennis with Anne Boleyn. They occupied his long isolated days on Sark until the very last of them was lost in the surf and left him bereft as though they were the last attributes of civilisation.

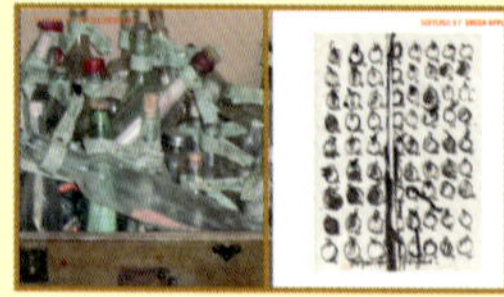

SUITCASE 66 BOTTLE MESSAGES

The South-West coastline of Sark was a terminus for bottled messages. They drifted across the Bay of Biscay from Spain and the Canary Isles, from the Mediterranean and the west coast of Africa, from the islands of the Atlantic and even from South America, floating east on the Gulf Stream. Luper collected them as indicators of the most extreme optimism.

SUITCASE 67 GREEN APPLES

A suitcase of green apples, the origin of the Fall of Man.

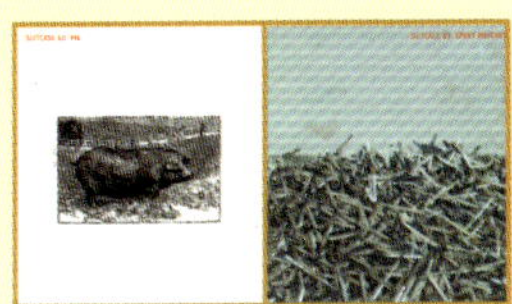

SUITCASE 68 PIG

An animal of high value, low esteem, religious taboo. Everything on a pig can be eaten or used with the exception of its squeal. No doubt someone will find a use for that too. Luper carried an effigy of a pig in a pigskin suitcase from Bilboa to Barcelona for Aristide Maillol. He killed a pig in the Mole Antonelliana in Turin and he and a cook and five orphans of the war lived on it for forty days.

SUITCASE 69 SPENT MATCHES

A suitcase of spent matches, indicative of profitless waste, and Luper's freezing days in the Mole Antonelliana in Turin.

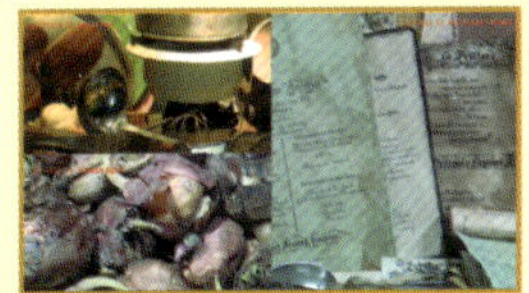

SUITCASE 70 SAUCEPANS

A suitcase of saucepans redolent of the memory of fine meals.

SUITCASE 71 FLOWER BULBS

A suitcase of flower bulbs. In wartime famine, Luper ate flower bulbs cooked such that his breath was scented with the smell of petals and he could imagine his intestines flowering. It was a powerful reminder of nutritious beauty regenerated in abject dearth.

SUITCASE 72 RESTAURANT MENUS

A collection of restaurant menus that grew into the Luper Cookbook, a record of 92 Luper meals.

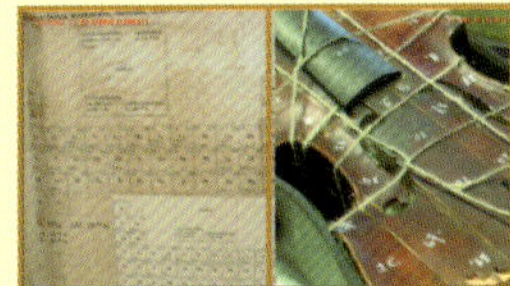

SUITCASE 73 92 ATOMIC ELEMENTS

A suitcase of symbols of the atomic elements, a present to Luper from Primo Levi in Turin.

SUITCASE 74 VIOLIN SPLINTERS

A suitcase of 92 violin splinters, symbol of needless destruction and the death of music.

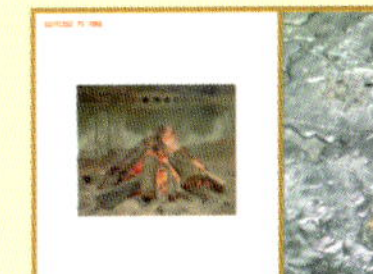

SUITCASE 75 FIRE

A suitcase containing highly combustible materials ready to be set alight, to remind us of how fire has ravaged the civilisations of man from the Burning of the Library at Alexandria to the burning of the martyr Joan of Arc to the burning of Dresden.

SUITCASE 76 LEAD

A suitcase of lead, the most stabile of elements and in constant competitive antithesis to uranium.

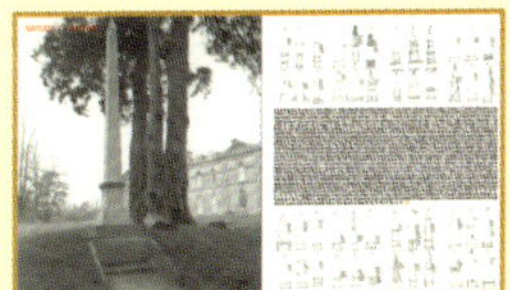

SUITCASE 77 OBELISKS

A suitcase of obelisks, monuments of perfect geometrical shape, the ancient world and longevity.

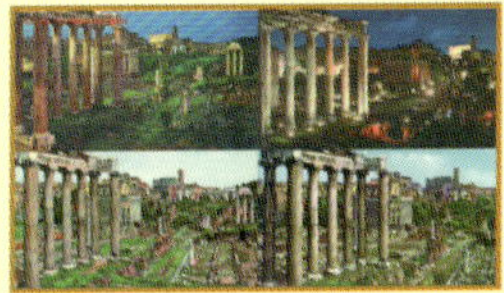

SUITCASE 78 ROMAN POSTCARDS

A suitcase of Roman postcards that pictorially record and link the buildings of Rome in journeys back and forth across the city.

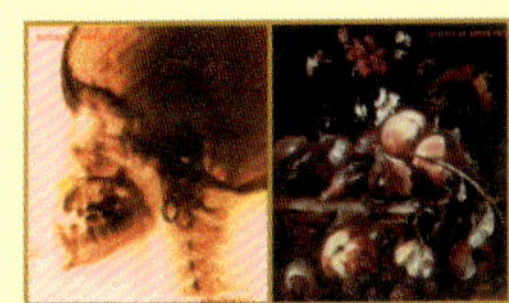

SUITCASE 79 HOLY EARTH

A suitcase of black earth stolen from the Capuchin Convent on The Via Veneto in Rome; the earth itself was stolen from Golgotha by monks in the 13th century.

SUITCASE 80 GREEN FIGS

A suitcase of green figs, most ancient biblical fruit, a ubiquitous vehicle for poisoners.

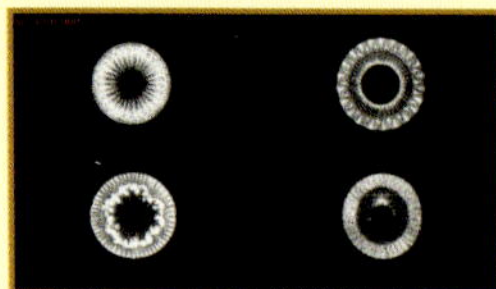

SUITCASE 81 LIGHT

A suitcase of light, emblematic of the power of Uranium, symbol of Pandora's power and the impudence of Prometheus.

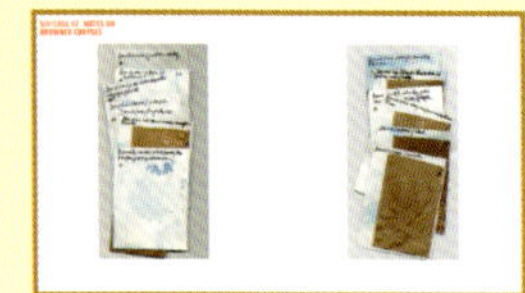

SUITCASE 82 NOTES ON DROWNED CORPSES

Luper feared death by drowning. Disturbed by the very early self-portrait photograph of Hippolyte Bayard as a drowned man, Luper wrote out his own mortuary notice of death by drowning in 92 different ways.

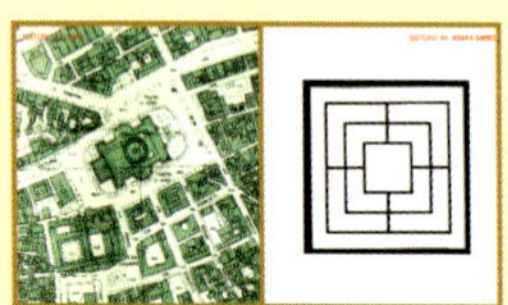

SUITCASE 83 MAPS

A suitcase of maps, supreme indicators of a scaled-down world, showing you where you have been, where you are, and where you could be.

SUITCASE 84 BOARD GAMES

A suitcase of board-games, both newly created and as old as history, all played according to the agreed rules of chance; conflict reduced to emblematic miniatures.

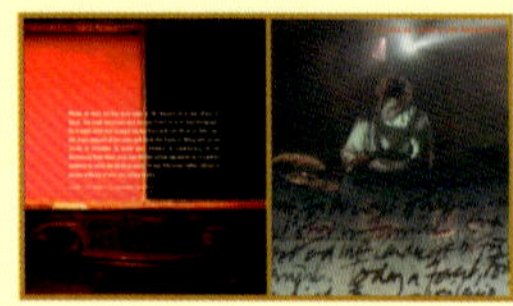

SUITCASE 85 INK & BLOOD

A suitcase of ink and blood. To represent the act of writing and all hand written and printed texts. To demonstrate the purveyance of knowledge and the channels of communication through ink. Ink can be seen to be the second blood of the world and as disposable.

SUITCASE 86 LUPER STORY MANUSCRIPTS

A suitcase of the manuscripts of Luper's 1001 stories written at a checkpoint border crossing between East and West Germany. Considering himself as a contemporary blackmailed Sherherazade, it was his attempt to rewrite the 1001 Arabian Nights, to stave off death and obscurity for as long as he could.

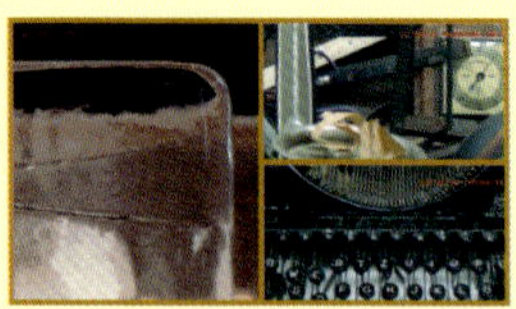

SUITCASE 87 ICE

A suitcase containing a block of ice, Luper's last object to represent the world, and the ultimate container of Passion, the beautiful woman who loved him so unwisely.

SUITCASE 88 MEASURING TOOLS

A suitcase of tape-measures, thermometers, slide-rules, clocks, watches, pedometers, egg-timers, the evidence of Luper's fascination with measuring.

SUITCASE 89 TYPEWRITER

A suitcase containing the typewriter that manufactured Luper and his world.

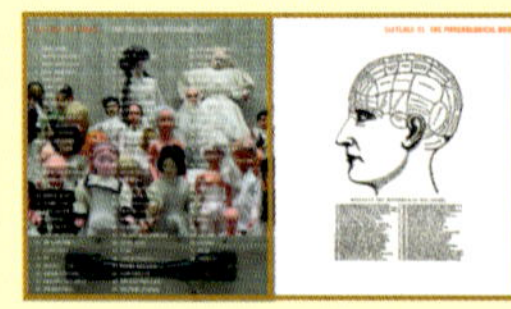

SUITCASE 90 DOLLS

A suitcase of 92 minature dolls, each doll representing a character in the life of Tulse Luper and ticketed with his or her name.

SUITCASE 91 THE PHRENOLOGICAL BOOK

A suitcase containing the pages of Martino Knockavelli's Phrenological Book, an illustrated volume that provided a catalogue for the anatomical details of Luper's friends, enemies, jailers and lovers.

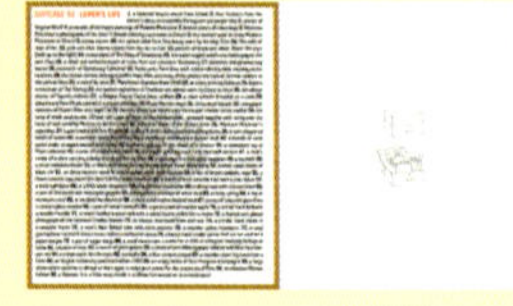

SUITCASE 92 LUPER'S LIFE

A suitcase of Luper's life-history.

SUITCASE 93 LIVE SQUID

A suitcase of live squid from Maxims in Paris apparently presented to Luper by General Foestling to demonstrate the excessive power of the occupying powers in France to obtain anything they wanted from anywhere.

SUITCASE 94 WHISTLES

A suitcase of whistles, symbol of imperative command and emblematic of Luper's favourite ghost story, 'Whistle, and I will come to you'. It was said that Luper hoped one day to whistle up death when he was ready for it.

SUITCASE 95 HUMAN ASH

A suitcase of cremated human ash and bone, collected from Hiroshima on August 8th 1945.

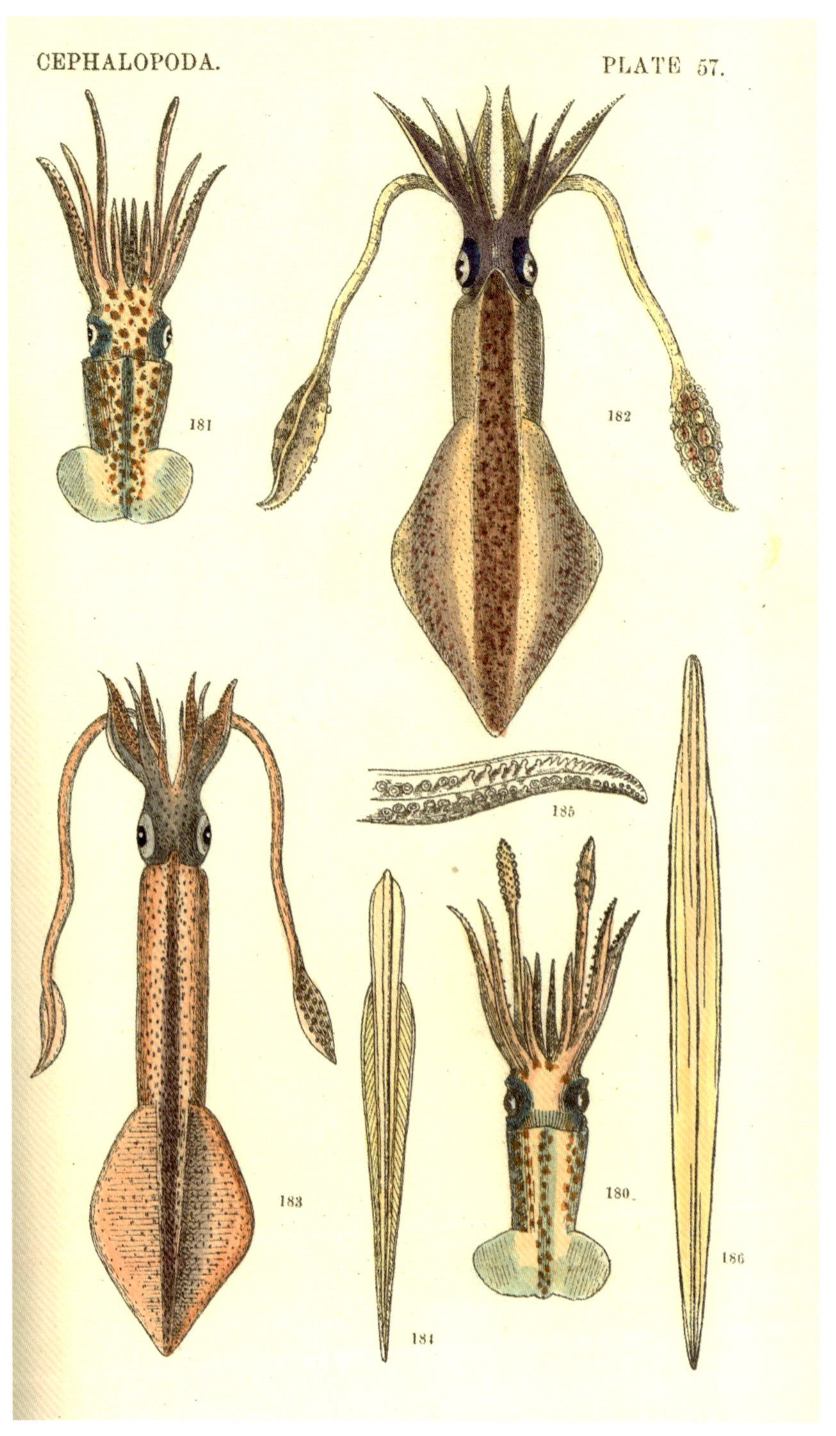
CEPHALOPODA.
PLATE 57.
181
182
183
184
185
186
180

LUPER AT COMPTON VERNEY

Director	Peter Greenaway
Assistant to Mr. Greenaway	Allard van der Werff
Design	Reinier van Brummelen
	Maarten Piersma
Light design	Reinier van Brummelen
Lighting technician	Joep Vermeulen
Lighting team	Harm Bredero
	Marc Dresens
	Peter van Deth
	Sebastiaan de Rooij
Construction manager	Maarten Piersma
Construction team	Lidewij Kapteijn
	Rob Duiker
	Ernst Paradies
Props master	Diana van de Vossenberg
Props assistants	Rosie Stapel
	Martine de Schipper
Production props	Eva Haak-Wegman
Props trainees	Solange Welch
	Rupert Rand
	Oskari Korenius
Wardrobe	Marrit van der Burgt
Video editor	Elmer Leupen
Assistant editor	Jaap Praamsma
Sound editors	Jef Grosfeld
	Mattijs Mollee
Projection technicians	Marc Thelosen
	Martijn van Bommel
	Manuel van Kraaij
Calligrapher	Brody Neuenschwander
Assistant to the calligrapher	Phil Duckworth
Production Compton Verney	John Leslie
	Antonia Harrison
Line producer	Jet Christiaanse
Production manager	Christophe Istace
Production assistants	Esther Thedinga
	Natasha Theunissen
	Meike van der Pol
Catering	Sara Synge
Producer	Kees Kasander/
	The Kasander Film Company

IMAGE CREDITS **cover**, installation view, Adam Hall, photo Hugo Glendinning | **inside flap**, installation view, grounds, photo Hugo Glendinning | **inside cover**, Compton Verney, the house and grounds, from an estate map by James Fish, 1736 | **page 1**, Peter Greenaway, suitcase drawings overlaying design for the great parlour at Compton Verney, by Robert Adam, courtesy of the Trustees of Sir John Soane's Museum | **page 2**, installation view grounds, photo Hugo Glendinning | **page 4**, installation view, main gallery, photo Hugo Glendinning | **page 11**, The Manchester Guardian, 1940 || PHOTOGRAPHIC CREDITS AND COMPARATIVE IMAGES **1. COAL** Installation (detail) photo Hugo Glendinning | **2. TOYS** Peter Greenaway, drawing | **3. LUPER PHOTOS** Installation (detail) photo Hugo Glendinning | **4. LOVE LETTERS** The Tulse Luper Suitcases, film still | **5 & 6. CLOTHES** Installation (detail) photo Hugo Glendinning | **7. VATICAN PORNOGRAPHY** Installation (detail) photo Hugo Glendinning | **8. FISH** Installation (detail) photo Hugo Glendinning | **9. PENCILS** Installation (detail) photo Hugo Glendinning | **10. HOLES** Installation (detail) photo Hugo Glendinning | **11. MOAB PHOTOGRAPHS** Peter Greenaway / The Kasander Film Company | **12. FROGS** The Tulse Luper Suitcases, film still | **13. FOOD DROP** Peter Greenaway, text | **14. DOLLARS** found image | **15. COINS** Peter Greenaway / The Kasander Film Company | **16. LUPER'S LOST FILMS** Installation (detail) photo Hugo Glendinning | **17. ALCOHOL** Installation (detail) photo Hugo Glendinning | **18. PERFUME** Installation (detail) photo Hugo Glendinning | **19. PASSPORTS** Peter Greenaway / The Kasander Film Company | **20. BLOODIED WALLPAPER** Installation (detail) photo Hugo Glendinning | **21. CLEANING FLUIDS** The Tulse Luper Suitcases, film still | **22. DENTAL TOOLS** The Tulse Luper Suitcases, film still and found images | **23. CHERRIES** found image | **24. HONEY** photo courtesy Denis N. Keyte | **25. NUMBERS & LETTERS** The Tulse Luper Suitcases, film still | **26. LUPER UNIFORMS** Installation (detail) photo Hugo Glendinning | **27. DOG BONES** Peter Greenaway / The Kasander Film Company | **28. LOCKS AND KEYS** Peter Greenaway / The Kasander Film Company | **29. LIGHT-BULBS** Peter Greenaway / The Kasander Film Company | **30. PLACE-NAMES** Peter Greenaway, text | **31. BOOTS AND SHOES** Heaps of shoes taken from the gassed inmates at Auschwitz, photo courtesy The Wiener Library | **32. ZOO ANIMALS ARK** Installation (detail) photo Hugo Glendinning | **33. IDEAS OF AMERICA** Installation (detail) photo Hugo Glendinning | **34. ANNA KARENINA NOVELS** Installation (detail) photo Hugo Glendinning | **35. CANDLES** Gerhard Richter, Two Candles, 1983 oil on canvas, courtesy Studio Richter | **36. RADIO EQUIPMENT** The Tulse Luper Suitcases, film still | **37. CLEAN LINEN** Installation (detail) photo Hugo Glendinning | **38. WATER** The Tulse Luper Suitcases, film still | **39. CODE** The Tulse Luper Suitcases, film still | **40. A SLEEPER** Goya, The Sleep of Reason © The Trustees of the British Museum | **41. EROTIC ENGRAVINGS** Installation (detail) photo Hugo Glendinning | **42. 92 OBJECTS TO REPRESENT THE WORLD** The Tulse Luper Suitcases, film still | **43. RAINBOWS** John Everett Millais, The Blind Girl, 1854-1856 © Birmingham Museums & Art Gallery | **44. PRISON MOVIE FILM-CLIPS** Installation (detail) photo Hugo Glendinning | **45. MANUSCRIPTS FOR THE BABY OF STRASBOURG** Peter Greenaway / The Kasander Film Company | **46. HOLOCAUST GOLD** Wolfgang Tillmans, Gold (b) 2002 courtesy Maureen Paley / Interim Art | **47. CHILDREN** The Tulse Luper Suitcases, film still | **48. DEAD ROSES** Installation (detail) photo Hugo Glendinning | **49. TRAINS** The Tulse Luper Suitcases, film still | **50. SEWING NEEDLES** Installation (detail) photo Hugo Glendinning | **51. SHOWER-HEADS** Installation view, photo Hugo Glendinning | **52. 55 MEN ON HORSEBACK** The Tulse Luper Suitcases, film still | **53. CHINA DOGS** The Tulse Luper Suitcases, film still | **54. BRUSHES** Installation (detail) photo Hugo Glendinning | **55. DRAWINGS OF LUPER** Installation (detail) photo Hugo Glendinning | **56. MUSICAL INSTRUMENTS** found image | **57. SMOKED CIGARS** The Tulse Luper Suitcases, film still | **58. BODY-PARTS** found image | **59. INGRES PAINTINGS** Installation (detail) photo Hugo Glendinning Ingres, Madame Moitessier seated, courtesy National Gallery, London | **60. BROKEN GLASS** Installation (detail) photo Hugo Glendinning | **61. MOITESSIER GOWNS** The Tulse Luper Suitcases, film still | **62. CRABCLAWS** found image | **63. FEATHERS AND EGGS** Peter Greenaway / Kasander Film Company | **64. YELLOW PAINT** Peter Greenaway, text | **65. TENNIS BALLS** Installation (detail) photo Hugo Glendinning | **66. BOTTLE MESSAGES** Installation (detail) photo Hugo Glendinning | **67. GREEN APPLES** Peter Greenaway, drawing | **68. PIG** found image | **69. SPENT MATCHES** Installation (detail) photo Hugo Glendinning | **70. SAUCEPANS** Installation (detail) photo Hugo Glendinning | **71. FLOWER BULBS** Installation (detail) photo Hugo Glendinning | **72. RESTAURANT MENUS** Installation (detail) photo Hugo Glendinning | **73. 92 ATOMIC ELEMENTS** Installation (detail) photo Ruth Inglefield | **74. VIOLIN SPLINTERS** Installation (detail) photo Hugo Glendinning | **75. FIRE** photo John Kippin, 2003 | **76. LEAD** Installation (detail) photo Hugo Glendinning | **77. OBELISKS** The obelisk, marking the family vault at Compton Verney, photo Malcolm Davies / Peter Greenaway, obelisk drawings | **78. ROMAN POSTCARDS** Peter Greenaway / The Kasander Film Company | **79. HOLY EARTH** Peter Greenaway / The Kasander Film Company | **80. GREEN FIGS** Michele Pace del Campidoglio, A melon, peaches, figs, mulberries, plums and carnations on a step on a rocky ledge oil on canvas, 17th century © Christie's Images Ltd 2003 | **81. LIGHT** Peter Greenaway, drawing | **82. NOTES ON DROWNED CORPSES** Installation (detail) photo Ruth Inglefield | **83. MAPS** found image | **84. BOARD GAMES** found image | **85. INK & BLOOD** Installation (detail) photo Hugo Glendinning | **86. LUPER STORY MANUSCRIPTS** The Tulse Luper Suitcases, film still | **87. ICE** Installation (detail) photo Hugo Glendinning | **88. MEASURING TOOLS** Installation (detail) photo Hugo Glendinning | **89. TYPEWRITER** Installation (detail) photo Hugo Glendinning | **90. DOLLS** Installation (detail) photo Hugo Glendinning | **91. THE PHRENOLOGICAL BOOK** found image | **92. LUPER'S LIFE** Peter Greenaway, text || SOME FAKE, APOCRYPHAL & UNAUTHENTICATED SUITCASES **93. LIVE SQUID** from Manual of conchology by George W. Tryon Vol. I Cephalopoda. Philadelphia: published by the author, 1879. © the Zoological Society of London.

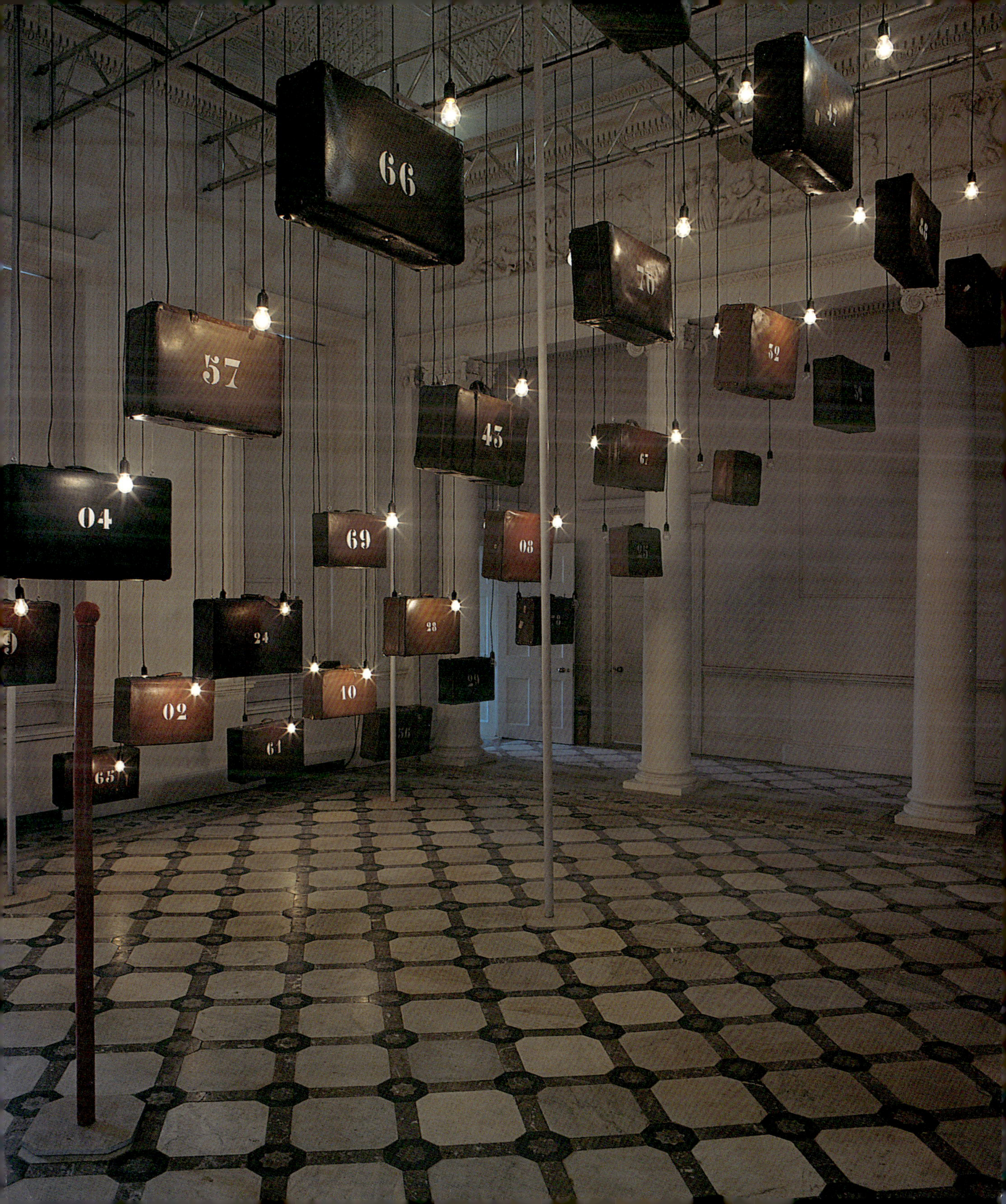
66
57
04
43
70
52
69
08
24
28
02
10
29
61
65
67

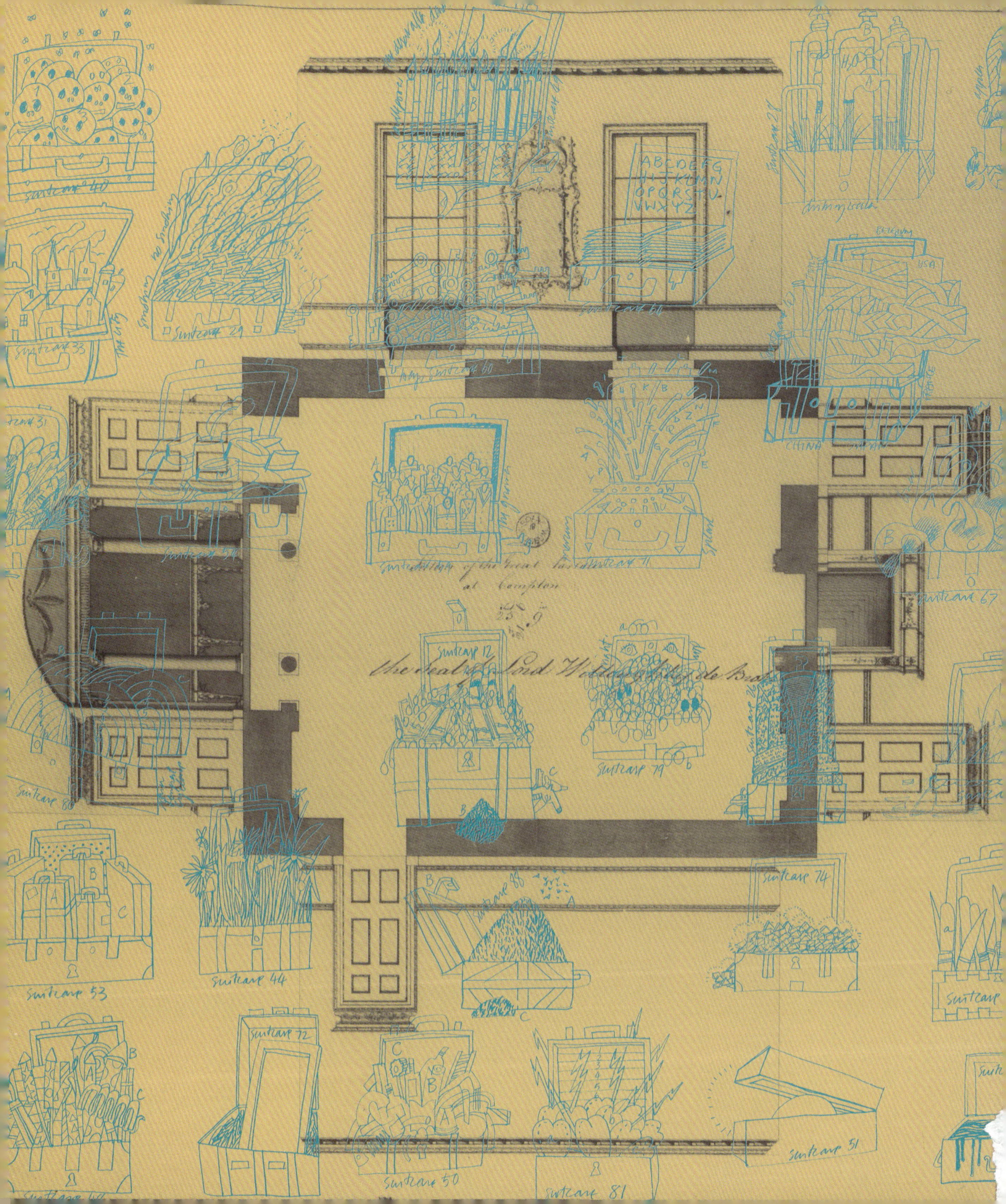
Suitcase 40
Suitcase 33
Suitcase 29
Suitcase 12
Suitcase 79
Suitcase 67
Suitcase 74
Suitcase 53
Suitcase 44
Suitcase 72
Suitcase 50
Suitcase 81
Suitcase 51
ABCDEFG
HIJKLMN
OPQRSTU
VWXYZ
CHINA
USA
the Seat of Lord Willoughby de Broke